Liberating Systems Theory

Contemporary Systems Thinking

Series Editor: Robert L. Flood
University of Hull
Hull, United Kingdom

LIBERATING SYSTEMS THEORY
Robert L. Flood

OPERATIONAL RESEARCH AND SYSTEMS: The Systemic
Nature of Operational Research
Paul Keys

A Continuation Order Plan is available for this series. A continuation order will bring delivery of each new volume immediately upon publication. Volumes are billed only upon actual shipment. For further information please contact the publisher.

Liberating Systems Theory

Robert L. Flood
University of Hull
Hull, United Kingdom

PLENUM PRESS • NEW YORK AND LONDON

Library of Congress Cataloging-in-Publication Data

Flood, Robert L.
    Liberating systems theory / Robert L. Flood.
        p.   cm. -- (Contemporary systems thinking)
    Includes bibliographical references and index.
    ISBN 0-306-43592-6
    1. System theory.   I. Title.   II. Series.
    HD38.F588   1990
    003--dc20   90-42963
                                                                    CIP

ISBN 0-306-43592-6

© 1990 Plenum Press, New York
A Division of Plenum Publishing Corporation
233 Spring Street, New York, N.Y. 10013

Printed in the United States of America

Dedicated to my great friend Mike

SERIES PREFACE

Contemporary Systems Thinking is a series of texts, each of which deals comparatively and/or critically with different aspects of holistic thinking at the frontiers of the discipline. Traditionally, writings by systems thinkers have been concerned with single theme propositions such as General Systems Theory, Cybernetics, Operations Research, System Dynamics, Soft Systems Methodology and many others. Recently there have been attempts to fulfil a different yet equally important role by comparative analyses of viewpoints and approaches, each addressing disparate areas of study such as: modeling and simulation, measurement, management, 'problem solving' methods, international relations, social theory and last, but not exhaustively or least, philosophy. In a recent book these were drawn together within a multiform framework as part of an eclectic discussion - a nearly impossible task as I discovered (see *Dealing With Complexity - An Introduction to the Theory and Application of Systems Science*, R. L. Flood and E. R. Carson, Plenum, New York, 1988). Nevertheless, bringing many sources together led to several achievements, among which was showing a great diversity of approaches, ideas and application areas that systems thinking contributes to (although often with difficulties remaining unresolved). More important, however, while working on that manuscript I became aware of the need for and potential value in a series of books, each focusing in detail on the study areas mentioned above. While modeling and simulation are served well in the scientific literature, this is not the case for systems thinking in management, 'problem solving' methods, social theory, or philosophy to name a handful. Each book in this series will make a contribution by concentrating on one of these topics. Each one will offer a further interest beyond other available books because of the inevitable tensions that authors will have to deal with, between contrasting approaches that have all too often met in nonreflective adversarial mode as specialist takes on specialist. There can be no genuine victors emerging from that style of intellectual debate.

Yet an alternative critical and comparative study poses an interesting difficulty for authors in this series. Each author must consider how they can best deal with contrasting approaches. There are two obvious options. First, by adopting a monolithic isolationist position that makes no real distinction between approaches which stand apart according to their own principles. Second, by taking the bold step of adopting a complementarist approach that operates at a meta-level and accepts fundamentally that different rationalities exist, each with its own theoretical and methodological legitimacies and limitations. I do not intend to dictate an isolationist or a complementarist position to the authors, but the reader's awareness of this issue sets up an extremely interesting tension that can be followed throughout the series.

Robert L. Flood
Hull, UK
June 1990

PREFACE

The argument of this book has no beginning and no end. This volume, therefore, was difficult to start and finish, which is inevitable for complex dependent thoughts set out in serial presentation. The argument is a 'system of thought', a highly integrated but not totalizing, closed, or complete whole. It is an unbounded one, an argument that awaits critique. Consequently, I thought that a useful way of entering the argument would be by reflecting upon the thesis that follows (a postscript titled 'Introduction') and an appropriate exit would be by outlining prospects arising from the thesis ('A Beginning'). So much for the diffuse edges.

The argument amounts to a general conception of 'Liberating Systems Theory' ('LST'): made up of two more specific conceptions, of Liberating 'Systems Theory' (L'ST' - about the liberation of systems theory) and 'Liberating Systems' Theory ('LS'T - about systems theory for liberation).

The thesis is organized in the following way.

CHAPTER 1   INTRODUCTION
            Entering the argument

START OF ARGUMENT

**SECTION 1 OF ARGUMENT - GENERAL - 'LIBERATING
SYSTEMS THEORY' ('LST')**
            An overview of 'system' and 'inquiry'

CHAPTER 2   LIBERATING SYSTEMS THEORY
            A general conception and two specific conceptions of
            Liberating Systems Theory. Four strands of study. An
            overview of the argument of the book

CHAPTER 3   INTERPRETIVE ANALYTICS AND KNOWLEDGE-
            CONSTITUTIVE INTERESTS: LIBERATE AND
            CRITIQUE
            A theory of discourse with a liberating rationale and a theory
            of the relationship between logical methodological rules and
            knowledge-constitutive interests. On unities opposing
            universals. A meta-unity of Interpretive Analytics and
            knowledge-constitutive interests

SECTION 2 OF ARGUMENT - SPECIFIC - LIBERATING
'SYSTEMS THEORY' (L'ST')
A critique of knowledges: articulation and release: against
universals

CHAPTER 4   ON 'SYSTEM': CONCEPTUAL ANTI-REFLEXIVITY
(*STRAND* 1)
The idea of a great natural systemic unification of knowledge
rejected

CHAPTER 5   ON 'SYSTEM': ABSTRACT AND PARADIGMATIC
CONCEPTIONS (*STRAND* 2)
Systems concepts take on differing meanings with different
rationalities. An investigation to seek out discontinuities
and breaks. An initial articulation of three rationalities and
their interpretation of 'system'

CHAPTER 6   ON 'SYSTEM': HISTORIES AND PROGRESSIONS OF
SYSTEMS THINKING (*STRAND* 3)
Discovering differing conceptions on the history and progress
of systems thinking. Liberating discourse, an example and
some ideas on legitimacies and limitations. The need for a
broad theory of legitimacies and limitations

SECTION 3 OF ARGUMENT - SPECIFIC - 'LIBERATING
SYSTEMS' THEORY ('LS'T)
A critique of knowledges: legitimacies and limitations:
against universals

CHAPTER 7   ON 'INQUIRY': SYSTEMS 'PROBLEM SOLVING'
(*STRAND* 4)
Establishing a complementarist vision and three
rationalities. A critique of the three rationalities in terms of
legitimacies and limitations

END OF ARGUMENT

CHAPTER 8   A BEGINNING
Exiting the argument

Some indication about how to read this volume will help the reader to
deal with the diverse nature of the content. In my view there are two

obvious ways. First, and perhaps the more difficult, is to focus on the interplay between the ideas of Foucault and Habermas, which leads to a critical theory defined by the process *'liberate* knowledges' and *'critique* knowledges' to tease out their theoretical and methodological legitimacies and limitations. This sets out a whole program of research that needs to develop the powerful idea of the respective yet dependent roles of Interpretive Analytics and knowledge-constitutive interests in advancing any theory, although in the case of this book the focus is systems theory.

A second and probably easier way of reading this book is as a history of systems thinking, and as an attempt to think out the relationship between the different strands that have emerged. Whichever way(s) you opt for, I hope that some value arises from your own interpretation(s).

A section at the end of this book, titled 'Terms and Concepts: Some Critical Observations', provides support that may help the reader who has had little exposure to social theory. This section was not misnamed 'Glossary', the latter being a misleading term which suggests a definitive or permanent account, as opposed to the more realistic idea that at best we can offer useful insights. 'Terms and Concepts' should help the reader to appreciate meanings that I wish to portray.

Liberating System Theory is an epistemological argument (developing the earlier work; Flood, 1990). The ideas appear elsewhere in a pragmatized but not compromised form (see R L Flood and M C Jackson, *Creative Problem Solving: Total Systems Intervention,* Wiley, Chichester, 1991a — briefly described in 'Terms and Concepts' and the 'Appendix'). The epistemological issues are also dealt with in a further volume (see R. L. Flood and M. C. Jackson, *Critical Systems Thinking: Directed Readings*, Wiley, Chichester, 1991b—where authors from diverse backgrounds contribute to a critically edited work). The reader can also consult the learned journal *Systems Practice* where issues arising from this book are discussed.

I thank the following people. For direct contributions: Werner Ulrich for allowing me to integrate our paper, 'Testament to conversations on Critical Systems Thinking between two systems practitioners', *Systems Practice*, Volume 3 Number 1, into Chapter 7; Wendy Gregory for allowing me to integrate our paper, 'Systems: Past, present and future', and Sionade Robinson for allowing me to integrate our paper, 'Whatever happened to General Systems Theory?' into Chapter 6 (both otherwise appearing in *Systems Prospects*, Plenum, New York, 1990, R. L. Flood, M. C. Jackson and P. Keys, eds.). Any distortions from the messages of the original works are my own choice and responsibility.

For indirect contributions: David Schecter for convincing me (at 2:00 A.M. on July 10 1988, in my garden shed during a rainstorm) of the value of the term 'Liberating Systems Theory'; Gary Wooliston whose unpublished summary of Habermas' knowledge-constitutive interests was of some use when writing Chapter 3; and Johnathon Calascione, with whom I enjoyed an ongoing dialogue on 'complexity' that must have contributed in some way to Chapter 5. All of those mentioned above, except Werner, 'are/have been' students that I have worked with. More generally, I am grateful to all the students who, more than most, have made my working life so interesting.

I thank Julie Harrison for preparing the manuscript, and Christopher Stevens for designing figures from crude drawings, producing the final layout, and for countless other ways in which he contributed to the realization of this book.

I thank the following readers for comments on the book: R. Cooper, R. Fuenmayor, M. C. Jackson, G. Midgley, J. Oliga, W. Ulrich.

This volume could not have been written without the love and patience of Mandy or the love and friendship of Ross.

Robert L. Flood
Hull, UK
May 1990

CONTENTS

CHAPTER 1
    INTRODUCTION   1
    INSIGHT 1 – FROM POSITIVISM TO CRITIQUE   3
    INSIGHT 2 – INTO CRITIQUE   4
    INSIGHT 3 – REFLECTIONS FOR THE
                AUTHOR AND READER   5
    INSIGHT 4 – BACK TO THE BEGINNING   6
    NOTES   6

START OF ARGUMENT

SECTION 1 OF ARGUMENT - GENERAL -
    'LIBERATING SYSTEMS THEORY' ('LST')

CHAPTER 2
    LIBERATING SYSTEMS THEORY   11
    2.1   INTRODUCTION   13
    2.2   SURVEY OF LIBERATING SYSTEMS
           THEORY I   14
           2.2.1 General Status   14
           2.2.2 Ideological Status   14
           2.2.3 That of Discourse - Seeking
                    Fundamental Satisfaction   14
           2.2.4 That Outside of Discourse - Seeking
                    General Utility   15
           2.2.5 Conclusion   15
    2.3   SURVEY OF SOCIAL THEORY - ON
           'TRUTH' AND 'MEANING'   16
           2.3.1 Introduction   16
           2.3.2 Foundationalism v. Anti-foundationalism   16
           2.3.3 Foundationalism   18
           2.3.4 Anti-foundationalism   20
           2.3.5 Scholars of Union   21
           2.3.6 Conclusion   22
    2.4   SURVEY OF LIBERATING SYSTEMS
           THEORY II   23
           2.4.1 Introduction   23
           2.4.2 On 'System': Conceptual Anti-reflexivity
                (Strand 1)   23

2.4.3   On 'System': Abstract and Paradigmatic
         Conceptions (Strand 2)   24
2.4.4   On 'System': Histories and Progressions
         of Systems Thinking (Strand 3)   25
2.4.5   On 'Inquiry': Systems 'Problem Solving'
         (Strand 4)   26
2.4.6   Conclusion   27
2.5   SURVEY OF LIBERATING SYSTEMS
         THEORY III   27
2.5.1   Introduction   27
2.5.2   Theoretical Status   28
2.5.3   Integrated Nature of Theory and Ideology   28
2.6   CONTEMPORARY SYSTEMS THINKING:
         SOCIAL THEORY AND THE CHALLENGE
         OF PRACTICE   29
2.7   CONCLUSION   31
NOTES   32

CHAPTER 3
INTERPRETIVE ANALYTICS AND
KNOWLEDGE-CONSTITUTIVE INTERESTS:
LIBERATE AND CRITIQUE   33
3.1   INTRODUCTION   35
3.2   KNOWLEDGE-CONSTITUTIVE INTERESTS   35
3.2.1   Introduction   35
3.2.2   Traditional and Critical Theories   37
3.2.3   Traditional and Hermeneutic Positivism:
         Isolationism   37
3.2.4   Knowledge-Constitutive Interests:
         Complementarism   38
3.2.5   Conclusion   41
3.3   INTERPRETIVE ANALYTICS   41
3.3.1   Introduction   41
3.3.2   An Interpretation of Foucault's Genealogy   42
         3.3.2.1   Introduction   42
         3.3.2.2   Living networks   42
         3.3.2.3   Conclusion   43
3.3.3   An Interpretation of Foucault's Critique   43
3.3.4   Conclusion   47
3.4   LIBERATE AND CRITIQUE   47
3.5   CONCLUSION   50
NOTES   51

SECTION 2 OF ARGUMENT - SPECIFIC - LIBERATING 'SYSTEMS THEORY' (L'ST')

CHAPTER 4
ON 'SYSTEM': CONCEPTUAL ANTI-REFLEXIVITY
(STRAND 1)   57
4.1   INTRODUCTION   59
4.2   DISCURSIVE EVIDENCE   59
4.3   'ANALYTICAL' EVIDENCE   63
4.4   CONCLUSION   65
NOTES   66

CHAPTER 5
ON 'SYSTEM': ABSTRACT AND PARADIGMATIC
CONCEPTIONS (STRAND 2)   69
5.1   INTRODUCTION   71
5.2   'SYSTEM': EVERYDAY CONTENTLESSNESS   71
5.3   'SYSTEM': ABSTRACT RICHNESS   72
       5.3.1 Introduction   72
       5.3.2 A 'First' Systems Struggle: Ontological
              Reconceptualization   72
       5.3.3 Systemic Metaphors   76
              5.3.3.1 Introduction   76
              5.3.3.2 Machine metaphor or 'closed
                       system' view   76
              5.3.3.3 Organic metaphor or 'open
                       system' view   77
              5.3.3.4 Autopoietic metaphor or 'self-
                       producing' view   77
              5.3.3.5 Neurocybernetic metaphor or
                       'viable system' view   78
              5.3.3.6 Culture metaphor   79
              5.3.3.7 Political metaphor   80
              5.3.3.8 Discussion   80
5.4   'SYSTEM' AND 'COMPLEXITY':
       PARADIGMATIC CONTENTFULNESS   81
       5.4.1 Introduction   81
       5.4.2 General Features of 'Complexity'   81
       5.4.3 A General Theoretical Framework   82
              5.4.3.1 Introduction   82
              5.4.3.2 Paradigmatic interpretations of
                       'system' and 'complexity'   84

| | 5.4.4 | Conclusion | 90 |

5.5 A 'SECOND' SYSTEMS STRUGGLE:
     A 'FIRST ' EPISTEMOLOGICAL BREAK   91
     5.5.1 Introduction   91
     5.5.2 Unleashing the Open System Metaphor   91
     5.5.3 Conclusion   92
5.6 THE NEED FOR A SUBSTANTIVE
     SUBJECTIVIST SYSTEMS LANGUAGE
     AND CONCEPTS   92
     5.6.1 Introduction   92
     5.6.2 Translating a Manuscript   93
     5.6.3 Discussion   98
5.7 A 'THIRD' SYSTEMS STRUGGLE: A 'SECOND'
     EPISTEMOLOGICAL BREAK   99
     5.7.1 Introduction   99
     5.7.2 Critical Systems Heuristics: Toward a
            Metaphysics of Design   99
            5.7.2.1 Introduction   99
            5.7.2.2 Ulrich's comment   101
            5.7.2.3 Social Systems Design   101
            5.7.2.4 'Second' epistemological break   103
     5.7.3 Conclusion   104
5.8 CONCLUSION   104
     NOTES   105

CHAPTER 6
ON 'SYSTEM': HISTORIES AND PROGRESSIONS
OF SYSTEMS THINKING (STRAND 3)   111
6.1 INTRODUCTION   113
6.2 VIEWS ON THE HISTORY AND
     PROGRESS OF SYSTEMS THINKING   113
     6.2.1 Introduction   113
     6.2.2 Ideas on the Nature of the History
            and Progress of Knowledge   114
     6.2.3 Approaches to the History and
            Progress of Systems Thinking   115
            6.2.3.1 Introduction   115
            6.2.3.2 Review   116
            6.2.3.4 Conclusion   119
6.3 ABANDON GENERAL SYSTEMS THEORY?
     AN INTERPRETIVE ANALYTICAL CRITIQUE   119
     6.3.1 Introduction   119

6.3.2   What is Meant by General Systems
        Theory?   121
6.3.3   Common Areas of Criticism   123
6.3.4   Reviewing the Philosophical Criticisms   124
        6.3.4.1   Introduction   124
        6.3.4.2   The positivist attack   124
        6.3.4.3   The neo-positivist attack   125
        6.3.4.4   The interpretive attack   127
6.3.5   Discussion   128
6.4   CONCLUSION   129

SECTION 3 OF ARGUMENT - SPECIFIC -
'LIBERATING SYSTEMS' THEORY ('LS'T)

CHAPTER 7
ON 'INQUIRY': SYSTEMS 'PROBLEM SOLVING'
(STRAND 4)   133
7.1   INTRODUCTION   135
7.2   GENERAL FRAMEWORK ON INQUIRY   136
        7.2.1   Introduction   136
        7.2.2   Four Principles, Six Styles   136
        7.2.3   The General Framework   137
        7.2.4   Comments on the Six Styles   138
                7.2.4.1   Pragmatism   138
                7.2.4.2   Complementarism   138
                7.2.4.3   Theoretical isolationism   139
                7.2.4.4   Methodological isolationism   140
                7.2.4.5   Methodological imperialism
                          (by subsumption)   140
                7.2.4.6   Methodological imperialism
                          (by annexation)   140
        7.2.5   Conclusion   140
7.3   SIX SCENARIOS FOR THE FUTURE OF
        SYSTEMS 'PROBLEM SOLVING'   141
        7.3.1   Introduction   141
        7.3.2   Pragmatic Approaches   143
        7.3.3   Isolationist Approaches   146
        7.3.4   Imperialist Approaches   147
        7.3.5   Complementarist Approaches   148
        7.3.6   Pursuing an Isolationist Approach   155
                7.3.6.1   Introduction   155
                7.3.6.2   Validation criteria   155
                7.3.6.3   Theory implied through language 157

　　　　　　　7.3.6.4　World-viewpoints: The answer
　　　　　　　　　　　 to the riddle?   158
　　　　7.3.7　Summary   161
7.4　THE NEED FOR A NEW EPISTEMOLOGY   161
7.5　TOWARD AN ADEQUATE EPISTEMOLOGY
　　　FOR SYSTEMS PRACTICE   162
　　　7.5.1　Introduction   162
　　　7.5.2　Contrasting Conceptions of Rationality:
　　　　　　　Legitimacies and Limitations   165
　　　　　　　7.5.2.1　Introduction   165
　　　　　　　7.5.2.2　On positivistic science/
　　　　　　　　　　　 rationality   166
　　　　　　　7.5.2.3　On interpretivistic science/
　　　　　　　　　　　 rationality   170
　　　　　　　7.5.2.4　On critical science/rationality 176
　　　　7.5.3　Conclusion   180
7.6　CONCLUSION   183
　　　NOTES   184

END OF ARGUMENT

CHAPTER 8
　　　A BEGINNING   195
　　　NOTES   199

TERMS AND CONCEPTS: SOME CRITICAL
　　　OBSERVATIONS   201

APPENDIX:
　　　A PRACTICAL FACE TO LIBERATING
　　　SYSTEMS THEORY   221
REFERENCES   229
INDEX   243

CHAPTER 1

INTRODUCTION

Entering the argument

I have decided to present four insights into Liberating Systems Theory prior to the thesis. Placing these at the end of the book would doom them to neglect, as if they belonged in some quiet backwater, and would miss an opportunity to reveal why the thesis was written. This may seem a little unorthodox, but an underlying purpose of my argument is to promote the idea of breaking away from accepted ways of discourse and other practices — in particular for systems thinking. To do this for the sake of being different would be worthless, but to show that challenge and liberation leads to an enriching of our intellectual and life-worlds is not.

INSIGHT 1 — FROM POSITIVISM TO CRITIQUE

For the past eight years, and probably more, I have tussled with ideas and concepts of systems thinking, particularly in social contexts, with the aim of assessing their practical utility. This odyssey has taken me across three paradigmatic continents: positivism (including its neo- and logical positivist regions), interpretivism, and critique. I explored each one, setting bearings and plotting new routes.

The intellectual port from which I departed is positioned deep in the positivistic continent, being a university department with a population who focus on empiricist and structuralist, systemic and scientific, methods applied in hard engineering and other contrasting fields of inquiry such as international relations. There was a suspicion in my homeland that if I traveled 'too far' (or was it 'far enough'?) on my exploration, I would 'go over the edge' since evidently the positivistic continent is flat. This myth restricted progress in the early years.

My first main break was to visit ports in the interpretivistic continent. Initially mutual distrust abounded, accentuated by the apparent difficulty of speaking different languages and by our different practical ways. Later, a few of these civilized intellects befriended me — the emigré. We were soon sharing jokes such as: 'Did you hear about the positivist who persistently argued that the nature of the social world is objective, only to turn around to an interpretivist adversary and say that the real pleasure of intellectual debate is that we all have different viewpoints (!)'. Yet even with this insight there was a sense of isolationism.

I continued to the critical continent having loaded my intellectual hold. I felt uncomfortable again, meeting another population whose language was similar to interpretivists, but whose practical methods had an emancipatory difference. With this liberating conviction I was able to appreciate the complementary nature of styles of thought from each continent, animated by critically self-reflective awareness.

This enlightening journey, from positivism to critique, led to the reasoning that holds together the words, concepts, arguments, and many questions that comprise Liberating Systems Theory.

INSIGHT 2 — INTO CRITIQUE

Not surprisingly, the intellectual exploration recounted in Insight 1 has been rewarding, but it has also been troublesome. I will tell you about a few unexpected moments.

The intellectual journey made me weary, therefore a place to stop and rest would have been welcomed. But as soon as I became convinced, oh sweet reason, that at last my intellectual foundations were in place, I experienced a new wavering as a previously not-to-be-thought-of mentation cast doubt on 'this' (or was it 'my'?) reckoned understanding. A healthy skeptical diet was maintained, although resisting temptation to 'relax into skepticism' by giving up led to some difficult tensions (as C. West Churchman has told us, there are no answers, always more questions). Methodologies or theories which merely cast doubt rather than reflection and 'the tangible moment', offer little more than principles of despair. They are also flawed because doubting everything signifies that doubt must be cast on the reasoning behind skepticism. At the other extreme, methodologies or theories designed to reveal tangible and objective knowledge are unbelievable. Pursuing this reasoning in social contexts fails to uncover absolute truths. For example, an objective empirically based social science makes reference to values that it was designed to eliminate — significance and worth. A path between the antonymous positions had to be carefully cut.

I particularly remember a student discussion along these lines that reminds us of contradiction in absolute positions.

Student Discussion about Systemic Scientific Knowledge

Student 1 to Student 2: "There is no doubt that there is no truth you know" (the authenticist who in his certainty admitted uncertainty).

Student 3 to Student 1: "Is it true that you mean — it is true that there is doubt?" (reformulating Student 1's statement).

Student 4 to (now puzzled) Student 1: "Well, I am doubtful that knowledge can be doubted" (the skeptic who in her disbelief denied skepticism).

Student 2 to All: "Such absolutisms are simplistic and trivialize the issues. At least ideals are equivalent to a backboard against which we are able to critique" (she must have been reading critical theory!).

I also discovered the rich ideas of critical theory and in these notions of immanent 'objectivity' and 'validity' ('truths'), and 'false consciousness' and 'illusions' ('untruths').

There are naturally implications for systems thinking based on critical theory. The emancipatory notion of openness and conciliation leads to a potentially shocking realization, that there cannot be a systems science based on any single set of rational rules. We need to know if this has been dealt with elsewhere.

There is some evidence that systems thinkers have broken away from traditional science. For example, Maturana proposed that we change the meaning of cybernetics to the science and art of understanding control and communication in man, animal and machine (art being an addition). Churchman (1979) argued that a main challenge for systems practice comes from anything that is beyond the reach of empirically based systems scientific rationality (e.g., the challenge of morality, religion, politics, and aesthetics). Although important, neither Maturana's nor Churchman's ideas go far enough. An adequate epistemology must accept alternative rationalities and adopt the idea of systems science*s*. I am not, of course, calling for irrationality[1]. Nor am I giving up. Indeed, to the contrary it is the nonreflective isolationist views that have given up.

INSIGHT 3 — REFLECTIONS FOR THE AUTHOR AND READER

Personally this text is a crux unravelled through self-reflection and by working out general intellectual frameworks. These frameworks were designed to help establish base-line complementarist understandings in systems thinking at a time when the trend and general view of holism has ironically been toward fragmentation indicating a weakness. Throughout this book we will find that there is in fact a diversity in systems thinking which can be harnessed to display strength. As Ramsés Fuenmayor pointed out, the essence of the following thesis is a cry against provincialism.

For the reader, the argument offers a transparadigmatic journey reflecting on fundamental issues confronting the systems science*s*. If the reader has undertaken such a passage before then I offer redolence, perhaps with some new insights since all intellectual explorations pursue different routes and lead to alternative views and horizons (I could learn much from your account). If, however, the thesis represents a new venture, then I am uncertain about what I offer. Since the unfamiliar idea of the argument is thinking between paradigms, then presumably this text might (a) illuminate 'and/or' (b) confuse.

If on account of the intellectual message the reader finds themself exclusively '(b)' (i.e., confused), they should try the passages again or resign themself to a lifetime of isolationist thinking. If the reader declares themself to be exclusively '(a)' (i.e., illuminated), they could not have struggled to intellectually liberate themself and are no more than an unaware '(b)'. If the reader finds themself to be '(a) and (b)' simultaneously, then I suspect that they have read in a critical spirit and will, as I, have been partially intellectually emancipated.

INSIGHT 4 — BACK TO THE BEGINNING

In the previous three insights I have introduced the idea of diversity and the need for complementarist thinking and frameworks, or maps of the intellectual world of systems thinking. These should be useful because maps help to set bearings and trace out possible new directions. Of course, I do not claim to have fully explored the three vast paradigmatic continents.

The beginning of the thesis starts in the next chapter where the ideas of Liberating Systems Theory and its many associated meanings set the background for the following chapters. The four brief insights now hand over to the thesis.

NOTES

(1) For example, if an empirical scientist says that an account of 'whatever' is irrational, that only states the account is not valid in terms of empirical rationality, and does not state the account is absolutely and in all senses irrational. Also note that *irrationality* refers to a perception of an argument that appears to be counter-logical, and must be distinguished from *nonrationality*, which refers to emotions, the subconscious, etc.

START OF ARGUMENT

SECTION 1 OF ARGUMENT

- GENERAL -

'LIBERATING SYSTEMS THEORY' ('LST')

An overview of 'system' and 'inquiry'

CHAPTER 2

LIBERATING SYSTEMS THEORY

A general conception and two specific conceptions of Liberating Systems Theory. Four strands of study. An overview of the argument of the book

2.1   INTRODUCTION

The aim of this chapter is to explore a number of possible interpretations of its title, 'Liberating Systems Theory' ('LST'). Each of these selected meanings represents a theme, or a strand of study, that will be developed in one of the following chapters. Particular points of focus are:

(a) Strand 1, the liberation of systems theory from a natural tendency toward self-imposed insularity (L'ST');
(b) Strand 2, the liberation of systems concepts from objectivist or subjectivist delusions (L'ST');
(c) Strand 3, the liberation of systems theory from internalized localized subjugations of discourse, (L'ST');
(d) Strand 4, systems theory for emancipation in response to domination and subjugation in work and social situations ('LS'T); but in broader terms the book as a whole is concerned with
(e) The liberation of systems theory in the sense of more cognitive illumination for the reader or prospective researcher or practitioner ('LST').

To help us understand how systems thinking can deal with worrying issues arising in the four strands, we will develop a view on truth and meaning to promote coherent argumentation. The view must be fundamentally satisfying and of general utility. This directs our interest to discourse (ideas, concepts, knowledges, etc.) and to the creators of discourse—the two being inextricably linked. By addressing the themes in terms of truth and meaning, this book synthesizes systems thinking and social theory.

This chapter is structured as follows. Initially the general status of Liberating Systems Theory is reviewed. The ideological status (political sense) is then declared. The inseparable, but more tricky, theoretical (epistemological and ontological) status is deferred to the end of the chapter. A survey on truth and meaning is presented in the third section. This leads us to the fourth section, which is an overview of the four strands of Liberating Systems Theory and the influence of the social theorists Habermas and Foucault. The structure of Chapter 2 is also an outline of the whole argument.

2.2   SURVEY OF LIBERATING SYSTEMS THEORY I

2.2.1   General Status

The title Liberating Systems Theory can and indeed should be interpreted in many ways. The intended meanings that I attach importance to are outlined in the introduction to this chapter. The idea of a plurality of intended meanings reflects diverse difficulties that are currently challenging the integrity of systems thinking. This demands at least an equal diversity in strands of research. Four are addressed in this book.

The convergent question 'What is Liberating Systems Theory?' is therefore misguided. It is not a distinct thing. It is not another systems methodology, model or meta-status offering. It is none of these typical outputs of systems research. Liberating Systems Theory is the basis of a sociological paradigm of thought with integrated epistemological, ontological, methodological, and ideological positions. The first three of these cannot easily be understood at the outset and are therefore dealt with toward the end of the chapter. This paradigm is also based fundamentally on the notion that various forms of the concept of 'system' can help us as abstract organizing structures to investigate, represent, and intervene in what we make to be systemic worlds understood through differing rationalities. We will now give thought to the ideological status.

2.2.2   Ideological Status

The ideology is nonconservative. The aim is to learn how to recognize all sorts of subjugation of knowledge and people, and then bring about liberation and emancipation respectively.

In this way, ideas, concepts, and discursivities may be liberated from microlevel procedures of power that constitute or subjugate discourse. Also, those in need of emancipation from power structures in organizations, institutions, societies, and other social groupings can be helped toward a greater degree of self-determination. We will discover later how Foucault and Habermas have influenced our ideology. Together they furnish the basis of a rationale behind liberating knowledges which unites with critiquing those knowledges, providing a basis for self-determination.

We will now consider how Liberating Systems Theory relates to that of discourse and that outside of discourse.

2.2.3   That of Discourse—Seeking Fundamental Satisfaction

Our interest in that of discourse amounts to a search for subjectively intended meaning, or truth, in written and spoken forms. The scientific investigation of the understanding of human communication labelled structuralism addressed this concern. More recent approaches concentrate on concepts and discursivities, for example the 'Archaeology' and 'Genealogy' of Foucault; together with metaphor and analogy, for example the 'Deconstruction Theory' of Derrida and 'Phenomenological Hermeneutics' of Ricoeur.

A critical concern with written discourse is naturally of great importance, since we frequently consult and make reference to academic writings, although we should not discount non academic literature. In this context Ackoff (1988) reminded me that 'When one characterises the position of another in terms of assumptions, beliefs, assertions, etc., one's formulation of these as well as one's perceptions of them are conditioned by one's own assumptions'.

We also need to be critically alert to spoken discourse, since we verbally communicate intellectual ideas when socializing in bars, pubs, at work in corridors, at conferences, and workshops, etc. A critical awareness is important because systems ideas and methods of any worth must portray or capture as far as possible the ideas, perceptions or viewpoints of human beings. False consciousness, however, is the deadly enemy of all interpreters of discourse. We therefore need to look for forms of misrepresentation outside of discourse.

2.2.4   That Outside of Discourse—Seeking General Utility

Our interest in discourse is fringed by a concern with power. By explaining power through nonsovereign influences in discourse, we can understand how some concepts, ideas and discursivities have emerged while others have not. Nonsovereign power relations are essentially the main focus of Foucault's Genealogy and critique. With his methodological ideas, dominance and subjugation can be explained and liberation of ideas, concepts, and discursivities can be achieved. For example, localized procedures of power effected at a microlevel may be traced upward revealing dominant cultures, as with the church's traceable position in the subjugation of the theory of evolution. The factors influential on discourse are naturally linked to human beings, the creators of discourse and give rise to 'social systems'.

2.2.5   Conclusion

This section has provided a survey of the general and ideological status of Liberating Systems Theory and our interest in discourse, but has left me with two further tasks:

    (a) to provide a concise survey of social theory in the area of truth and meaning so that the theoretical basis of Liberating Systems Theory can be better understood (dealt with in Section 2.3); and

Table 2.1

Summary of some main schools of thought from a general survey
on notions of 'truth' and 'meaning'

	FOUNDATIONALISM	ANTI-FOUNDATIONALISM
INFLUENTIAL PHILOSOPHERS	Immanuel Kant	David Hume
SCHOOLS OF THOUGHT	Structuralism Post-structuralism Hermeneutic Theory ('of reason') • phenomenological symbolic interactionism • ethnomethodology • existentialism • phenomenology	Deconstruction Theory Hermeneutic Philosophy
	UNIONISM	
	Genealogy and critique/Interpretive Analytics	
	Critical Hermeneutics/knowledge-constitutive interests	

(b) to elaborate on the research strands of Liberating Systems Theory,
and to expand on the ideas of social theorists who have
fundamentally influenced this thinking (dealt with in Section 2.4).

2.3   SURVEY OF SOCIAL THEORY – ON 'TRUTH' AND 'MEANING'

2.3.1   Introduction

In this section I shall present a survey of social theory, discussing the
main areas of study on truth and meaning insofar as they are relevant to this
thesis (summarized in Table 2.1). I will then be in a position to present four
strands of Liberating Systems Theory in outline without fearing that their
theoretical bases will be misunderstood. We will start with the main
contemporary polemical debate.

2.3.2   Foundationalism v. Anti-foundationalism

Roderick (1986, Chapter 1), in accordance with the literature of social
theory, has identified 'early' Foundationalism with the writings of the
eighteenth-century philosopher Immanuel Kant. Kant introduced the idea
that man is a unique being, totally involved in nature (the body), society
(historical, economic, and political relations), and language. These are
integral with the meaning-giving organizing activity of man (Dreyfus and

Rabinow, 1982). Kant wished to redeem philosophy from the radical skepticism of the British Empiricist Hume, who was unsuccessful at revealing a link between laws of thought and the nature of real-life events and experience. Hume finally concluded that it was not possible to have definite self-validating knowledge of the external world (Norris, 1982). For Hume, almost nothing about existence could be demonstrated, hence we could link him to Anti-foundationalism. Kant, however, believed that knowledge is a product of the mind and thus the world can be 'known', although only through interpretation. Consciousness could not know the world in a direct form—the mind could not '...deliver it up in all its pristine reality' (Norris, 1982, p. 4).

Kant agreed with Hume's conclusions. He found Hume's early search for such a reality a hopeless cause, yet was equally opposed to the resulting skeptical position. Kant's proposition was that there are deep regularities, *a priori* truths in the transcendental subject that are the essence of human understanding. This is the Kantian subject/object division. Fundamentally, Kant disagreed with the Empiricist's view that concepts arise from impressions, as if reality is scribed on our minds through tangible experiences. The counter proposition states that it is the other way round, that '...impressions had to be formed in accordance with our innate intuitions of space and time in order to be *experienced* at all.' (Trusted, 1981, p. 187).

> Kant saw that our understanding confronted a difficulty similar to that faced by any producer who seeks to impose a particular form on unyielding matter. The 'Critique' ('of Pure Reason') begins from the fact that only an incoherent profusion of impressions or sensations are given in perception. Since, on the other hand, we always perceive the world as a world of ordered things, it must be our faculty of perception itself which produces order out of the variety of impressions. This is the decisive work of perception: the production of possible objects of knowledge out of the given material of impressions. The faculty of perception produces, not indeed reality itself, but the mode in which reality appears to us. Things are 'constituted' by us in the sense that we can know them only through certain *a priori* forms or 'categories' which are embedded in the human subject. (Connerton, 1976, p.17).

Developed from this theme, Foundationalism attempts to provide knowledge with a justification where possible and a critique where none is possible. The aim is to ensure that our knowledge is set on firm, indubitable and unshakable foundations. Anti-foundationalism proposes a theory about intersubjectively shared practices of language, against the notion of indubitable ideas of the individual thinking subject. It attempts to establish that there can be no absolutely neutral standpoint for inquiry outside ongoing interpretations, values, and interests of actual communities of inquirers at work in current social practices (Roderick, 1986, p. 8). We will now consider the apparently oppositional nature of the polemical debate.

2.3.3 Foundationalism

Several schools of thought fall within this general class. We will consider only Structuralism and Hermeneutic Theory. We can work on these to dig out the core notions of Foundationalism with the advantage of brevity (for a broader insight into Foundationalism see Roderick, 1986; and into Hermeneutics as such; see Bleicher, 1980; Dreyfus and Rabinow, 1982).

Structuralism in the study of language was envisaged by Saussure as being truly scientific, so that human communication could be understood in general in terms of verbal and nonverbal forms. The 'science of signs', labeled 'semiology', argues that knowledge of the world is ultimately inextricably shaped and conditioned by the language which serves to represent it (Strickland, 1981). Saussure argued that language precedes the existence of independent entities, rather than providing a set of labels for entities which exist independently in the world. Thus the world becomes understandable through the differentiation of concepts (Belsey, 1980). In this we find a Kantian link.

Structuralism is a simultaneous attempt to do away with meaning and the subject by finding objective laws that govern all human activity. It attempts to treat human activity scientifically by finding basic elements (concepts, actions, classes of words) and rules or practices by which they are combined (Dreyfus and Rabinow, 1982).

The ideas of Structuralism are evident in positivistic cybernetic thinking, where the elements and rules take on the form of structured relationships that purport to represent reality.

To summarize, the basic relativity of thought and meaning is the starting point of Structuralist theory, the Kantian link. Structuralism, however, can be thought of as Kantianism without the transcendental subject (Norris, 1982).

Hermeneutics is opposed to Structuralism. It is generally defined as the theory and/or philosophy of the interpretation of meaning (Bauman, 1978; Bleicher, 1980). It is thus of central concern to literary criticism (see Strickland, 1981) as well as to the philosophies of the social sciences, art, and language.

Hermeneutics can be thought of in terms of different types. Heidegger, for example, thought in terms of two types of Hermeneutic inquiry. For 'Type 1' Heidegger argued that understanding in everyday practices and discourse is not complete and must be assumed distorted. 'Type 1' inquiry seeks to uncover meaning which if pointed out to us we would be able to recognize. It is a 'Hermeneutics of reason'. With 'Type 2' Heidegger suggests something a little more sinister: that 'Type 1' interpretation should not necessarily be accepted at face value since there might be a motivated masking of the truth. This points to a 'Hermeneutics of suspicion' (Ricoeur, 1975).

Bleicher (1980) argues for three incompatible groups with conflicting views: Hermeneutic Theory, Hermeneutic Philosophy, and Critical Hermeneutics. Hermeneutic Theory focuses on the problematic of a general theory of interpretation as the scientific methodology for the human sciences. Hermeneutic Philosophy asserts that the interpreter and object are linked by a context of tradition and rejects as objectivism scientific investigation of meaning. An interpreter is assumed to have an *a priori* understanding of the object and cannot meaningfully claim neutrality of the mind. Hermeneutic Theory can therefore be linked to Foundationalism, and Hermeneutic Philosophy to Anti-foundationalism. Critical Hermeneutics will be discussed later as a form of union in the polemical debate.

Hermeneutic Theory has a number of distinct interpretive approaches according to Oliga (1988, see Table 2.1). For a brief discussion of each one see Oliga (1988, p. 97–98), and for an in-depth discussion refer to Burrell and Morgan (1979). Currently we need only consider Edmund Husserl's Transcendental Phenomenology, to develop a sketch which simultaneously highlights a distinct ontological break with empiricist methodologies toward subjective meaning and intention, and an epistemological unity with empiricism in terms of objectivist aspirations in the production of knowledge (Oliga, 1988).

Husserl's phenomenological reduction wants to draw away human consciousness from its intricate interweaving with the social and historical. It therefore emerges as '...an absolute; when consciousness becomes the sole world left at the end of reduction, all beings will become meanings for consciousness.' (Bauman, 1978).

Another way of describing this, is that we close our eyes for a moment, and then reopen them, starting afresh and cleansed in an effort to explain our 'looking out' (our thoughts and the external world). Husserl argued that this liberation is essential for true noncontingent meaning to be attained, and proposed a cleansing of psychological connotations from the process of understanding since thoughts are historical phenomena (Bauman, 1978). This turned out to be a tricky and difficult procedure. Indeed, in his later works Husserl recognized a number of fundamental difficulties with his transcendental reduction and tried to build a bridge between the phenomenologically reduced to the 'life-world'.

We have developed an appreciation of Foundationalist thought, and will now carry out a similarly leveled investigation into Anti-foundationalist thought.

2.3.4   Anti-foundationalism

Several schools of thought fall into this general class. We will consider Hermeneutic Philosophy and Deconstruction Theory, and work on these to dig out the core notions of Anti-foundationalism, while maintaining the advantage of brevity (see Table 2.1).

Hermeneutic Philosophy wants us to turn away from the objectivism of Foundationalist thinking because, it is argued, an interpreter has a preunderstanding of any object approached. The interpreter and object are assumed to be linked by a context of tradition.   There can be no object in itself, no theory-neutrality or value-freedom. Instead, with an openness of tradition, historical reality is realized

> ...through a process of dialogical relationship between the subject and the object...and [with] the dialectic between question and answer, the corresponding traditions become integrated....With [Hermeneutic Philosophy] consciousness and experience can never be complete, being limited by our historicality. (Oliga, 1988, p. 99–100, that in brackets added)

A routing attack on Foundationalism has been leveled through Deconstruction Theory (Derrida, 1972, 1980 and 1981), which shares the sentiment of Hume's conclusions on skepticism. It is the '...antithesis of everything that criticism ought to be if one accepts its traditional values and concepts' (Norris, 1982, p. xii).

It suspends all that we take for granted about language, experience, and the traditional possibilities of human communication.   It takes away the assumed correspondence between mind, meaning, and the concept of method that claims to unite them. Skepticism might well be an incurable ailment that will not leave us, according to Hume (Norris, 1982). The implications of adopting Deconstruction Theory extend well beyond literature, making social criticism of history and philosophy virtually impossible (Goodheart, 1984).

Derrida may be thought of as the learned father of contemporary Deconstructionist thinking (see Norris, 1982). He stressed that there is no language so vigilant and self-aware that it can effectively escape the conditions placed upon thought by its own prehistory and metaphysics. On this basis he made an unreserved critique of philosophy, anthropology, linguistics, and indeed human sciences in general.

We have now established the polemical debate as Foundationalism v. Anti-foundationalism.   There are writers, however, who adopt a complementarist approach in the face of this apparent contradiction. We will now consider these unionist tendencies.

2.3.5   Scholars of Union

Evidence that there are scholars of union[1] can be found in several review articles where attempts to bisect social theory falter. Marsh (1988) attempts to contrast Modernist with Post-modernist thinking (which is similar to the Foundationalist/Anti-foundationalist debate).   Yet Marsh's self-confessed inability to find consistency of some researchers in one or other paradigm highlights unionist tendencies.   In some cases he found strong Modernist influences coexisting with Post-modernist ones. Roderick's (1986) attempt to separate out contrasting strands was more successful, since he made a point of using his debate to indicate open and conciliatory, or unionist interests[2].

Marsh (1988) and Roderick (1986) identify Habermas' (1971) knowledge-constitutive interests with complementarity. Marsh writes about Habermas' acknowledgment of Post-modernism's reminder to Modernism of the necessary complementarity between reason and eros, politics and aesthetics, and reflection and sensuality.   Roderick writes about Habermas' acceptance of the critique of Foundationalism and the Anti-foundationalist's view that there can be no timeless and absolutely neutral standpoints for inquiry.   Critical Hermeneutics was mentioned earlier, and Habermas' multifarious project has been given status under this label by Bleicher (1980).

While Hermeneutic Philosophy and Theory focus on the mediation of tradition and subjectively-intended meaning, differing on how understanding is possible and to what degree it might be objective, Critical Hermeneutics additionally focuses on the content of the object of interpretation. It thus concerns synthesizing explanatory and interpretive procedures to help actors appreciate why they thought what they thought, for what reasons these perceptions might have been erroneous and how any such errors, or false consciousness, might be dealt with. Psychoanalysis engages in this type of examination.   Freud's psychoanalytic theory centers on a plurality of plausible interpretations, offering methodological guidelines to tackle deceptive understandings. Freud's ideas have been extensively integrated into critical thought (see Habermas, 1970, 1971a in Chapter 12; Lorenzer, 1970).

Psychoanalysis is a psychoanalytic technique that intervenes in the balance between rationality and emotion on a nonrational level. It breaks away from the notion of one past history by deconstructing the perceived history, and then by reconstructing and incorporating new findings. By repeating this process a pluralist picture is constructed which indicates that there are many possible historical explanations. This counters the traditional idea of one totalizing history dominated by special traumatic and heroic events. Psychoanalytic ideas naturally can be extended to the notion of many histories relating to dynamics of discourse. This provides us with a stepping-stone onto the works of Michel Foucault.

Foucault's ideas defy easy classification with Modernist/ Foundationalist v. Post-modernist/Anti-foundationalist schemes. He is accused of being a Structuralist or Post-structuralist by some authors. For example, Bleicher (1980) briefly discusses Lorenzer's critique of the contrasting conceptions of Structuralism as represented by Lacan, Althusser, and Foucault. Conversely, both Norris (1982) and Strickland (1981) link the works of Foucault and Derrida and thus find some relationship between Interpretive Analytics and Deconstruction Theory. Dreyfus and Rabinow (1982) declare Foucault's propositions as *Beyond Structuralism and Hermeneutics*, linking his work to these theories by way of his proposed Archaeological analysis that maintains its distance from Structuralism, which is thoroughly mixed with an interpretive flavor of Hermeneutical insight. In labeling Foucault's work Interpretive Analytics, Dreyfus and Rabinow described it as an approach

> ...which explains the logic of Structuralism's claim to be objective science and also the apparent validity of the Hermeneutic counter-claim that the human sciences can only legitimately proceed by understanding the deepest meaning of the subject and his tradition. (Dreyfus and Rabinow, 1982, p. viii)

We may conclude that Habermas and Foucault have either implicitly or explicitly reasoned for unities. This proposition will be explored in detail in Chapter 3.

2.3.6   Conclusion

In this section we initially reviewed Foundationalism and Anti-foundationalism as a polemical debate. This set up the discussion about Habermas and Foucault who defy such barriers. With each of these unionist works, we have experienced tensions generated by forced relations of methodologically irrelative rules drawn together through meta-theoretical reasoning. In two varying ways we have come across the idea of theoretical commensurability. Cooper and Burrell (1988) point out these variations, noting that Habermas has been vigorous in his criticisms of Foucault and that the groundings appear to conflict. From another angle, however, a commonality that turns out to be a linchpin in the following studies, can be found at a meta-level, and is characterized as an open and conciliatory approach to competing views and traditions. In this book we will be handling tensions that arise in and between the works of Habermas and Foucault, but we will always work toward unities and oppose universals. By drawing together Interpretive Analytics and knowledge-constitutive interests, we will create a methodological approach to liberating and critiquing knowledges. This prepares us for critical application of systems approaches to 'problem solving'.

In the following section four strands of Liberating Systems Theory are outlined. The two scholars of union identified above are shown to have influenced much of this early thinking. Their works are discussed in detail in the next chapter.

2.4   SURVEY OF   LIBERATING SYSTEMS THEORY II
2.4.1   Introduction

This section is a general survey of the four strands of Liberating Systems Theory mentioned earlier. Focusing on 'system' we will consider conceptual anti-reflexivity, abstract and paradigmatic conceptions, and histories and progressions of systems thinking.   On 'inquiry' we will consider systems 'problem solving'. This presentation is equally an outline of the way the remainder of the book is organized. The separate outline discussions of each strand in this chapter will be adapted to act as introductions to respective chapters as they occur.

2.4.2   On 'System': Conceptual Anti-reflexitivity (Strand 1)

A unique feature of holism is the possibility of, and natural tendency toward, describing everything in systems terms. This can be explained by its early development within the forced confines of a realist inclined General Systems Theory. We can choose to consider any situation as a system and know that of course it is also a sub- and a supra-system ...'Is it not?' That is, unless the Universe is the system in focus, which is naturally heralded as the ultimate supra-system. Apparently there is no need to look beyond the horizons of this closed set of concepts... 'Can this be so?' I think not.

We might propose two lessons that would counter such an impoverished view (worked out in Chapter 3 but given here in reverse order).

Lesson 1: Systems thinking has a natural tendency to be conceptually reflexive (or autopoietic; i.e., there merely to confirm and recreate itself) and would benefit by looking beyond its own horizons.

A lesson from Lesson 1 is that we need to look beyond the ideas of systems thinking, to promote a proper use of them in social contexts. This relates to our second lesson.

Lesson 2: The study of (systems) concepts requires an 'historical and developmental' investigation that attempts to deal with the subjectively intended meaning of authors.

Developing these arguments will cast doubt on the possibility for and will stand against the desirability of, conceptual reflexivity in systems thinking. This principle will be better advanced if we consider, 'What in detail is this abstract idea of system?' and, 'In what ways do contrasting paradigmatic viewpoints influence our use of systems concepts?'

2.4.3   On 'System': Abstract and Paradigmatic Conceptions (Strand 2)

The notion of 'system' as a status, or essentialistic, representation is a consequence of accepting 'system' as an abstract term without reference to inevitable paradigmatic forces. When considering social reality, status questions must be considered as normative questions in disguise. It is therefore important to distinguish between abstract and paradigmatic definitions of 'system'. The task for this investigation is threefold.

First of all we must deal with the everyday contentless use of the term 'system'. We are continually confronted by as many desolate labels as you wish to dream up with the word 'system' tagged on. You know how it is: education system, political system, and endless other general labels; central heating system, the complete system to treat your hair, and endless other specific labels. Our everyday understanding of 'system' is contentless. We need to liberate our thinking from this snare of denaturing and stripping of meaning. This can be achieved by showing value in notions of 'system', by developing a proper understanding of its abstract richness and paradigmatic contentfulness.

Second, abstract richness needs to be fully appreciated. This can be achieved if we accept that there is no single metaphorical/analogical term which is 'system'. Such singularity would clearly be nonsense. In the last forty or so years there has been considerable redefinition through analogical reasoning. There are various abstractions relating to an organic natural world. These deal with traditionally conceived passive ideas of feedback in organisms, ecology, and evolution. Additionally, types of relationship between organisms have been theorized, such as the idea of autopoiesis and the active feedforward conception of the brain of man. More recently, systemic metaphors relating to culture, politics, and psychic prisons have surfaced. We can work out paradigmatic understandings of these abstract conceptions.

Third, then, is the issue of paradigmatic contentfulness. This refers to the realization, or understanding, of abstract systemic metaphors in terms of the fundamental tenets of coherent theories. For instance, 'How might we understand and treat social reality if we hold an objective view of the world?' On the other hand, 'In what way would systemic metaphors help us to appreciate social reality if we accept a subjectivist stance?' Further, what ideological notions are grounded in each theory; 'Ideas of conservativism or ones of fundamental change?' These deep understandings lead to contentful appreciations of systemic ideas.

If we apply paradigmatic analysis to discourses of systems thinking, we locate a major rupture in the traditional line with the development of an interpretevistic view. This discontinuity marks a first epistemological break in systems thinking, where the 'system' metaphor has been unleashed from a concrete realist world to become a structure for organizing our thoughts about social reality, or indeed the external natural world if that is our interest. This discourse brings with it the need for new terms and ways to articulate different concepts. There is a requirement for a substantive subjectivist oriented systems language to support the discourse.

These issues can be brought together within a study of histories and progressions of systems thinking. For example, we could ask 'How can we explain epistemological breaks in systems thinking?' and 'What about the validity of the various understandings that have been offered as explanations?'

2.4.4   On 'System': Histories and Progressions of Systems Thinking (Strand 3)

The idea of a history of knowledge is in itself contentious. In the argument of this book we identify four different approaches to the history and progress of systems thinking.

There are two which are of a positivistic nature. A linear sequential approach suggests that ideas develop in a cumulative fashion; while structuralism involves the use of scientific models that also give rise to systemic explanations in terms of cumulative progression, but through deep behavioral characteristics of a model.

Of an interpretivistic nature there is a world-view approach. The notion of normal science is introduced in a novel non-Popperian way. Stress associated with anomalies of a normal science leads to periods of extraordinary science. Knowledge is not cumulative here since the world-view is said to be changing in a nonincremental fashion.

Of a critical nature we can draw upon Genealogism. This is an explanation of discursive formations and statements, or concepts, articulated through the form of networks that cut across sentences and other discourse. These formations are understood as dynamic and are shaped by localized power relations which are reflected in social groupings. The use of critique in seeking out subjugation and liberating discourse is an important step forward that arises from this approach.

One feature of the survey of historical analyses of systems thinking discussed in Chapter 6 is striking. Only in exceptional cases has any notion of power been introduced into theoretical explanations. The lack of attention paid to the forces of power is a matter of some concern, particularly within the thesis of this book which accepts possibilities of subjugation and domination in promoting a liberating rationale. Foucault's critique can help us out.

A powerful critical approach to history of knowledge arises from conceptions of Foucault's Archaeology, Genealogy and critique. Foucault's critique offers an approach to oppositional thinking. It is an instrument for fighters and resistors to deny assumed truths and is of a liberating rationale. This is important in terms of emancipating knowledges from subjugating criticism based on untenable or impoverished epistemologies.

Adopting a Foucaulvian approach enables us to question commonplace contentions like, systems thinking is recognized as coming together 40 to 50 years ago. Instead we may argue that histories are a dialogue between past and present, between the events of the past and progressively emerging future ends. This is explained by localized forces. Thus the genealogy of the descent of systems thinking and the issues relating to emerging trends such as Critical Systems Thinking are part of one process with no clear origins or terminal points.

Applying Foucault's critique to systems thinking is enlightening. For example, we can challenge the reasoning behind the forces that have led to ruptures and discontinuities, such as the breakaway from the heroic age of analogy and General Systems Theory. Recognition of these breaks helps us to apprehend differing rationalities in systems 'problem solving'. But the debate between complementarity and contradiction arises, and we have to consider in detail legitimacies and limitations of theories and methodologies. This refers us to inquiry and 'problem solving'.

2.4.5   On 'Inquiry': Systems 'Problem Solving' (Strand 4)

Debates in systems thinking have been dominated for the past 15 years or so by the merits and worth of hard v. soft ideas. 'Is hard a subset of soft?'

'Is soft a subset of hard?' 'Are hard and soft distinct?' These debates are of a paradigmatic nature; hard relating to nonreflective positivistic and soft relating to nonreflective interpretivistic theories. Hard is typified by quantitative approaches that have raised much contention in social contexts. Soft places emphasis on a qualitative action-research approach seeking to generate mutual understanding in social contexts. The discourse of soft systems thinking has effectively led to the routing of hard systems thinking. Thankfully, these outdated isolationist and adversarial debates now face and need to be overcome by a higher-level complementarist argument.

The key observations for recognizing complementarism are methodological incommensurability and theoretical commensurability. Knowledge of the world is associated with fundamental human interests. The practical relevance of methodologies logically derived from these interests is assessed in terms of the possibilities of bringing about desired change in problematic situations. This contrasts with isolationism where theoretical incommensurability and methodological commensurability are assumed. Methodologies are taken as working from one theoretical world-viewpoint. Concepts from an inferior paradigm are accepted after being denatured by the tenets of the superior paradigm.

I will argue in some detail in Chapter 7 that complementarism leads to diversity and strength in systems 'problem solving', whereas isolationism leads to fragmentation and weakness.

Knowledge-constitutive interests in Habermas' critical theory reflects complementarism because of its open and conciliatory approach toward competing views. Similarly to complementarism, Habermas sets out to assimilate seemingly disparate approaches through Kantian, Hegelian, and Marxian poles in his thought. The emergence of this critical notion in the debate about 'Which systems methodology is appropriate when?' is an extremely important turn for systems practice.

2.4.6   Conclusion

Four strands of Liberating Systems Theory have been introduced in this section. They are discussed in detail in following chapters. We are now in a position to tie up this chapter by undertaking our third brief survey of Liberating Systems Theory, addressing the theoretical status.

2.5   SURVEY OF   LIBERATING SYSTEMS THEORY III

2.5.1   Introduction

The general and ideological status of Liberating Systems Theory were presented at the outset of this chapter. The tricky theoretical ideas have since been discussed within an overview of the four strands of Liberating

Systems Theory considered in this book. We will draw these together below and then stress the importance of recognizing the integrated nature of theory and ideology in social affairs.

2.5.2 Theoretical Status

The theoretical basis of Liberating Systems Theory incorporates the basic tenets of interpretivistic thinking. A social world that cannot be known as a concrete and tangible structure is assumed. Knowledge is subjective, but simply interpreting this world as if there are no forces of distortion would be naive. Critical reasoning is necessary to help overcome false consciousness, the consequence of forces at work on knowledges and our self-determination. With the critical view it is necessary to accept 'the positivist moment' to enable action to come about, and to learn to work with tensions of theoretical commensurability and methodological irrelativity. Openness and conciliation between theoretical paradigms is necessary, but methodologies can do no more than legitimately contribute in areas of specific context. Evidently, the ideological and theoretical status of Liberating Systems Theory demands that we work out a comprehensive liberating rationality. This needs to extend well beyond the narrowly bounded interest in 'problem solving' that a significant proportion of the systems community is currently stuck to.

2.5.3 Integrated Nature of Theory and Ideology

Systems approaches to 'problem solving' have traditionally been assumed neutral. With positivistic approaches, ideas are presented as a rational means for making correct and optimal decisions in an impartial way. Yet there can be no value-freedom since there is always an underlying attitude toward social 'problems'. For example, when discussing policy science (instrumental reasoning) in the political arena, Fay (1975, p.60), noted that such an approach accepts '...certain basic social arrangements as necessarily the way they are and, by making...proposals in terms of their continued existence... unwittingly act to support those very arrangements'.

This refers to an ideological bias, one of conservatism that supports forms of social order as they are found. Similar observations can be made about interpretivist thinkers whose tendency is to reconcile people to their social order. In fact, there is always conservative or radical bias, whether the researcher claims neutrality or not.

With positivistic, interpretivistic or any other theoretical approach, there is no escape from ideology. A most worrying aspect of systems practice based on these largely nonreflective theories, is the ideological dishonesty shown toward those captured in a problem situation. The ideological component of 'problem-solving' activities are wittingly or unwittingly hushed up. With a critical approach the ideology is necessarily and explicitly declared at the outset.

We will now consider some of these issues in relation to contemporary systems thinking.

2.6   CONTEMPORARY SYSTEMS THINKING: SOCIAL THEORY AND THE CHALLENGE OF PRACTICE

The debates in social theory briefly presented in this chapter are well rehearsed in journals and other literature. For instance, Fay's (1975) accessible work *Social Theory and Political Practice* more or less summarizes the theoretical debate that is currently prevalent in the domain of systems 'problem solving' more than a decade later. He discusses and critiques positivist and interpretive social sciences and supports the development of a critical social science—in our debates we overwrite 'social' with 'systems'.

While it is true that systems thinking is a theoretical late comer, it is equally true that systems 'problem solving' is traditionally a practice driven venture where social theory is not. Practice has long been accepted as the challenge for systems intervention, albeit traditionally in a pragmatic and heuristic, positivistic or interpretivistic fashion. Theory has largely been neglected. The misnamed Systems Theory or Control Theory is a construction and manipulation of mathematical notations that makes little reference to epistemological or ontological issues. This mathematical adoption gripped within an invisible positivistic epistemology, alongside the meta-concept 'system', has led to an excessive interest in meta-status studies that have nowhere to go in the social sciences. Such systemic representations are repetitiously reproduced in unexceptional diagrammatic or equation form. This work has virtually and rightly been ignored by the community of reason in the social sciences.

This combination of heuristic practice nonexplicitly associated with positivistic theoretical underpinnings was thankfully challenged with a well reasoned alternative titled Soft Systems Thinking. Jackson (1982) drew together the works of Ackoff, Churchman, and Checkland within one general soft system framework, a lasting contribution of critical and referential value. Checkland and colleagues have explicitly replaced the interest in traditional positivistic thinking through the adoption of phenomenological and hermeneutic, or more broadly, interpretivistic thinking. This practically based effort has led to the development of Soft Systems Methodology (SSM, Checkland, 1981), a landmark in the development of applied systems methods. In my view soft systems thinking saved the movement from a path to inevitable extinction. This is no mean achievement.

Interpretive thinking does, however, attract powerful criticism. Fay (1975) has discussed these criticisms in detail in the realm of nonsystems social sciences. We have found that they are at least partially substantiated in systems practice (see for example Flood and Gaisford, 1989). Unfortunately, Checkland has failed to *fully* respond to the relevance and implications of the criticisms of interpretivistic thinking in his work. He chooses to ignore, or has not recognized, the integral nature of theory and ideology in social practice. Presumably he maintains to have conceived a meta-methodology suited or adaptable to all social situational contexts, convertible to work in principle with any mode of social rationality. The work of Habermas comes nearest to having achieved this in a complementarist critical theory—but Habermas works in the spirit of complementarism whereas Checkland writes in the spirit of isolationism. Habermas has recognized that it is useful to think in terms of three knowledge-constitutive interests. He reckons that there are three different and revealing ways, or rationalities, of conceiving and understanding reality, rather than the partial totalizing interpretivistic view Checkland has subscribed to. There is little evidence of this aspect of Habermas' work in Checkland's writings, and Checkland needs to have worked out such ideas in his own domain before claiming too much 'in principle' (see Checkland, 1981, p. 283).

We could liken Checkland's appraisal of SSM to the view of some hypothetical inventor of a knife. The inventor might maintain that a knife is a neutral artifact usable constructively or destructively. The criticism leveled at the inventoir is that by admission (s)he has developed an artifact that could be used in devastating fashion (a methodology rather than an artifact with SSM). This stance of ideological neutrality is not acceptable and is outside the discourse of a critically oriented thinker, where the potential consequences are thought out *a priori* through heuristic interpretation of the theoretical and ideological underpinnings. The critical ideology relates to liberation and emancipation. A key feature of the critical approach is the nonneutral explicitly worked out relationship between ideology, theory, and practice; that not only should theories be seen as agents of fundamental change in social situations, but the method of testing the truth of such theories necessitates assessing that the theory is practically relevant to those changes (it would be, not could be). Checkland's neglect of ideology masks the issues of fundamental social change. SSM is dangerous in the hands of the powerful, the managers and other elites. Far better that this issue be cleared up with some deep theoretical studies, rather than arguing incorrectly that we need to undertake empirically based studies with a heuristic faith of confirming in principle intuition (as some of Checkland's disciples do).

One final related point. The notion that validation of practical efforts in social contexts is not achievable is a natural outcome of interpretive isolationist thinking. A reconceptualization of the term (partially achieved in Flood and Robinson, 1988; Robinson, 1990) suggests that validation should be possible by immanent means (also see Oliga, 1988). There is not a once-and-for-all concrete positivistic validation. Rather, validation is made by reference to the inherent assumptions of the adopted theory, or rationality. For example, with interpretivism validity implies a guarantee of participation. In this immanent way actions and outcomes are valid according to theoretical and ideological tenets.

The critical model attempts to integrate theory and practice consistently with an inherent underlying view of the nature of social reality. Critical theory is seen as an

> ...analysis of a social situation in terms of those features...which can be altered in order to eliminate certain frustrations which members...are experiencing, and [the critical] method of testing the 'truth' of a social scientific theory consists partially of asserting the theory's practical relevance in leading to the satisfaction of human needs and purposes. (Fay, 1975, that in brackets added).

Let us now summarize the main points of discussion emerging from this overview of Liberating Systems Theory.

2.7   CONCLUSION

The thesis of this book has been introduced in this chapter. I have shown that there are competing approaches in traditional social and systems thinking. It is not necessary for us to treat them that way. A more helpful procedure arises when we move away from the acceptance of fragmentation and weakness, to diversity and strength. I have introduced Habermas' knowledge-constitutive interests, each of the three understandable through differing, relevant and therefore legitimate rationalities. I have also introduced Foucault's critique, a means of identifing breaks in rationalities articulated by ruptures and discontinuities in discourse and maintained by micropolitical procedures. For this reason I have proposed undertaking critical analysis where localized forces lead to a dominant discourse. This should be undertaken in the spirit of a liberating rationale. These ideas have been discussed in four areas of Liberating Systems Theory: on 'system' – conceptual anti-reflexivity, abstract and paradigmatic conceptions and histories and progressions of systems thinking; and on 'inquiry' – systems 'problem solving'. In this chapter some propositions about systems thinking for liberation of knowledge and emancipation of those in need at work and in other social situations have been launched.

The core of the argument of this book, that makes Liberating Systems Theory an unusually powerful critical approach, is the meta-unity of Foucault's Interpretive Analytics and Habermas' knowledge-constitutive interests. The essence of this argument is acceptance of unities as critical, but rejection of universals as totalizing. This gives rise to tensions at the unity and meta-unity level. The next chapter works out how we can ride on these tensions and establish Liberating Systems Theory through sound reasoning.

NOTES

(1) The importance of tensions generated by the scholars of union are similar to those which arise when optimistic and pessimistic perceptions of the world rub against each other. If we are exclusively optimistic, if we are privileged enough, we might assume that the world offers aesthetic pleasures on a grand scale, as with the 'grace of the wildcats' for example. Or we may indulge in human fancifulness and tease our five senses. These are the seeds of decadence and a perception of a world where we would be deaf to the screams of the pessimists, who see only pain and suffering as beast (wildcat, say) devours beast (antelope, say) and who watch mankind in true animalistic clothing degrade and destroy all (Zola, 1962, constructed a similar view about human relationships in terms of Naturalism). In the first case there is naivity like the Structuralists' in the sense of a sham on meaning, in the last case there is despair as with the skeptics, where all is lost. Together there is a synergy of 'hope tempered by fear', of 'fear overcome by hope'. It is with such tensions that Liberating Systems Theory operates.

(2) Relevant to this debate is Burrell's (1988) caution that concepts like modernity are frequently defined in incompatible ways.

CHAPTER 3

INTERPRETIVE ANALYTICS AND KNOWLEDGE - CONSTITUTIVE INTERESTS: LIBERATE AND CRITIQUE

A theory of discourse with a liberating rationale and a theory of the relationship between logical methodological rules and knowledge-constitutive interests. On unities opposing universals. A meta-unity of Interpretive Analytics and knowledge-constitutive interests

3.1 INTRODUCTION

In the preceding chapter we underwent a first indulgence with the whole argument of this book. This comprised ascertaining the theoretical and ideological status of Liberating Systems Theory, identifying the intellectual grounding of this sociological paradigm and then surveying four strands of thinking. The remainder of this book consists of expanding upon the main issues arising from that presentation.

While further chapters systematically work through the four main strands of Liberating Systems Theory, we will be concerned now with working out the details of the intellectual groundings on which the four strands are based. We will consider how to achieve a form of meta-unity between Interpretive Analytics and knowledge-constitutive interests. This leads to new tensions, but if we can ride with these then we will achieve a new and valuable position. It is conceivable that with this meta-unity, we will have at our disposal chances to liberate knowledges that have been suppressed or dominated by positions that are epistemologically untenable or impoverished. With an adequate epistemology, developed from Habermas' knowledge-constitutive interests, we can then satisfactorily critique the rationalities teasing out legitimacies and limitations. Our overall achievement will be a methodological process that promotes a liberating critique of extant and dominated discourses of systems thinking, followed by a critical examination of the ideas and concepts of each one according to adequate epistemological principles. This chapter first details an interpretation of Habermas' knowledge-constitutive interests, then Foucault's Interpretive Analytics, and makes a case for an adequate and consistent meta-unity of the two.

3.2 KNOWLEDGE-CONSTITUTIVE INTERESTS

3.2.1 Introduction

Knowledge-constitutive interests in Habermas' critical theory reflects complementarism, because of its open and conciliatory approach toward competing views. Similarly to complementarism, Habermas sets out to assimilate seemingly disparate approaches through Kantian, Hegelian, and Marxian poles in his thought. In order that we may grasp a better understanding of Habermas' ideas, we will first of all undertake a study of relevant portions of his work before moving on to specifically consider knowledge-constitutive interests.[1,2]

There are two important contributions from Habermas of interest to us. First, that accounts of social practice may be thought of in terms of labor and interaction. The production and reproduction of human lives occurs through the transformation of nature with the aid of technical rules and procedures, and through communication of needs and interests in the context of rule-governed institutions. This is an extension of thinking from a 'linguistic turn' to include a 'social turn' (the latter was introduced into epistemology by Marx; Ulrich, 1983). Abstracting from either in isolation is distorted and mistaken. Dialogue is always dominated by social constraints and power relations. Social theory must therefore be critical, and must by definition be judged by possibilities of turning theory into practice. This point is argued by Fay (1975), who writes that not only should theories analyze a social situation in terms of what might be altered, but the method of testing the truths of this theory should also embrace an analysis of the theory's practical relevance in bringing about those changes. I would argue that this analysis should be extended to a methodological level where practical concern is with systems-based intervention.

The second contribution is Habermas' attempt to find a foundation for critical social theory, while accepting the Anti-foundationalist notion that there are no theory-neutral facts for inquiry. Habermas proposes that rationally motivated agreement among participants in argumentation is the only foundation. Although this ground is arguably unsettled, Habermas still rejects the extension of this uncertainty toward a skeptical abandoning of the search for justification and theoretical grounding, which can be sought after in ethical and cognitive stances (a modern skepticism Habermas says). These foundations can be established by analysis of perceptions of communication. Social theory, therefore, must be critical so that fundamental norms that guide theory may be reconstructed (communicative rationality, see Habermas, 1976, for example). Accepting this, Habermas has attempted to develop a foundation for a critical social theory by examining the presuppositions of communication which reveal a rational dimension within the conversation itself, and which can be reconstructed using Kant's transcendental mode of posing questions. A rational consensus is only achieved through free and equal discussions, within a framework of an ideal speech situation, which implies truth, freedom, and justice. This also assumes a process free of unnecessary domination in all its forms. In this Habermas offers the notion of legitimate authority, which poses a significant challenge to systems practice and practitioners (see Fairtlough, 1989).

Let us now look in detail at the idea of knowledge-constitutive interests. This is achieved through a partial reconstruction of Habermas' Appendix of *Knowledge and Human Interests* (1971a, p. 301–317).

3.2.2   Traditional and Critical Theories

In an attempt to build up a substantive critical theory based on Horkheimer's (1968) essay *Traditional and Critical Theories*, Habermas set up the following proposition to refute: '...the only knowledge that can truly orient action is knowledge that frees itself from 'mere' human interests and is based on ideas, which states that knowledge has taken a theoretical attitude.'

According to Horkheimer, theory in a traditional sense is like 'looking-on' where we abandon ourselves to the events. In philosophical language, we abandon ourselves to contemplation of the cosmos. Theory can, therefore, enter the conduct of life and molds life to its form. For instance we may assume: 'that is the way of nature', 'I am of nature' and through this position find that theory is reflected in the conduct of those who subject themselves to its discipline. If we contemplate the cosmos then our soul might be likened to motions of nature.

This is a conception that places life in theory, that inevitably leads to isolationist stances and, it has been argued, has defined philosophy since its beginnings. It should not be surprising, then, to find that any isolationist position is characterized by such strong intellectual forces, which are hard to escape from without fundamental reconceptualization.

Habermas made much use of contrasting Horkeimer's essay with Husserl's (1950) *The Crisis of European Sciences*, these appearing at about the same time. Husserl's crisis was degeneration of advanced disciplines from the status of true theory. This is a crisis of science where it has nothing to say to us, as if the information content of theories produces scientific culture. An alternative critical view is that scientific culture is produced by the formation among theorists of a thoughtful way and enlightened mode of life. This last position is the basis of knowledge-constitutive interests.

3.2.3   Traditional and Hermeneutic Positivism: Isolationism

Habermas made a further proposition for our consideration, that '...there is a real connection between the positivistic self-understanding of the sciences and traditional ontology'. With empirical-analytical sciences theories are developed in a self-understanding, through dogmatic association with the natural interests of life. This science has the cosmological intention of describing the Universe theoretically in its law like order, just as it is (which in contemporary times is reminiscent of Stephen Hawkins', 1988, drive for a universal theory of physics).

With historical-hermeneutic sciences the concern is with transitory things and mere opinion. Yet it shares the tradition of noncritical theory even though it has nothing to do with cosmology. Approaches to historical-hermeneutics comprise a scientistic consciousness based on the model of science, that is, we do not understand science as one form of possible knowledge, but rather must identify knowledge with science. In this sense we are dealing with an isolationist stance, one which introduces another form of positivism.

As much as the cultural sciences may comprehend facts through understanding and little though they may be concerned with discovering general laws, these sciences share with the empirical-analytical sciences a methodological consciousness of describing a structured reality within the horizon of the theoretical attitude. As Habermas said, historicism had become the positivism of the cultural and social sciences.

Positivism, it was argued, had permeated the self-understanding of social sciences: whether they obey the methodological demands of empirical-analytical science or orient themselves to the pattern of normative-analytical science.

In essence, this concept of value-freedom promotes psychologically an unconditional commitment to theory and epistemologically the severance of knowledge from interest. It prevents consciousness of the interlocking of knowledge with interests from the life-world.

There is much more to say about this issue of value-freedom and positions of positivism, interpretivism and critical theories. The development of an adequate epistemology toward the end of the book, in Chapter 7, deals with many of the emerging issues. The following reasoning for complementarism is a response to the isolationist forces highlighted above.

3.2.4   Knowledge-Constitutive Interests: Complementarism

Three categories, proposed by Habermas, comprise the relationship between logical methodological rules and knowledge-constitutive interests. Three fundamental knowledge-interests are seen as presuppositions for the possibility of a differentiated constitution of meaning of possible objects of experience. These are, in fact, nonreducible quasi-transcendental cognitive interests, to which we will now turn our attention.

A central idea of Habermas is that orientation toward technical control, mutual understanding in the conduct of life and emancipation, establish viewpoints from which we may apprehend reality in any way whatsoever.

Respectively, the cognitive interests are technical, practical, and critically self-reflective; which are exhibited in the paradigms of empirical-analytical, historical-hermeneutic, and emancipatory sciences. The first two represent the dichotomy between natural sciences v. humanities, that we are struggling to avoid. The third category is Habermas' creation.

To tie up this complementarist vision, Habermas (1971a) drew up five theses on the relationship between knowledge and interests. These are described below and the page numbers where they appear are given in brackets.

It was found that Kantian transcendentalism is not appropriate since the distinction between the transcendental analytic and dialectic cannot hold: it is not possible to show that *a priori* concepts are strictly universal. We therefore need quasi-transcendental forms that are relative to other concepts (Ulrich, 1983, p. 177). Quasi-transcendental conditions constitute a form of human interest based in the natural history of the species. This natural history submits standards that cannot be logically deduced, only critically assessed. This leads us to:

Thesis 1: The achievements of the (quasi-)transcendental subject have their base in the natural history of the human species (p. 312).

We may now consider the evolution of human interests through natural history and social 'systems'. Self-preservation is seen as a process with natural origins, but deeply embedded in the forms of work and intersubjective communication. This leads us to:

Thesis 2: Knowledge equally serves as an instrument and transcends mere self-preservation (p. 313).

Specific viewpoints can be related to a social media, through which each cognitive interest seeks to secure its existence. Cognitive interests that use information to expand technical control use the medium of work; interpretations allowing orientation of action with tradition acts through language; emancipating interests, relieving consciousness from hypostatical powers, mediates through power structures. This leads us to:

Thesis 3: Knowledge-constitutive interests take form in the medium of work, language, and power (p. 313).

Autonomy and responsibility are the only *a priori* possessions posited
from language, representing the only familiarization with nature. These
a priori factors are congruent with self-reflection. This leads us to:

> **Thesis 4:** In the power of self-reflection, knowledge and interest are
> one (p. 314).

There is strength in the unity of knowledge and interest. Evolution
toward autonomy and responsibility enhances the potential for rational

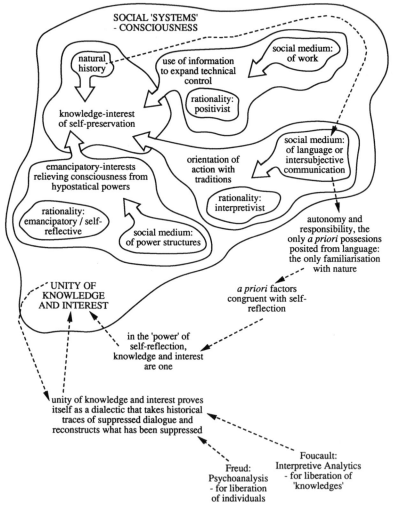

A general thesis for knowledge-constitutive interests: complementarism

Figure 3.1

consensus which needs to be established through a historical dialectic pronouncing distorted communication. This leads us to:

Thesis 5: Unity of knowledge and interest proves itself in a dialectic that takes the historical traces of suppressed dialogue and reconstructs what has been suppressed (p. 315).

These five theses are combined in the representation of Figure 3.1

3.2.5   Conclusion

We have seen that Habermas' notion of knowledge-constitutive interests is a sophisticated complementarist response to the powerful forces of isolationist thinking. Each of the three categories are encouraged, but systems methods based on them will have to be subject to critical reflection.   In the past, theories have been suppressed by untenable (nonreflective positivistic) and/or impoverished (nonreflective interpretivistic) discourse. While we have the basis for being critically reflective with Habermas' complementarism, we as yet have no worked-out means by which we can liberate knowledges from the type of domination referred to above. This is the task for the next section.

3.3   INTERPRETIVE ANALYTICS
3.3.1   Introduction

There are various views on how and why theories or knowledges come into focus or slip away from dominant positions. We are interested in these perceptions of the past, present, and future of systems thinking. Some have argued that the history of knowledge is characterized by a natural linear or holistic progression, while others forward the idea that world-views emerge according to scientific revolution when the strain of anomalies of old world-views can no longer be resisted. There is, in my opinion, a fourth and more realistic means of explanation relating to the constituting and suppression of discourse from which knowledges can be said to have a current, active and wide existence, or not. These four positions are discussed in Chapter 6. The last is characterized by the difficult and exhilarating works of Michel Foucault (labeled Interpretive Analytics by Dreyfus and Rabinow, 1982) which will be reviewed below, but after all deliberations I will only claim to have achieved one personal, biased interpretation of Foucaulvian analysis. In the end it might not be Foucaulvian. I will leave that for others to judge but it does not matter for my argument.

3.3.2   An Interpretation of Foucault's Genealogy

3.3.2.1 Introduction

Michel Foucault's notion of Genealogy considers descent, or origin, and emergence of concepts through what he termed an *Archaeology of Knowledge* (Foucault, 1974). This acts as a methodology to support genealogical principles that were developed later (e.g., Foucault, 1980). Emergence of knowledge in accidental manifestations is explained as a consequence of domination at local discursivity levels imposed by nondiscursive subjugators. Thus there are forces holding together discursive formations, which gives rise to a situation of conflict that leads to the rising of some and the subjugation of other knowledges, and thus to resistance and relations of power. Historical succession of discursive formations becomes a matter of contests and struggles over systems of rules (i.e., interpretations and networks).

The following is a portrayal of Foucault's Archaeology and Genealogy in the form of a metaphor (but also see Smart, 1983, 1985; Dreyfus and Rabinow, 1982; Burrell, 1988).

3.3.2.2 Living networks

If you can imagine in some enormity of space and time, a dynamic nexus of 'cables of knowledge' (they are not of epistemology but a part of an archaeology that may give rise to epistemological figures). These cables can be thought of as statements, where a statement is a function of existence that belongs to signs (indicative of quality or state) that cut across a domain of structures (sentences and so on) and reveal in them concrete contents in space and time (i.e., there is objectivity in this shared subjectivity).

If you can imagine, at any one time, that the connectedness of these cables represents a structure of thought (among many), or an episteme. With this episteme there are a set of relations that unite, at a particular temporal point, discursive practices that give rise to epistemological figures and to sciences: where episteme is not therefore a form of knowledge.

Then the connectedness of the cables is equivalent to a network, a network that amounts to a group of statements that belong to a discursive formation. Concepts facilitate analysis of the domain of statements.

Yet these discursive formations are dynamic networks. Terminal points between statements may break off (become uncoupled or cut off) and seek other connections or drift away (by neglect or forced isolation) from the discursive formations into a proximal void. New statements (cables) drift in or are forcefully connected, and become involved in the connectedness of the living network. The general system of the formation and transformation of the statements (cables) is then the archive, there is the possibility for a temporal record. Ruptures and discontinuities in the archive articulate discursive formations (the loss, repair, and reformation of cables).

In this sense, Foucault's Archaeology is a description of the archive that documents the conditions of existence. Genealogy on the other hand accepts a notion of power, extending the archaeological ideas into a discursive *plus* nondiscursive domain.

Genealogy considers descent, or origin, and emergence through the archaeological framework. Descent is considered as a plurality, or multiplicity, of accidental (i.e., not inevitable) connections of statements (cables). The temporal features of any episteme suggests local discursivities from descendant points. Emergence of knowledge arises because of domination at local discursivity and episteme levels. There are forces holding together discursive formations: a situation that leads to subjugation and thus to resistance and relations of power.

This is an anti-realist or nominalist position, because the existence of discourse independent objects is denied. Objects are discursive whose appearance and disappearance is dependent on discursive rules (Freundlieb, 1989).

Power (the forces) can be understood as strategies, manoeuvres, tactics, and techniques (not repression and domination as normally understood). Power circulates through living networks that are organized in a netlike fashion in which we are mostly caught.

Genealogy, then, is an analysis of the development of humanity, as a series of interpretations emerging from a relationship between power and knowledge in discursive and nondiscursive relations. It is the task of Genealogy to record this.

3.3.2.3   Conclusion

We have now developed an understanding of the term network and have introduced a theory of their dynamics. This will influence the findings of following chapters on the possibility for conceptual reflexivity in systemic thought, issues of abstract and paradigmatic conceptions of system, histories and progressions of systems thinking and indeed shapes the outlook of the book. We need to go a little further yet in qualifying these ideas and to develop a critique in the form of methodological principles.

3.3.3   An Interpretation of Foucault's Critique

Essentially, Foucault reckoned that power and knowledge are intricately linked, which inevitably leads to many suppressed knowledges. With the absence of alternative discourses, or merely having other dominated weak ones, there are limitations for articulating resistance to knowledge as captured by the dominant discourse. Foucault's critique is about strengthening the resistance.

Critique is an important part of Foucault's work. The aim is to provide the possibility for discursivities to be liberated, that are otherwise prevented from being 'seen or heard', known or even formed (e.g., in our time local discursivities have been pervaded by the methods and criteria of positivism and scientism).

Foucault's (1979, 1980) critique offers a number of methodological precautions or principles that promote resistance. We will address these a little later, but first it is necessary to develop an understanding of Foucault's notion of power (helped by Smart, 1983).

Power is rejected in the conceptual form of right, sovereignty, and obedience and as being like a commodity. The idea that power is descending and negative, as would be the sovereign case, is replaced by an idea of ascension and positiveness. Power is constructed and functions on the basis of particular micropowers and is productive in the way that it produces reality (i.e., domains of objects and rituals of thoughts). These are not autonomous or independent, being integral with a series of broad historical processes.

Emergence of knowledge is explained as a consequence of domination at local discursivity levels, imposed by nondiscursive subjugators. There are forces holding together discursive formations. A situation of conflict leads to the rising of some and the subjugation of other knowledges and thus to resistance and relations of power. Historical succession of discursive formations becomes a matter of contests and struggles over systems of rules, or interpretive discourse.

In order that critical analysis of power is correctly focused on domination and subjugation, rather than sovereignty, Foucault provided five mutually anticipating methodological precautions, or principles (see Smart, 1983, p. 82–84) and claimed neutrality in this reasoning. The principles are summarized as follows.

(1) Avoid an analysis of power in terms of sovereignty and obedience. Rather than focusing on regulated, legitimate, and centralized forms of power, be concerned with power at the extremities, with its regional and local forms, where it becomes less legal.

(2) Rather than concentrating on conscious intention in the analysis of power, look for the point of application, where it is in direct relationship with its object. So questions like 'Who has the power?' or 'What intentions or aims do power holders have?' would be replaced by interest in how things work at the level of ongoing subjugation, of

continuous and uninterrupted processes that subject our bodies, govern our gestures, dictate our behavior, etc. (Foucault, 1980). Attention should therefore be focused on the process by which subjects are constituted as effects of power rather than issues of motivated interest of particular groups, classes, or individuals in the exercise of domination, or on the constitution of an all-powerful state or sovereign.

(3) Power ought not to be conceptualized as being attributable to individuals or classes. It is not a commodity. Rather it is of a network which, as described above, can grow and pervade and become strong. Individuals do not possess power, rather they constitute its effects.

(4) Analysis of power should proceed up from a microlevel and seek to reveal how mechanisms of power have been colonized by more general or macro forms of domination. This requires an examination of how the techniques and procedures of power that operate routinely at the level of everyday life have been engaged by more general powers of economic interest. It is not the other way around. This is, in other words, an analysis of the individual mechanisms, histories, and trajectories of the micro-powers which then proceeds to a documentation of the manner and method of their colonization.

(5) The exercise of power is accompanied or paralleled by the production of apparatuses of knowledge.

The mechanisms that we will be concerned with relate to discursive formations, written, verbal, and nonverbal. Commonality of expression gives rise to domination, but only when this occurs in the mediums and forums which have an acceptance as constituted by discourse. New concepts may be articulated by changes in the discursive formations, but challenging ones are mainly, invisibly and silently denatured by integrating procedures when they are in force, and lost in isolation.

Setting up new, or revitalizing other, discourse requires a confidence and a risk. Confidence can be promoted through critique where a liberating rationale opens up new possibilities. The new mediums and forums are at risk, their viability will be in question, in doubt, and in dispute. The liberation of infant or dormant discourses which have the potential to constitute mediums and forums, leads naturally to external forces of resistance. Points of discontinuity articulate the history and succession of these battles. The success of forces of resistance relate to a colonization of the mechanisms. Discontinuities and recolonization are features of one process of resistance and counter-resistance.

At any one time there may be many local discursivities, but networks are understood as generalizations of these. Admittedly, there are many ways of generalizing, but it is the network that underwells the widest, whose currents and forces are the strongest, whose constitutive capabilities are the most secure and thus which is overall most resistant, which pose the greatest concern to critique.

In modern times we are dominated by empirical-analytical and structuralist sciences which relate to a network of discourse, an apparatus characterized by positivist assumptions. A reaction against an isolationist positivistically oriented approach to science, as we have discussed, came in the form of Critical Theory. Interpretive Analytics has something to say about the rise of this German Sociological position, in particular in relation to the colonization of the mechanisms of power that give rise to dominant discourse. For not only was there the emergence of the Institute for Social Research in Weimar, Germany (directed by Max Horkheimer from 1930), but more importantly there were the constitutional forces in the activity of critique. Connerton (1976, p. 16) noted that this activity became first directly and then indirectly political (to which we would attach Foucault's notion of power):

> In salons, clubs, lodges and coffee-houses a new moral authority, the public, found its earliest institutions. Critique became one of its slogans and an endless stream of books and essays included the words 'critique' or 'critical' in their title.

The colonization had begun. We can learn more by reflecting further on the dominant positivistic approach that Critical Theory so vehemently rejected.

The contemporary general dominant discourse is supported through a command over texts with language and concept articulation that assumes positivism and structuralism. This is evidenced in the propaganda of school teaching, which includes the coerced input of religion, the fact-based examination process as a punishment-reward system, the characterization, image building, and immortalization of the wise men of this scientific means of assumption, and acceptable and confirmatory jokery. This also involves the inaccessibility for the everyday person of jargonese, in the fights for discontinuity and the trivializing of these disputes in reports to laypeople who are subject to an installed rationality in mind and in their texts on the shelves. The mind is conditioned by the rationality, the body is understood through the rationality but more importantly is subject to a social world constituted by the knowledge. The social world is maintained by a written, verbal, and nonverbal discourse, an acceptable conversation in a native language. Like Habermas, Foucault was concerned about the shaping of our existence according to theoretical attitude.

There are several discourses underwelling the local domain of systems thinking, each of which traditionally clash and repel each other. They are formulations of statements which articulate isolationistic forcing concepts. Generalization of these local discourses form networks of resistance. One case analyzed in Chapter 6 is the positivistic (classical- and neo-positivist) and interpretivistic resistance to General Systems Theory.

3.3.4   Conclusion

We have now discussed Interpretive Analytics and knowledge-constitutive interests as separate and, we might be asked to suppose, adversarial theories. Now I wish to explore them at once to find a synthetic singularity, a meta-unity that proposes a set of theoretical and methodological principles which integrate the propositions of the remaining chapters.

3.4   LIBERATE AND CRITIQUE

Smart (1983), in his book *Foucault, Marxism and Critique*, notes that reflections on genealogical analysis show commitment to critical analysis by revealing subjugated knowledges that have either been lost or suppressed. Smart points out that Foucault identifies '...centralizing powers ... linked to the institution and functioning of organized scientific discourse' (Foucault, 1980, p. 84). Throughout his book, Smart wishes to realize a common denominator for Foucault's studies and declares that (p. 123) this factor is '...a critical concern with the questions of the relationship between forms of rationality and forms of power'. He compares this with the works of the Frankfurt School (as well as Weber) and in particular notes that '... it is the presence of a critique of instrumental rationality at the very foundation of critical theory which has prompted comparison with the work of Foucault' (p. 132).

A little later (p. 135), however, Smart argues a point made by Gordon (1979) that Foucault's conception of power-knowledge relations does not incorporate a relationship between knowledge and ideology. If taken as read then, there would be a fundamental irreconcilable difference between Foucault's work and that of the Frankfurt School and Habermas.

In the previous section we noted that the central notion to critical theory and consequently new critical systems 'problem solving', is the idea where theory and ideology are integrated. Smart (1983, p. 155) therefore goes on to point out that the concept of critique has at least two different meanings (similarly we might reflect on the many interpretations of Liberating Systems Theory, some of which are set out in this book). The first, based on this notion of theory-ideology, is that relating to Habermas' work. The second meaning considers Foucault's critique as oppositional thinking, an instrument for fighters and resisters to deny assumed-as-being commonplace truths— it is of a liberating rationality.

Instrumental scientific rationality as a starting point is a common opposition of these critiques. Science can be linked to control in the human condition, by extending the idea of power to control the natural world, to the power of science that gives rise to technology and social structures that control our working and social lives. It is the domination of instrumental reasoning, of scientific rationality, that has created the forces of subjugation over other forms of reasoning.

We therefore find that the wider use which the term critical theory is acquiring is captured under the umbrella title Liberating Systems Theory,[3] at least insofar as the two meanings knowledge-constitutive interests and Interpretive Analytics are outlined above (a similar suggestion was made by Fay, 1975, p. 93).

In this sense, then, there must be a more proper way of relating knowledge-constitutive interests and Interpretive Analytics. Foucault's critique can release subjugated ideas of discourse. We will see later that releasing all systems-based knowledge and methodological principles breaks away from ideas of fragmentation, weakness, and even conflict. Diversity is seen as a strength. Interpretive Analytics can release rationalities, thus helping to grow diversity. Habermas' critical theory accepts openness and conciliation and welcomes this diversity. Knowledge-constitutive interests then deals critically with the tensions between rationalities.

On the one hand, with Foucault, we acknowledge and attempt to deal with forces of isolationism through a liberating rationale; on the other hand, with Habermas, we work against those forces by seeking epistemological and methodological legitimacies and limitations in order to deal with the complexities that ultimately must have given rise to such diversity.

There is, however, a fundamental difficulty that we need to consider, that relates to contradictions between the works of Foucault and Habermas. We cannot simply add one unity to the other to achieve a cumulative meta-unity that underpins Liberating Systems Theory. We must be cautioned by Habermas' (1985) powerful criticism of Foucault's notion of the history of knowledge (supported in the writings of Honneth, 1985 and Fraser, 1981). This debate has been usefully dealt with by Freundlieb (1989), which will be drawn upon in our search to discover how the difficulties might be adequately resolved.

Let us recount certain details of Foucault's argument. Archaeology was conceived as an analysis of the history of discursive formations, explained as the anonymous systems of rules which allegedly form the conceptual and institutional conditions for the possibility of scientific statements. These rules act as historical *a prioris* that determine what can be thought and stated within a discourse, what objects can be theorized and what will be accepted as true or valid.

The response of Habermas (and Honneth) was to ask how it might be possible to reconstruct in an historical analysis what those historical *a prioris* are, from within a present neutral discourse, which *by definition* must have its own rules of the constitution of objects and of inclusion and exclusion.

This criticism is supported by the natural development of the thesis of this book. Rules necessarily have been defined in the argument for an adequate epistemology for systems practice (presented in Chapter 7). With this, statements of discourse may be said to be true within the rules of a discursive formation, but cannot themselves be given a true or false, valid or invalid, rational or irrational status from an external or objective point. While this is the case, our position as per the rules of the adequate epistemology is to insure that rationality and irrationality of knowledges are critically assessed, although this is not a search for ultimate truth or falseness, validity or invalidity. So, I do not claim to have achieved the nonideological approach that Foucault seems to declare that he has achieved with Interpretive Analytics.

Genealogy was a move away from the Archaeological project and involved an abandoning of the idea of autonomy of discursive formations. This new effort attempted to account for the emergence and disappearance of discourse by an analysis of contingent and external historical circumstances which bring about an interaction of, or a contact between, discursive practices. Discourse now incorporates the idea of apparatuses, these being conceived of as discursive as well as nondiscursive practices, but like the discursive formations the apparatus is assumed to play an objective-constitutive role.

On this issue Habermas criticized Foucault's concept of power since it played a dual and irreconcilable role in his work: power is constitutive, a transcendental condition for the possibility of truth and knowledge; which is contradicted by power as a purely descriptive term in historical analyses.

Reflecting upon our own interpretation of Genealogy, it is the former role that has surfaced as important, which again succumbs to the wish to liberate and critique. This does not, however, overcome the contradiction between Habermas and Foucault on the fundamental conception of power. Broadly speaking, power might be considered to be that which allows a subject to affect objects in successful actions. In Habermas' terms this is dependant on the truth of the judgment that informs the actions. For Foucault it is the other way around since he makes truth dependent on power, which then allows for an uncoupling of power from competences and intentions of individual agents.

This is an extremely difficult contradiction to overcome. Our goal is to end up with an adequate epistemology that is constructed from the complementarist ideas of Foucault's Interpretive Analytics and Habermas' knowledge-constitutive interests. This can, however, be achieved via the notion that truth is dependent on power and that there is a need to liberate discourse. We then employ Habermas' ideal by looking for the truth of judgement according to our interests, explicit ideology and critical analysis. In this process, however, we drop the idea that truth comes about from the force of the better argument. Ideology, for example, can never be said to be absolutely right, although many may find a particular position desirable.

Finally, Habermas has argued that Genealogy is crypto-normative, it cannot say on what grounds its critical rhetoric should be accepted. Decisions have to be made on the basis of certain cognitive and moral values and norms. The choice, then, that has to be made is between a crypto-normativism that refuses to discuss its assumptions and an approach which opens those norms up for critical discussion and assessment.

In respect to this, it should by now be clear that Liberating Systems Theory has an inherent position of openness. Statements have been made about the rules for discourse analysis, they have been stated as emancipatory and they come from an epistemology that declares certain others to be untenable or impoverished. What is important, however, is that this whole effort is indeed up for critical discussion and assessment. As Connerton (1976, p. 22) points out, the only unchanging basic thesis of critical thinking is that it is itself changeable.

3.5   CONCLUSION

The aim of this chapter has been to work out the intellectual groundings on which the four main strands of the argument of this book are based. In particular, we wanted to achieve a form of meta-unity between Interpretive Analytics and knowledge-constitutive interests that would offer a way forward in terms of liberating and offering a critique for discourse. In other words, Liberating 'Systems Theory'. That achieved, it would be appropriate and meaningful to consider issues of 'Liberating Systems' Theory, the use of systems ideas for liberation of the human condition.

Such a meta-unity, or synthetic plurality, is not easily achieved. After presenting the main ideas of each approach, a number of points of contradiction were identified, but each of these were then shown to have been adequately dealt with in the main thesis of this work. This has required concessions to be made from the critical positions of Foucault and Habermas. It does not mean, let us be reminded, that a universal position has been realized. Rather, the argument is that a meta-unity of critical thinking has been formed that is itself open to critique. We do, however, have a set of well-reasoned ideas that intellectually support the two general and four specific conceptions of Liberating Systems Theory which follow.

NOTES

(1) Necessarily in a short book such as this, Habermas' basic position is accepted in a somewhat unsupported way. Support is partially covered elsewhere, for example with Ulrich (1983) and Jackson (1985a, 1987a, 1987b), who explain why Habermas is highly relevant to systems theory. For a contrasting view see Luhman (1970, 1973).

(2) A comprehensive study on meta-science can be found in Radnitzky (1970). From page 59, Radnitzky undertakes a thorough and informative study of complementarism, that precedes Habermas' knowledge-constitutive interests. There is no room in this focused thesis to recount such an analysis, however, a brief insight into Apel's (1965) argument is important.

Radnitzky (1970), in preparing us for Apel's key arguments on complementarity of the hermeneutic and naturalistic approaches, underlined the difficulty of moving between traditions. 'There is no lazy way, nor short-cut to overcome the ethnocentricity of scientific subcultures expressed and reinforced by the special sublanguages'. (Radnitzky, 1970, p. 59). An understanding depends on ideas of dialectic mediation, complementarity and polarity.

Dialectics plays a role in the development of totalities and their parts. Bohr's complementarity thesis is the classical model which inaugurated the application of the dialectic method. Complementarity does not imply presupposition between theories of each other. Different viewpoints make us see different aspects of a theory. No single theory can help us catch all aspects of a section of reality, the idea of a complete description is elliptic. Aspects of each theory may complement each other and together give an ever fuller picture. Bohr, for example, argued that the wave and particle theory aspect of elementary particle phenomena complement each other in this way.

Radnitzky continues, that the impression of polarity of two theories or of their base explanatory models, typically is due to the totalization of either, that is the claim for each model that it has a universal application within the sector of reality concerned. Tension between knowledge-systems or theories in polarity is a crisis, it is not merely a dialectical tension such as thesis-antithesis, but a logical contradiction.

Apel's complementarity thesis is directed against totalization, considering knowledge-systems as complementary, and that we can use them to round and fill our picture of man. Apel states that natural science and human science — in the science of man — and quasi-naturalistic and hermeneutic approaches — in human science — are mediating each other, so that in each the developments of knowledge proceed in a continuous tacking between the two approaches or levels. This is a move toward detotalization.

While Apel provides an appealing notion of complementarity, it is Habermas' knowledge-constitutive interests that turns the argument toward a sound epistemological position.

(3) The discussion about a range of meanings has also been addressed by Connerton (1976, p. 16–22). In his introduction to the collected works *Critical Sociology* he noted that the Frankfurt School of Sociologists had broadly shown an allegiance to Enlightenment. Within this can be found a commitment to critique, an oppositional thinking, an activity of unveiling or debunking, as Connerton points out particularly for the works of Horkheimer and Habermas. It was further stressed, however, that the Frankfurt School are equally indebted to two new senses of critique in which the heritage of Enlightenment has assimilated and reformulated.

Reconstruction is one, where critique denotes reflection on the conditions for possible knowledge, and the potential abilities of human beings possessing the faculties of knowing, speaking and acting. This, Connerton argued, has its roots in Kant's *Critique of Pure Reason*.

Criticism is the second, where critique denotes reflection on a system of constraints which are humanly produced, being distorted pressures to which individuals, or a group of individuals, or indeed the human race as a whole, succumb to their process of self-reformation. This holds the idea of liberation from coercive illusions such as Hegel's notion of the experience of the slave overcoming resistance and the Master-Slave relation understood in terms of their connection with material things.

Connerton's thinking behind distinguishing the two commitments to critique is summarized and put together in Table 3.1. He also surfaced the idea that the scholars of the Frankfurt School have not made this distinction sufficiently clear. The argument of this book purposely

Table 3.1
Reconstruction contrasted with Criticism

RECONSTRUCTION	CRITICISM
Reflection on the conditions of possible knowledge.	Analysis of constraints of which classes of individuals are subject.
Understanding of anonymous systems of rules that can be followed by a competent subject.	Criticism is brought to bear on something, not anonymous but particular, such as the shaping of an individual's or a group's identity. In this way there is explicit reference to a subject.
Based on data considered to be objective and relating to conscious operations of the human actor (i.e., sentences, actions, cognitive insights).	Criticism is brought to bear on objects of experience. It seeks to remove degrees of deformity that masquarade as reality and thereby to make possible the liberation of what has been distorted. There is a conception of emancipation.
Considers what is correct knowledge (e.g., what is necessary to operate the rules previously suggested in a competent manner).	Aims to change or remove the conditions of what is considered to be a false or distorted consciousness.
Reconstruction, by explaining the rules that we follow implicitly, may lead to broadening of the range and a greater sophistication in the prossession of our theoretical knowledge.	Criticism renders transparent what had previously been hidden and in doing so it initiates a process of self-reflection, in individuals or groups, designed to achieve a liberation from the dominant or past constraints.

makes such a distinction. With respect to Liberating Systems Theory, the ideas of Criticism have been used to enrich the basic notions of Reconstruction in order to add a clearer liberating rationale. Furthermore, it has also been necessary to bring the two commitments together in terms of products of scholars of union, neither Foundationalist nor Anti-Foundationalist. This is particularly helpful because Reconstruction as Connerton has defined it (see Table 3.1) is hyper-rational. In fact, what has been carried out in the structuring of the argument herein, is a ready acceptance of Criticism more or less as Connerton proposes the position, alongside a rethinking about the second commitment (because of the hyper-rationalism) with Foucault's ideas.

Now, of course, this meta-unity must differ from that of any other meta-unity such as the one proposed by Connerton on behalf of the

Frankfurt School. It invites new tensions to be set up and requires that new resolutions are proposed. We will shortly be facing a number of these in the bringing together of Interpretive Analytics and knowledge-constitutive interests.

SECTION 2 OF ARGUMENT

- SPECIFIC -

LIBERATING 'SYSTEMS THEORY' (L'ST')

A critique of knowledges: articulation and release: against universals

CHAPTER 4

ON 'SYSTEM': CONCEPTUAL ANTI-REFLEXIVITY (STRAND 1)

The idea of a great natural systemic unification of knowledge rejected

4.1   INTRODUCTION

A unique feature of holism is the possibility of and tendency toward describing everything in systems terms. This can be explained by its early development within the forced confines of a nonreflective positivistically oriented General Systems Theory. We can choose to consider any situation as a system and know that, of course, it is also a sub- and supra-system ....'Is it not?' That is unless the Universe is the system in focus, which is naturally heralded as the ultimate supra-system. Apparently there is no need to look beyond the horizon of this closed set of concepts....'Can this be so?'

This issue is explored below in two fashions. First, through a discursive investigation based in the broad area of understanding meaning. This draws out two general lessons supporting a move toward conceptual anti-reflexivity. Second, two further aspects relating to the need for conceptual anti-reflexivity are then considered analytically. These are captured in the essence of the two general lessons. The necessary conditions for conceptual reflexivity to hold are also uncovered and refuted.[1] In carrying this out the importance of understanding abstract and paradigmatic conceptions of 'system' are uncovered.

4.2   DISCURSIVE EVIDENCE

It was not until I worked on a book review of the *Systems and Control Encyclopaedia*, edited by M. G. Singh (1987), that I recognized the dangers of conceptual reflexivity.[2] The volumes contain articles on systems thinking and related concepts of control. Some articles are two or three lines long, others spread over as many pages or more. They are presented alphabetically and are cross-referenced. Although there are approximately 20,000 entries, a relatively small portion of these form a set of systemic concepts, the remainder being essentially systematic and technical terms. My starting point was to 'play around' with an earlier review on the same volumes authored by a colleague of mine, M. S. Leaning. My aim was to get a handle on some issues that were troubling me. In his review Leaning (1987) wrote that:

> ...in a real sense...[there] is a contradiction in terms. An encyclopaedia divides a department of knowledge into its elements, whereas 'systems

and control' aims to unify or fuse knowledge into a whole....The
references at the end of each article link the reader to related items....In
this way the encyclopaedia is efficient to use and retains a systemic
structure...

Let us reprove the reviewer for a number of contradictory statements
(i.e., deconstruct the review).[3]

Leaning suggests that in contradiction to reductionism ('dividing a
department of knowledge into its elements') are unification and the fusing of
knowledge. In a dictionary sense unifying is reduction to unity or uniformity,
which in itself is dividing knowledge into unities or, perhaps, one ultimate
universal (i.e., an absolute, which might relate to some early aspirations of
a General Systems Theory) from many possibilities (a variety reduction in
terms of potentiality). This is self-contradictory and perhaps even
paradoxical (i.e., 'systems and control' is assumed to be both holistic and
reductionistic at once).   Furthermore, and using a dictionary based
metaphorical extension, the notion of fusing knowledge into a whole is
inconsistent since 'the melting together' of knowledge elements (and if left
to cool and harden as required by a fusing procedure) will result in a closed
(in this frozen state) and rather unappealing notion of what Leaning also
claims (at least in Singh's case) is systemic in structure and thus should be
open.

This may be so, but let us invert and test the criticism by asking a
number of fundamental questions on my own analysis of the review in
question. Let us be skeptical.

'How can I be confident about my interpretation?' 'Did I not use my own
metaphorical extension?' 'Have I fairly represented Leaning's subjectively
intended meaning (a hermeneutic concept)?' 'How can I be sure that the
contradictions identified are logically correct from Leaning's argument and
are not a complete misrepresentation of his intentions?' 'Systemic in
structure automatically implies openness to me, but should it necessarily to
Leaning?' 'What other deconstructive themes might there be and on what
grounds should I select a representative one?'   For example, the
deconstruction outlined above merely casts back a reductionistic and closed-
system interpretation to Leaning's writing.

Such deconstructive observations lead me to conclude in this instance
of skepticism, that without additional intellectual means I cannot state my
case categorically. This is a crucial point because we are concerned with the
idea of understanding meaning in general, particularly the concepts of
'systems and control' with respect to the encyclopaedia, and specifically in
the context of this chapter, systemic concepts as such.

Yet Singh's unresolved difficulty and our dilemma as the systems community is that in eight volumes he has only presented an ABC... 'single-author single-concept' type approach to understanding sometimes sophisticated 'systems and control' concepts. At least in some cases these undoubtedly have various subjectively intended meanings in their historical use: which are inextricably linked to the use, the users and the context. There are two lessons to be drawn from this.

Lesson 1: The study of (systems) concepts requires an historical and developmental investigation that attempts to deal with the subjectively intended meaning of authors.

The difficulties outlined above might not be so acute for much of Singh's work (as hinted) since the theoretical basis of 'systems and control' is largely mathematical and deals with concepts that are legitimately used as carefully defined technical terms with precise meanings (in the manner discussed by Checkland, 1988a). For instance, the 'angle of attack' (p. 290) is defined as: '...the angle between the direction of the wind at infinity and a reference chord of the wing, at a specified distance from the fuselage' and 'program compilers' (p. 3892), we are reliably told, '...translate a source program, which is in a high-level language such as FORTRAN or PL/1, into an object or target program, which is in a low-level language such as an assembly language.'

These are pristine in their clarity. This is not however an exclusive let-off for Singh since, as Leaning points out, the more difficult terminology of Checkland's (1981) Soft Systems Methodology and social systems thinking are not dealt with.[4] This is despite Singh mentioning, for example, social systems, management systems and social effects of automation in his introduction. These are references to the murky back-street alleys where the difficult shop-soiled words and concepts that Checkland (1988a) refers to and where paradigmatic influences lurk. Respectively, those concepts dirtied in everyday use and those with multi-meanings, that we will attempt to unravel through the frameworks of this book.

A lesson from Lesson 1, then, is that we need to look beyond the ideas of traditional systems science in order to promote an understanding of them in social contexts. This is a point that Leaning among many others apparently does not see the importance of. He is relieved to find an efficient systemic structure to the encyclopaedia (mind, even given the open view of this chapter, it can only be understood as systemic in a primitive sense). There is, however, a glaring danger in the presumption that we can analyze and base our understanding of systems science through systems science. This is insular, hardly testing and suggests that the systems discipline has developed a set of self-contained concepts that, paradoxically for contemporary holists, must be conceived of as the sort of closed system referred to above. Systems scientists need to seek recourse from other areas of intellect.

What is particularly troubling is that the so-called systems community[5] is sufficiently large to support annual conferences and a number of mainly systemic-theoretic journals, at and in which systems concepts are worked over endlessly and kneaded into further meta-status offerings. These merely pose essentialistic questions while neglecting or hiding the normative component. Such efforts nowadays only occasionally result in some minor abstract or analogical development. These are then applied in another disciplinary area without considering the wealth of research in that particular field. This is equivalent to the transfer of an analogy with very little analogical and no paradigmatic reasoning.

Such arrogance warrants and receives little attention. 'Is it not self-preserving, self-interested, self-indulgent and ultimately self-defeating?' The systems community 'will' (or should it be 'has') isolate(d) itself by continuing in this fashion.

A number of others have expressed a similar concern. Notably, Ulrich (1983, p. 139) politely pointed out that:

> ...for a research programme under the title of 'systems practice'- we should develop a conceptual framework that would:
> (a) assign an adequate place and yield proper standards of improvement from all kinds of systems methodologies...;
> (b) help us to deal critically with the theories of social reality and corresponding concepts of rational social action, implied by each type of systems methodology; and
> (c) finally, embed the application of these tools within well defined institutional and procedural arrangements for rational debate amongst the various parties involved in and affected by a decision.

Ulrich then immediately went on to state that (and here the emphasis is mine) 'Such a programme of research will *require the systems movement to expand considerably its universe of discourse'.*

In order to open up systems to traditions of thought that promise to offer methodological support for the task of mediating between systems concepts and the life-practical concerns of the 'enemies' (i.e., life-worlds of politics, morality, religion and aesthetics), Ulrich proposed that we seek recourse from practical philosophy.[6] In this he suggests that the 'enemies' are evidently beyond the capacity of the explanatory power of any closed set of systemic concepts.[7]

On the account of philosophy as such, I could be directed to Laszlo's (1972) volume as so-called systems philosophy. Yet I rest my case on the evidence offered in the message of a rave-review on its jacket (at least on the edition that I consulted), where J. E. Smith says that the book is '...a much needed antidote to the excessive interest of contemporary philosophers in the analysis of language.'

More fool the reviewer. We cannot afford to immunize ourselves against such revealing thinking, as witnessed earlier in this chapter and played on there by setting up a tension by mixing the debate between critical and deconstructionist theories. That is not to say the 'linguistic turn' is all. In critical theory we have already noted the work of the Frankfurt School of Sociology and Habermas who also include a 'social turn'. This, then, brings us to the second lesson mentioned earlier.

Lesson 2: Systems thinking has a 'natural' tendency to be conceptually reflexive (or 'autopoietic') and would benefit by looking beyond its own horizons.

This discursive argument has cast doubt on the possibility for conceptual reflexivity in systems thinking from many angles. The following section seeks to make further refutation while also introducing a number of important concepts that will take us forward to Chapter 5 and beyond.

4.3   'ANALYTICAL' EVIDENCE

There are two aspects of the conceptual anti-reflexivity issue, captured in the essence of the two general lessons above, that I think need to be drawn out. The first is that systemic concepts developed from Bertalanffy's era are of the abstract (i.e., they are transportable meta-analogies). The second is, that what we choose to do with these abstract notions is of paradigmatic concern and not primarily a matter of systems theory (the conceptually reflexive notion). In recognizing this we have to acknowledge two ways of defining systemic concepts: abstract and paradigmatic conceptions.[8, 9, 10]

Abstract conceptions deal with the core ideas of systems thinking and, although their development has undoubtedly been world referential (analogical), they can be developed in thought rather than practice. For example, the open system metaphor is an abstract conception. Fundamental understanding at this level can and does change. This is shown to be the case in the next chapter, where a first systems struggle is shown to be of this nature. Briefly, an example is the shift in meaning from understanding in abstract 'system' as an aggregate with cumulative properties, to one where it is understood as a whole with synergistic properties.

Paradigmatic conceptions are specifically world-referential, or at least have a position in this respect depending on the paradigmatic outlook, and are therefore inextricably linked to views on what is, how we can represent and disseminate knowledge of what is, how we might go about investigating, representing, and intervening in situations, and what value-based ideas ought to be introduced into an inquiry.

Given this background, we are now in a position to consider analytical refutation of the notion of an acceptable conceptual reflexivity in systems thinking.

There might be three possibilities for reflexivity to hold given the following sets of conditions (assuming constancy in current abstract conceptions and implicitly accepting that language is related to theory):

(a) that concepts must be clearly and singularly definable and articulated through a single cluster (or network) of compatible, consistent, and coherent statements, or if not then

(b) the plurality of meanings of many concepts must be clearly separated and articulated through clusters (or networks) of compatible, consistent and coherent statements

and if (a) then

(c) (i) nothing 'in reality' must be uncovered that is beyond the feasible explanatory power of the single freeze-frame network (as organized at a point in time),

but if (b) then

(ii) nothing 'in reality' must be uncovered that is beyond the capacity of the feasible explanatory power of the favored (or according to Interpretive Analytics the dominant) freeze-frame network (as organized at a point in time),

or if (b) then

(d) nothing 'in reality' must be uncovered that is beyond the feasible explanatory power of the clusters in combination (dominant and dominated).

Now, put in other terms we can deduce three possibilities:

(a*) if (a) and (c)(i) then there is the possibility for a singular final form for General Systems Theory, or (b*) if (b) and (c)(ii) then there are competing paradigms of which one is found to be superior or dominant, or

(c*) if (b) and (d) then there is the possibility for paradigm commensurability.

In fact, since analogical (i.e., abstract) conceptions are assumed constant, then if (b) rather than (a) is satisfied we must have identified some form of paradigmatic reconceptualization. I have suggested in the previous section that there are some difficult terms lurking about and such a reconceptualization refers explicitly to this difficulty. Further to this I shall show comprehensively in the next chapter that (a) cannot hold. Multi-theoretical standpoints can be uncovered. Fundamental notions of interpretation and criticism therefore help us to recognize contrasting tenets to those of positivism. Positivism does not question its own theoretical construction and so it is only with the blindness of this convergent yet dominant view that conceptual reflexivity could be given any credence. Only from this position is the idea of a concrete world of systems assumed to be provable by taking the study of holonomics to its supposed final conclusion, uncovering through scientific study all the laws of social reality. In other words I am saying that (a*) in traditional clothes is misconceived. As soon as this reflexive construction is challenged and the blindfold is removed, then brand-new theoretical and ideological issues surface. Systems concepts are seen to be tied up with value constructions of politics, religion, morality, and aesthetics, and are shown 'for what they are': abstract organizing structures through which we can conceive of a world around us and which can help us to critically organize our thoughts on matters of action in the world of natural and social dynamics.

Up to this point we have still not refuted possibilities (b*) or (c*); however, later on in Chapter 5 I shall show quite comprehensively that (b*) is not acceptable, leaving only (c*), which in itself is too archaeological and absolute and needs to be dealt with under the critical eye of an adequate epistemology for systems practice (but is at least moving in the right direction).

4.4   CONCLUSION

In this chapter evidence against the possibility and desirability of conceptual reflexivity in systems thinking has been presented. This has to a large extent tackled the need to respect the idea of subjectively intended meaning and to refute the impoverished notion that systems thinking has developed a set of self-contained and adequate concepts which are transportable across disciplines. One task emerging out of this study is the need to clarify, 'What in more detail is this idea of an abstract conception?'

and 'Exactly what is meant by systems analogy or systems metaphor?' We must also explore the idea of paradigmatic conceptions by asking: 'In what ways do contrasting theoretical viewpoints influence our use of systems concepts?' These are tasks for the next chapter.

NOTES

(1)   This debate is clearly related to issues of epistemology and ontology, but such issues are deferred for explicit discussion until the next chapter. Here we are interested in pursuing a discursive and mixed look at the anti-reflexivity issue.

(2)   The book review was published in *Systems Practice* (Flood, 1988a) and forms the basis of much of the first part of this chapter.

(3)   Deconstruction is used in the spirit of the idea put forward by Derrida (e.g., 1972, 1980, 1981), although I have made no attempt to be methodologically consistent with his thinking in this short exercise.

(4)   Measurement and control in social contexts are of concern to our community, but the application of such ideas needs careful rethinking. I would point the interested reader to an early text on Management Science, where Beer (1967) sets out some fundamental ideas in terms of measurement and control, although it is done in a positivistic way.

(5)   I say 'so-called' since the community considers itself to be fragmented.

(6)   In my view Ulrich can hardly be faulted on these points (as long as the complementarist position is not neglected). I believe that the contents of this book are fundamental to such endeavors. For instance, in (b) above Ulrich calls for us to deal critically with the theories of social reality implied by each type of systems methodology.

(7)   Ulrich's position on systems thinking is constructed from the philosophy of Immanuel Kant which, Ulrich (1983) believes, were lost in the emergence of General Systems Theory and have been regained only partially through the work of C. West Churchman (e.g., 1968a, 1968b, 1971, 1977, 1979, 1981). We will confront Ulrich's position head-on in the next chapter, when the idea of a 'third systems struggle' (a 'second' epistemological break) is put into the context of these historical dynamics.

(8)   We will see the relevance of distinguishing between 'abstract' and 'paradigmatic' definitions in the next chapter, where paradigmatic

interplay between the concepts 'system' and 'complexity' is the dialectical focus.

(9)   It is evident that Maturana and Varella have found it necessary to draw up a similar distinction in order to explain their theory of autopoiesis (discussed in the next chapter where full references are given). Mingers (1989) expresses this distinction well in his excellent introduction to their largely difficult to access writings. Accordingly, an important distinction is made between the structure and organization of a unity. Very broadly and respectively, the distinction is between the reality of an actual example and the abstract generality lying behind all such examples. Mingers also pointed out Giddens (1976) similar distinction between system (the observable interactions between actors) and structure (the unobservable set of rules and resources). These have some similarities to the notion of paradigmatic and abstract conceptions, respectively in both examples. I have drawn attention to these expressions of comparison in order to encourage:

(a)   recognition of the general need to use distinctions in systemic thought [also see Note (10)], but

(b)   to help the reader appreciate the similitude by the differences, that is the differences between my own needs and meaning and those in other developments in systemic thought.

(10)   Which also brings me to the point that the abstractions of nonreflective positivistic General Systems Theory have similarities with ideas of 'particulars' and 'universals'. Let us take, for example, Plato's notions. Universals are his highest grade of knowledge, being immaterial and completely independent entities that exist in an immaterial world of universals. This world and the universals of which it is comprised, are the ultimate and objective reality. Plato's view is a realist one concerning the nature of universals. With this view particulars can be known in the world of sight . Particular mountains and particular horses exist in virtue of their resemblance to the universal mountain and universal horse. That is, there is a permanence in the universal horse that has attributes which are essential to the nature of all horses and there is change in the particular horse that has ever-dynamic attributes. In Plato's view sense perception is not a basis for knowledge, but we can aspire to knowledge asymptotically toward the universals through similarities and patterns that build up via sensations.

A nominalist view of universals endorses them simply as a name for a group of particulars that it subsumes. They are catalogues or lists with subsidiary lists corresponding to subsidiary universals.

An empiricist philosopher's view leads to an understanding of universals as abstract ideas that approximate our modern notion of concept (for further discussions on universals and particulars see Trusted, 1981).

This does raise the important issue about how we accept holonomic ideas into our thinking . General Systems Theory suggests real immaterial universals, that once discovered by empirical, inductive, and deductive means, offer us the highest grade of knowledge. We might ask, 'Are universals merely cataloguing devices?', 'Or are they abstract ideas or organizing concepts?'

We have now dealt with universals and particulars, and have seen how General Systems Theory compares with other centuries old ideas on epistemology.

CHAPTER 5

ON 'SYSTEM': ABSTRACT AND PARADIGMATIC CONCEPTIONS (STRAND 2)

Systems concepts take on differing meanings with different rationalities. An investigation to seek out discontinuities and breaks. An initial articulation of three rationalities and their interpretation of 'system'

5.1   INTRODUCTION

In the previous chapter I noted the importance of distinguishing between abstract and paradigmatic definitions of 'system'. In this chapter I shall deal with both of these intellectual matters in order to clarify the point further, and to focus on the implications of this for understanding 'system'. There is, however, a third significant yet contentless custom for the term 'system'. That concerns a nonintellectual everyday use. What follows is in three parts. First, the trivialized everyday use will be quickly dealt with and disposed of. Second, the historical development of abstract notions of 'system' will be explored and a broad range of conceptions in the form of systemic metaphors will be discussed. Third, a general framework is described and drawn upon to show how a variety of paradigmatic definitions of 'system' and the oft-related concept 'complexity' can be explored. Through this analysis we will uncover an epistemological break in systems thinking and will consider the implications of this, before moving on to consider the need for a further epistemological break.

5.2   'SYSTEM': EVERYDAY CONTENTLESSNESS

In everyday life we are confronted with catch-phrases aimed at drawing our attention to a particular product or service. There is one type of phrase, however, that is most troublesome and unsatisfactory. 'How many of the following have you been subjected to over the past few weeks[1]: Acme Computer Systems, Newtown Hi-Fi and Video Systems, John's Complete Kitchen Systems, etc.?' In my local town we even have a salesroom called Road Systems — 'Does the word car no longer hold utility?'

It was not long ago that the public at large was relatively safe from such empty generalized labels. Now, through the adoption of the word 'system' by industry, commerce, advertising, and other groups, that term has effectively been rendered meaningless. Our everyday understanding of 'system' is contentless. The stark reality that consequently confronts us in systems thinking is the daunting task of 'spreading the word' to societies that, following mass saturation, have been trained to respond to 'system' by hiring or buying something.

It is perfectly possible to bring in Interpretive Analytics here. One important notion of such Foucaulvian analysis relates to the colonization of the mechanisms of localized points of power. In this case we have seen society at large enter into discourse through all sorts of media, ranging from news reports to the many outlets of advertising. The 'systems' age, through these processes, has become part of a barren discourse where there are no concepts articulated and there is no useful or meaningful discourse. This appears to be protected from a wider influence. If there is any content that penetrates to the general public, it is of the systematic adjective sense of 'system' and the machine view that accompanies it.

In a serious tone, Checkland (1988a) made a further case. He noted the '...casual way the word is used in everyday chat. 'The education system', we say casually, or 'the legal system' or 'health-care system', using system as a label for a recognisable bit of the world's complexity.' Checkland also commented that 'Alas, Bertalanffy used 'system' as the name for the abstract concept of a whole and immediately began to refer to things in the world as systems.' Checkland expressed an opinion that this was a semantic disaster that has led to confusion forty years on.[2]

The disaster in my view was more fundamental than that, since Bertalanffy's use of the term was a meaningful way of putting across this new conceptualization in terms of the dominant theoretical underpinnings of his time. In other words, it was an epistemological disaster that had semantic consequences. Nevertheless, this is a matter of grave concern and one that has no simple remedy.

The following sections are put together to show a strength and richness in notions of 'system' in abstract, and that there is contentfullness through paradigmatic interpretations.

5.3 'SYSTEM': ABSTRACT RICHNESS

5.3.1 Introduction

Initially I shall consider the development of some general systemic concepts, resultant abstract redefinitions that have arisen through analogical reasoning. Then I shall move on to describe how these can be specifically realized in various systemic metaphors.[3]

5.3.2 A 'First' Systems Struggle: Ontological Reconceptualization

What I term the 'first' systems struggle is, I suspect, rather what Ackoff (1974) meant in his notion of a transition from a 'machine age' to a 'systems age'. We are certainly referring to the same discontinuity and to a point when systems ideas emerged in a dominant way (to technology and, in a more barren way, to society at large). We agree that the origins are hard to find, which is no surprise bearing in mind that in this thesis there is an acceptance of a Foucaulvian notion of the history of knowledge.

This 'first' systems struggle was not, however, characterized by an epistemological break since, as we will discover elsewhere in this book, the ideas remained firmly embedded in positivistic thought. It would be more appropriate to consider the 'first' struggle as analogical, focusing on ontological reconceptualization. It was the realist nature of the position concerning *what is* that underwent fundamental questioning. The machine view of reality was replaced by a systems view (hence Ackoff's two ages) and emerging out of this ontological debate, that was largely held in the domain of the natural living world, came abstract redefinitions. The proposal was that these could be used for general transportability, to be applied in other contexts of the natural and social world.

In fact, one of the most fascinating studies of systems thinking from an historical perspective, is to investigate the intellectually based analogical struggle that gave rise to the discourse in which the 'open system' concept was articulated in Western thinking (i.e., the genealogical explanation). Bertalanffy's (1950) General Systems Theory is often hailed as the coming together of this struggle, although a genealogical survey would not accept such 'heroic' moments.

Systems thinking was a response to the dominant conceptualization of living beings as 'closed systems' or machines. The discourse relating to the latter was already in conflict with that of vitalism, even before the 'first' systems struggle.

Vitalists believed that a mysterious vital force characterized organisms and even objects (a view that is called animism). Mechanists believed that everything which occurred was completely determined by something that preceded it. Vitalism was refuted, being thought of as mystical following developments in scientific study that led to explanations of causal relationships. This involved reductionist thinking: where all objects and events, their properties and our knowledge of them are made up of ultimate elements (Ackoff, 1974). Analytic study naturally complements reductionist thinking and leads to the view that the Universe and everything in it are best considered as a machine. Such an ideal has been proposed as applicable to organisms, organizations, and even societies. This traditionally scientific rational view proceeds from the assumption that goals are easy to define and therefore organisms, organizations and even societies can be seen as machines seeking to achieve these goals with a minimum use of resources (Clemson and Jackson, 1988). The holistic perspective that subsequently emerged can be seen as a response to the increasing fragmentation of science that characterized the search for ultimate elements.

The systemic ideas of this revolutionary new discourse cast a different light on the mechanist-vitalist debate, since holism went a long way toward explaining certain phenomena of living things that a mechanistic rationality could not. By the articulation of concepts that helped to explain such phenomena as emergence, the discourse of holism finally snuffed out the last embers of vitalism and paved the way for the replacement of mechanism as a dominant view of living and social things. The forces of the scientistic view would, however, prevent an epistemological break from happening in systems thinking at that time.

Whether Bogdanov's (1922) *tektology* was the realization of a similar Soviet struggle is difficult to know in the West, since we must rely on brief and valuable appraisals such as that by Gorelik (1975) and the informative book reviews of Banathy and Banathy (1989) and Checkland (1989) as well as honest appraisals such as that of Kiss (1989). These cannot, however, provide us with access to the discourse of which Bogdanov's work must have been a part. Interestingly, there is a hint in Mattesich (1978) that Bertalanffy could have been aware of Bogdanov's work, although this is speculative. In cybernetics too, there is an East European forerunner to the Western European conceptualization, in the work of Trentowski, although no suggestion of cross-fertilization of discourse has been made here. Even so, investigating the Western discourse, as it is substantively documented, is in itself an absorbing study. Witness this below in the appraisal of some example works.

Two sources of reading that consider texts relating to the early discourse of the systems view are Emery's (1969) collection of articles and Lilienfeld's (1979, Chapter 1) discussion on anticipations of systems theory. We will now consider some issues of the 'first' struggle that surface in these readings.

Koehler (1938) argued forcefully against an equilibrium theory to explain the behaviour of organisms. While he recognized that the two principal ideas of machine theory, the Second Law of Thermodynamics and the Law of Dynamic Direction, are compatible with dynamic or functional notions to which equilibrium theory applies, he argued that unless a broader view of these two functional principles is taken, an equilibrium theory of organic regulation is misleading. The three main points were as follows.

(a) No organism is detached from the rest of the world, thus the principles are not directly applicable to living systems — they are not closed.

(b) Organisms are not in equilibrium with their immediate environment — at rest many organisms are in an unstable position.

(c) From the point of view of physics, it is difficult to explain the apparent increase in human stores of energy, from say a baby to a teenager — development of life is associated with an *increase* in energy (negentropic).

Henderson based his sociological thinking on biochemical and physiological analogies (refer to Barber, 1970, for selected readings of Henderson). He represented social processes in systems terms and is noted for his notion of equilibrium (i.e., an organism possesses a self-regulating mechanism where the goal is the maintenance of equilibrium or health). Here, the meaning of equilibrium encompasses a broad view such as that for which Koehler (1938) argued. Cannon (1932) has been attributed with an early and clear account of homeostasis (i.e., where a variety of mechanisms work toward the maintenance of various analytes so that these are constant in identity yet changing in constituents).

Angyal (1941) attempted to develop some concepts that would be useful for understanding the structure of wholes. He defined through his writings a new understanding of the concept 'relationship'. A relationship in the then-traditional scientific thinking required two and only two relata between which a relation could be established. Conventional thinking of the time assumed that a complex relation, where there are many relata, could always be analyzed into pairs. Angyal argued however that a 'system' is not a complex relation that can be analyzed in such a way. The term 'system' as understood today is at variance with the view of Angyal's time, where 'system' implied an aggregate of elements considered together with relationships holding among them. Angyal's struggle was to argue that the type of connection in a whole is very different from those in an aggregate.

Feibleman and Friend (1945) offered some methodological thinking for empirical analysis of organization, in the form of a search for a common structure and function. Fundamental to their thesis was a distinction between 'static' and 'dynamic' viewpoints. Statics, the dominant view, would treat organizations as independent of their environment (here we can imagine the theoretical construct of a 'closed system'). Dynamics, the then-novel view, would treat them as dependent to some extent and therefore interactive with other organizations. As Lilienfeld (1979) and others pointed out, it was not until Bertalanffy (1950) published *The Theory of Open Systems in Physics and Biology* that the 'open systems' view could claim to have been established (the new discourse promised to force its way to the surface).

There are many other publications where the struggle toward an 'open system' view can be witnessed. Many of these are difficult to comprehend without substantial exposure to the discourse through which the new concepts were articulated. We must be very careful when interpreting old concepts through today's means of articulation.

The intellectual foundations of the 'open system' view are thus clearly marked by discontinuities of discourse. In many cases these ontological breaks are evidenced by reconceptualizations of old concepts (e.g., Angyal redefined 'relationship' and 'system', Koehler and Henderson redefined 'equilibrium', and so on). This 'first' struggle revolutionized Western thinking.

We will now consider the way in which the 'system' concept casts understanding on the social world.

5.3.3   Systemic   Metaphors

5.3.3.1   Introduction

Arising out of the 'first' analogical and ontological struggle were a number of systemic metaphors, some of which have played an important role in the development of well-received strands of systems thinking. These have been expanded quite considerably. The resulting abstract and rich definitions are based on fundamental ideas such as complex networks, control and communication. They have been drawn upon widely as a means of conceptualizing both the natural and social world, such as biological, organizational, and social sciences (see Mangham, 1979; Morgan, 1986). We are mainly concerned here with the abstract richness of 'system' in many metaphorical guises as structures for organizing our thoughts about social reality (the pragmatic utility of these metaphors is discussed by Flood and Jackson, 1991a). We will not deal with theoretical issues at this point. Matters of ontology and epistemology are explicitly dealt with in the next section on paradigmatic contentfulness.

5.3.3.2 Machine metaphor or 'closed system' view

It will be useful initially to consider this 'presystems' view. A machine metaphor reflects a technical apparatus that has several often standardized parts each with a definite function. Emphasis is placed on efficiency of parts. Routine and repetitive operation captures the essence of this metaphor, with the performance of predetermined sets of activities seeking the rational and efficient means of reaching preset goals and objectives. Internal control stresses the importance of the return of state variables or processes to set-points (i.e., to a normal state of functioning). Environment is hardly considered, so that external events are virtually ignored — hence the alternative label 'closed system'. Equilibrium refers to the state of maximum entropy or total disorder and so the Second Law of Thermodynamics is particularly relevant to the machine view. Entropy in a 'closed system' never decreases.   As with thermodynamics, entropic processes are naturally irreversible.

5.3.3.3 Organic metaphor or 'open system' view

The organic view incorporates ideas from several 'levels of resolution' (a systemic view of hierarchy). The cell represents the high-resolution end of the spectrum, followed by complex organisms and ecosystems toward the low-resolution end. A metaphor that extracts concepts from these biological phenomena and through which they can be generalized and made transportable, is the 'open system' view (abstracted from the reconceptualizations discussed above and further modernized).   The essential ideas are familiar: a complex network of elements and relationships that interact forming highly organized positive and negative feedback loops, immersed in an environment from which inputs and outputs are exchanged.   An 'open system' is homeostatic, it is self-regulatory. Where 'a machine' suffers from wear–and–tear (or entropy) an organic-like system temporarily offsets degradation by importing and putting to use matter and energy (negentropic).   Survival and adaptability are organic concepts which promote the ideas of other open systems metaphors such as ecological and evolutionary systems.

We will pick out two life-based metaphors for individual attention below, since they have been well received and widely discussed in the scientific literature.

5.3.3.4 Autopoietic metaphor or 'self-producing' view

The works of Maturana and Varella (e.g., Maturana, 1980; Varella, 1979; Maturana and Varella, 1975, 1980) have been prime in constituting a theory of self-producing organizations, or autopoiesis. Mingers (1989) opened up this difficult-to-access theory and his explication has been drawn upon below.

An autopoietic system is dynamic and is a unity of parts that may be considered as a network of productions and components that interact, giving rise to recursive regeneration of the network of productions that produce them (i.e., self-production). The network is realized as a unity in the space in which it exists by composing the form of its boundaries as distinct from the background by preferential interactions within the network (i.e., boundary production). Three types of relation enrich this abstract idea. Relations of constitution is the idea that components are a necessary distance from each other and that they are the required shapes and sizes. Relations of order refer to the correctness of the processes (rates, time and so on). Relations of specification determine that components which are generated by the various production processes conform to the specification for the continuation of autopoiesis.

The structure of an autopoietic system is 'plastic', existing in an environment with which it imports and exports matter and/or energy, and that inflicts perturbations. The sequence of states that an autopoietic system follows however, is primarily determined by their structure and only triggered by the environment. Relationship with the environment is therefore strange and unusual compared to other systems views, since an environment does not give rise to changes in a system, rather it selects states from those made possible at any instant by the system's structure. Relations with the environment arise from the system and its own identity. Further, if the environment offers recurring states then successful autopoiesis of the system will give rise to a suitable structure for that environment (i.e., structural coupling). In the previous organic view we noted the importance of the concept 'adaption'. Structural coupling is a related concept, but where the environment is not the specifier. Changes either occur or they do not, as Mingers notes. Structural coupling may be related to the medium in which the autopoietic system lives or to other possibly autopoietic systems with which it interacts.

The richness of the 'originality and beauty' of the ideas of autopoiesis (as Mingers describes it) can be more fully appreciated elsewhere (see Mingers, 1989; Morgan, 1986; Robb, 1989). A second life-based metaphor that warrants individual attention is the 'viable system' view.

5.3.3.5 Neurocybernetic metaphor or 'viable system' view

Systems thinking incorporates the cybernetic perspective . Autopoiesis is usually considered a cybernetic theory. The neurocybernetic view (see Beer, 1979, 1981, 1985) is a second important cybernetic view that deals with ideas of viability, particularly with active learning and control rather than passive adaptability that characterizes, for example, a traditional view of control in low-order life. Apart from Beer's work, viable systems is usefully dealt with by Clemson (1984), Espejo (1979, 1987), Espejo and Harnden (1989), and Flood and Jackson (1988). This approach looks to the brain of man for a well tried-and-tested control system. The idea is founded on communication and learning.

A standard cybernetic model has a control process (that which is being controlled), an information system (that relates information about the controlled process to a control unit), a control unit (that compares the actual to a desired state of the controlled process), and an activating unit (that brings about changes in the controlled process according to instructions from the control unit). Control can only be successful if the variety of the controller is equal to or greater than that which is being controlled. In addition to this classical cybernetic view, the viable system view stresses the importance of learning. This means accepting dynamic rather than static aims and objectives (i.e., they are time-varying). This amounts to self-questioning rather than self-regulating.

Beer's Viable System Model introduces the unique feature of recursivity. The same basic model can represent, say, an organization, a division of that organization, or may itself represent a division of a larger organization. The Viable System Model is an arrangement of five functional elements. There are parts that are directly concerned with implementation (System 1). Each viable organization has levels of control, from coordination of short-term local internal stability (System 2), to control of overall internal stability (System 3), to control of internal-external homeostasis (System 4), to policymaking (System 5). The organization of these functions allows for self-questioning.

The metaphors presented so far have drawn upon ideas from the natural sciences. At this juncture Laing (1967, p. 25) adequately deals with where we have been, where we should go and why:

We have had accounts of men as animals, men as machines, men as biochemical complexes with certain ways of their own, but there remains the greatest difficulty in achieving a human understanding of man in human terms.

The following metaphors offer a start.

5.3.3.6 Culture metaphor

Culture is a phenomenon that reflects many shared immaterial characteristics among conscious interacting parts and is typified by kinds of cohesiveness in communities. Studies in international relations (see Reynolds, 1971) point to people in cultures sharing language and/or religion and/or history (common descent). Culture therefore is better explained in terms of membership according to a sense of belonging, rather than statehood (membership according to sovereign rule). Culture refers to shared, or socially constructed, reality in terms of values and beliefs which dictate that certain social rules and practices are normal, acceptable and desirable, while other contrasting practices are apparently none of these. Social practices are underpinned by social rules that explain particular actions. Constitutive meaning, or world-view, puts all such actions and explanations into a meaningful context. Actions that do not conform to a shared reality are seen as peculiar, often threatening and are frequently rejected, repressed, or isolated from the cohesiveness of the community.

5.3.3.7 Political metaphor

A political metaphor characterizes organizational-individual relationships in a similar way to state-individual relationships (i.e., through sovereign control).   In industrial relations theory there are broadly three contrasting views on the character of any political situation (i.e., relationships between participants).   These are unitary (a perception of full agreement), conflictual (often termed pluralist - a perception of disagreement) and coercive (a perception of explicit or hidden disagreement resolved through power relations)   (that in brackets developed from Midgley, 1989b).   The political metaphor focuses on issues of interest, conflict, and power. The political character of a situation   is characterized by these issues. With coercive contexts cohesiveness is distorted by masked communication so that the whole is characterized by parts with irreconcilable and adversarial differences.

5.3.3.8 Discussion

The systems metaphors described above are examples of the rich abstract output of a 'first' systems   struggle that lead largely to ontological reconceptualization (in particular those from the natural sciences). Admittedly, the metaphors reflecting developments in the natural sciences are most easily seen as systemic, they have a tradition to support that conception.   The metaphors relating to ideas of 'consciousness'   can be clearly understood in systemic terms since they enable us to see our lives as socially constructed wholes, as interrelations between interpretations, but we must be careful not to denature them by just manipulating basic systems ideas of wholeness from the natural sciences in, for example, the manner of Atkinson and Checkland (1988).   They constructed straight forward organic relations between wholes, which are built on notions of the 'open system' view. These do not adequately help us to understand social rationality and irrationality.   In Chapter 7 we will consider in detail the idea of an interpretivistic rationality which cannot be   represented by making up metaphors from   natural science building blocks as Atkinson and Checkland suggest.   Their effort   would be of major concern to literary critics such as Black (1962) and Boyd (1979) who stress how metaphors elicit creative thought by calling forth insight and understanding.   Literary metaphors are deeply textual whereas Atkinson and Checkland have developed metaphor that are abstract and artificial.   A surer account of analogy and metaphor in systems thinking and practice can be found in Robinson (1990).

In application, the mixing of metaphors of the natural and social worlds can promote 'problem solving' as a means of contributing to appreciation of situations (see Flood and Jackson's, 1991a, *Total Systems Intervention*, which is a pragmatization of some of the ideas discussed in this book).

In this section we have developed an enriched view of 'system' over that of the everyday contentless use discussed earlier. This reflects the great achievements of the 'first' systems struggle. Now it is necessary to face theoretical issues head on. If we are to find a satisfactory way forward for systems inquiry then we must progress on from this abstract richness (and away from abstract artificiality) to realise paradigmatic contentfulness.

5.4 'SYSTEM' AND 'COMPLEXITY': PARADIGMATIC CONTENTFULNESS

5.4.1 Introduction

While the previous section outlined a 'first' systems struggle in terms of analogical and ontological developments, this section leads us to a 'second' systems struggle: toward the idea of a 'first' epistemological break and its incompleteness. This can be recognized through paradigmatic redefinition of systems ideas. To help us understand this with clarity, a general theoretical framework will be constructed. With this it is possible to build a strong argument by explaining a plurality of theoretically logical relationships between conceptions of 'system' and 'complexity'.

5.4.2 General Features of 'Complexity'

In an earlier book (Flood and Carson, 1988, Chapter 2) I tackled the impossible task of defining complexity once and for all. In that work a fragment was presented, as I now realize. There are many other ways of thinking about complexity. Nevertheless, some useful features are presented therein, ones that will be helpful in the following attempt to organize our ideas in a plurality of partial understandings. Each partial view will be found coherent in terms of its own theoretical underpinnings in which it is rooted. Each will have implications for how we might shape inquiry. The remainder of this section is a much abridged and generalized version of a development of the former work.

We might consider complexity to be related to anything we find difficult to understand. This suggests that complexity can be related to we, us, or people; and things, so-called objects, or preferably for our line of thinking systems (ontological presuppositions must be refrained from at this point). Significant for our study and relating to people and consciousness are: psychological factors such as notions, perceptions, interests, and capabilities; cultural factors such as values and beliefs; and political factors such as interests, conflict and power.

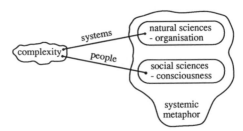

Complexity and systemic metaphor
Figure 5.1

Also significant and relating to 'system' and 'complexity' are features such as, number of parts, number of relationships and attributes of these such as nonlinearity, asymmetry, and nonholonomic constraints. The nature of these attributes is largely determined by the systemic abstraction, or metaphor, which is adopted (refer to Figure 5.1). Metaphor relating to 'system' are abstracted from natural sciences, while those relating to 'people' are abstracted from social sciences. More generally they refer to organization and consciousness respectively.

We will now consider the general theoretical framework through which notions of 'system' and 'complexity' will be explored.

5.4.3   A General Theoretical Framework

5.4.3.1   Introduction

Considering theoretical issues is vital if DeVries and Hezerwijk (1978) are to be believed. They were concerned that systems theory has dealt mostly with 'what is' status, or so-called essentialistic, questions that at best lead to classifications and/or taxonomies, but never lead to deeper explanations. The descriptive disassembly of complexity reviewed above could be labeled as yet another status representation if I were not to be explicit about possible normative interpretations. When considering social reality, status questions must be considered normative questions in disguise. What I am saying is that we must 'see through' status and uncover normative implications. In this section we shall be considering how the apparent status representation of complexity given above does, in fact, have many possible normative interpretations. We will be considering and relating normative, or paradigmatic, definitions of 'system' and 'complexity'.

In a very broad overview, Churchman's (1977) *Philosophy for Complexity* focuses explicitly on three paradigmatic issues: of ontology, epistemology, and ethics (we will return to Churchman's ideas later). We clearly need a framework through which we can focus on these issues so that we may work out a number of paradigmatic interpretations, as we have previously declared our interest. One was developed by Burrell and Morgan (1979) which identifies four sociological paradigms according to two dimensions: a theoretical dimension (ontological and epistemological, with extremes of objective and subjective); and an ideological dimension (with a political essence and extremes of order and conflict). These are shown in Figure 5.2. The integral nature of theory and ideology is an important feature of this ideal type framework. We will temporarily leave out ideological considerations, concentrating on the objective to subjective extremes of ontology (realism to nominalism) and those of epistemology (positivism to anti-positivism).

There is good justification for initially studying this dimension, because in our context of concern (i.e., 'system' and 'complexity') there are writings, such as that of Klir (1985), which do not simultaneously fit into the subjective/objective dichotomy on ontological and epistemological criteria (Klir appears to argue both an ontological realist and epistemological anti-positivist stance before disappearing into abstractness). In order to overcome this difficulty a more general theoretical framework can be developed, one that encompasses all possible combinations of the four: ontological realism or nominalism and/or epistemological positivism or anti-positivism. A simple diagrammatic representation of this framework is shown in Figure 5.3. There are eight possible theoretical windows assuming that ontology and epistemology can only be classified as subjective or objective. My claim with this framework is only that it is more comprehensive than that of Figure 5.2 with respect to theoretical considerations. I do not say that each of the eight possibilities is evidenced elsewhere, just that no possibility is excluded.

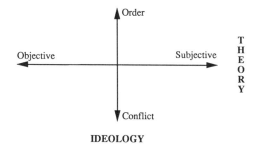

IDEOLOGY

A simple representation of Burrell and Morgan's (1979)
two dimensions of theory and ideology

Figure 5.2

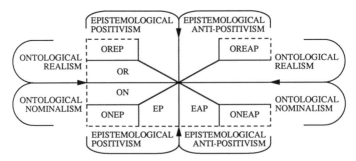

A simple representation of two dimensions of ontology and epistemology
and eight possible theoretical windows

Figure 5.3

5.4.3.2   Paradigmatic interpretations of 'system' and 'complexity'

We will be considering the possibility of understanding 'complexity' and 'system' through portions of these theoretical windows.   Let me first introduce a metaphor that I think will help to make the following discussion clearer (while admittedly narrowing consideration to only five possibilities), one relating to ontology and the other to epistemology . This will help us to get a handle on the framework of Figure 5.3 (but will not explain every bit of it) and will direct us toward related conceptions of 'system' and 'complexity' and to discontinuities, or breaks, between a number of these conceptions.

The metaphor that will be used is of a person or group observing a 'ship' ('ship' representing social reality) by looking out to sea (refer to Figure 5.4).

Very strong realists might say that social reality is virtually self-evident and obvious in its pristine clarity — because of its concreteness we can expect to see it like watching a ship sail close to shore where all its details and dimensions are observable. This is the *Close Ontologist.*

A less strong realist might say that social reality is evidently there, it is concrete but some genuine difficulties are encountered when attempting to get to grips with it — it would be like watching a distant ship where the observable details are often less than pristine, and the ship is difficult to know in all its dimensions. This is the *Distant Ontologist.*

A weak realist might, however, claim little or no observable evidence of an assumed concrete social reality — looking far out to sea the ship remains always beyond the horizon, only known through conceptualizations of what it must be like (using very special measuring devices). Nevertheless, the ship can be known by the community of which the weak realist is a member. This is the *Beyond the Horizon Ontologist.*

On the other hand some, who we call nominalists, have abandoned the idea of a social reality, one that 'is out there' and can be known by observation. Rather, they suggest, there are many human interpretations and social realities, each being equally 'valid' and 'objective' through the agreement of negotiation (i.e., objectivity arises through shared subjectivities and is of consciousness). This is the *Visionary Ontologist.* With this view there is no such thing as a 'ship' (i.e., one singularly definable social reality) unless a group of negotiators or actors agree upon such a reality. It is evidently not a realist position. This view assumes that there is no 'ship' in external objective reality and so if the group of negotiators were eliminated 'ships' would no longer be negotiated and would not be an issue or real. On the contrary, a realist position would maintain that any group of humans might equally well replace the lost one and continue observational exercises of getting to know 'ship' as it is.

A more extreme subjectivist position might give rise to the view that any conceptualization is the intellectual property of an individual consciousness. There is no way that we could logically argue for anything beyond the individual psychic knowing. This is the *Psychic Prison Ontologist.*

Given that there are at least these varying views on 'what is', we must accept that there are also various ways of reflecting on the validity of

Five possible ways of viewing 'ship' (or social reality)

Figure 5.4

representation and dissemination of knowledge from those contrasting positions. The problem of epistemology, then, is how the subject(s) can appreciate and know reality. The following discussion should be understood in these terms. These issues of sociological epistemology may be elucidated by extending the metaphor. 'Given the above positions on social reality, or 'ship', what 'visual resolution' can we genuinely attain?'

The Close Ontologist may well assume that high resolution is, at least in principle, achievable since social reality is clearly definable 'as it is'. Hence, the only real issue of representation concerns what degree of resolution is required so that social reality is sufficiently well understood, according to some purpose. Isomorphic representations are possible, but might be unnecessarily complicated for given intents. Some lower level of resolution might be found to be sufficiently detailed. Resolution may be varied from completeness to less complete. This is the *High-Resolution Epistemologist*.

The Distant Ontologist does not have the luxury of choice of resolution since the position dictates that this is problematic. The main goal, then, is to direct all efforts toward increasing the validity of knowledge by seeking ways of maximizing the naturally poor resolution. The aim is to work asymptotically toward representing social reality in as much detail as demanded by given intents and purposes. This is the *Low-Resolution Epistemologist*.

In counter-distinction, Beyond The Horizon Ontologists have abandoned trying to represent reality in its natural form, assuming that only 'radar' images of reality are feasible and hence the validity of knowledge gained can only be enhanced. This is the *Image Epistemologist*.

Of further contrast, the Visionary Ontologist has accepted that social reality is not a tangible real entity, in fact it is not even an intangible one. Knowledge relating to the visions comes through participation in negotiation, or the interrelation of interpretations where agreements may be achieved. This is the *Negotiation Epistemologist*.

Lastly, although not exhaustively in this analogy, is the *Psychic Prison Ontologist*, whose position of despair is epistemologically reaffirmed, since there is nothing to know beyond 'my own' reasoning. Validity is therefore problematic since dissemination is not considered possible. This is the *Individualistic Epistemologist*.

These five types of onto-epistemology, labeled I—V respectively, tend to place emphasis on particular issues of, or concerns about, theories. The five views and their primary concerns are summarized in Table 5.1. It is easy to comprehend why all eight possibilities are allowed for by relating this back to Figure 5.3. In some cases ontological and epistemological

Table 5.1
Five onto-epistemological views and primary concerns/issues

TYPE	ONTOLOGY Social reality is -	EPISTEMOLOGY Validity of knowledge of social reality is -	PRIMARY CONCERN / ISSUE
I	close and real. REALIST (strong)	of high resolution, but may be equally valid on lower resolution if intent and purposes are satisfied. POSITIVIST	Since reality is close and real and can be known 'as it is', there are no concerning issues except, perhaps, methodology: ie., which methodology is most flexible and accurate in leading resolution variation to purpose/ intent.
II	distant and real. REALIST (less strong)	of low resolution, but with a view to working on increasing validity. POSITIVIST	Since reality is real but distant, the validity of knowledge is a main concern (ie., epistemology) and so is the means by which we can improve understanding and representation (i.e., methodology).
III	beyond the horizon but real. REALIST (weak)	only in terms of images of which we may attempt to enhance. ANTI-POSITIVIST (weak)	Acceptance of reality is only important in so far as we are led to question the utility of the images in forwarding useful ways of reasoning about that reality (both epistemology and methodology are prime).
IV	visionary and transferable. NOMINALIST	in terms of many equally valid views of what reality is, that are open to negotiation. ANTI-POSITIVIST (less weak)	Since we only know a world through relations of labels in consciousness, of which there are many views, the main concern must be with proper handling of those views (through methodology, which is prime) at which point we may claim to have achieved valid representation (epistemology).
V	only in 'my own mind' and is like a psychic prison. NOMINALIST	that only I can know 'my own reality'. ANTI-POSITIVIST (strong)	Since reality is individualistic and unsharable the primary concern is of despair.

considerations might be given equal importance, in other cases either one or the other might be assumed as prime and could be considered singularly important. Once we have reasoned a theoretical position we will naturally prefer to use logically related methodological principles.

In summary, a general theoretical framework that caters for diversity and therefore promotes rich studying has been developed. It should not be used simply as a universal tool. Rather, its utility can only be drawn out if it is recognized as an ideal type, designed to promote debate and understanding, such as through the 'ship' metaphor.

We are now in a position to generate a number of contrasting conceptions of 'system' and 'complexity'. Let me quickly remind us that we shall be considering 'complexity' in terms of 'people related' and 'system related' features and mainly with respect to the 'open system' metaphor as the abstract notion of 'system'. We will now consider Types I—V respectively.

Type I: Close Ontologist, High-Resolution Epistemologist

Adopting this position, social systems are taken for granted as real and tangible. The traditional scientific method of observation would therefore seem ideal, it is generally accepted as singularly important. This science helps us to identify causal links and so social systems science is a matter of relating sets of variables and wholes. Boundary decision making is self-evident. The scientific methods of verification or falsification are appropriate means of validation.

Complexity is 'simple' with a Type I view. It is measurable or assessable in terms of number of parts, number of relationships, stability according to roots of characteristic equations (i.e., imaginary numbers with respect to oscillation, and the sign of the real root with respect to growth or decay), hierarchy and the ease with which decomposition techniques can be used to promote manageability among other characteristics (see Albin and Gottinger, 1983; Ando and Fischer, 1963; Courtois, 1977, 1985; Courtois and Semal, 1975; Klir, 1985; Simon and Ando, 1961, for decomposition and reconstruction techniques).

Given this reasoning, 'complexity' and 'system' are synonymous in a real way. The notion of 'system' is prime over 'people'. The latter are merely formed into social systems. These are said to exist despite metaphysical issues, which are deemed to be irrelevant to the facts and even misleading, clouding over the realness of social systems.

Type II: Distant Ontologist, Low-Resolution Epistemologist

A similar position to that of Type I is adopted, although much more emphasis is placed on the validity of knowledge. This instigates a higher degree of competitiveness among methods of inquiry, 'Simply which version of the scientifically based methodological principles is optimal in terms of falsifiability and verifiability?'. 'Which one leads to the realization of valid maximised resolution?' This must involve good boundary judgments. 'System' and 'complexity' are synonymous in a real sense, although part of the complication is the 'distance' between them that has to be contended with. The notion of 'system' remains prime over 'people' and no additional reasoning beyond Type I is required.

Type III: Beyond the Horizon Ontologist, Image Epistemologist

This position also promotes the idea that social systems are of the world, they are real but due to difficulties of accessibility their dimensions are hardly tangible. The reality is only knowable through impressions on the senses, what we make of those impressions and other *a priori* factors relating to reason (the radar image interpretation and *a priori* decisions on what we will scan for — following the earlier metaphors). Somewhere in the measurements are clues about the social reality. Subjectivity of *a priori* or indeed *a posteriori* components is assumed and so competing theories, ideas, or just plain opinions or intuitions will be forwarded.

'Complexity', then, is not only associated with the features of system based models but also with 'people' issues, involving psychological factors such as interests and capabilities. 'Complexity' and 'system' are not synonymous because human factors are assumed to be muddling the 'system' realization. Issues of interpretation cannot be easily overcome by turning a blind eye to all that is not real or objective. It is frustrating that the reality always lies just 'out of reach'. Neither 'people' nor 'system' can therefore be considered prime.

Type IV: Visionary Ontologist, Negotiation Epistemologist

The realness of social 'systems' is questioned. 'Systems' are identified through actions, social rules, and practices that define those actions (i.e., a set of socially generated rules that define the practices) and the constitutive meaning behind the social practices (i.e., what makes the social practice meaningful). Any possible 'system' is said to be identifiable with respect to action oriented interpretations and world-views, being an 'objective' agreement between a group of subjective interpreters. Take away the 'people' and the so-called 'system' vanishes. 'Complexity' can only be explained through human factors (psychological, cultural, and political). 'Complexity' and 'system' therefore have no clear relationship other than, I note, via the creators of 'complexity', who may or may not choose to unravel that 'complexity' by drawing upon abstract organizing structures such as systemic metaphors. That is, the idea of 'system' offering a partial means of conceptualizing the information that we receive.

Type V: Psychic Prison Ontologist, Individualistic Epistemologist

This is an extreme subjectivist position that only takes the arguments for Type IV farther away from any of the realist positions. 'Complexity' is absolutely of 'people', or more accurately 'myself'.

5.4.4   Conclusion

The discussion about the five positions is summarized in Table 5.2. This demonstrates the integral and difficult nature of the relationship between notions of 'system' and 'complexity' through paradigmatically contentful definitions. The 'ship' metaphor served this purpose well. There are, however, endless ways that the general theoretical framework of Figure 5.3 could be appreciated. I am saying that the metaphorical discussion above should not dictate a circumscribed means of thought. Nevertheless, even with this partial view we can begin to understand how issues of 'system' and 'complexity' lead naturally to approaches to inquiry. To make this point, let us consider two extreme observations on 'system' and 'complexity' that are extracted from the above discussion.

'System': 'Is it of the real world?' If yes then we require a methodology for optimal system identification. If no, it is of consciousness, then we need to use the abstract notion 'system' to help organize our thoughts and develop meaningful appreciations.

'Complexity': 'Is it of the real world?' If yes, then we need suitable methods to decompose to aid manageability, which may be carried out according to knowledge of weak links between variables. If no, it is of consciousness, then methodologies should encourage participation so that

Table 5.2

Five onto-epistemological views on 'system' and 'complexity'

TYPE	I	II	III	IV	V
ISSUE					
Relationship between 'system' and 'complexity'	Synonymous in a real sense.	Synonymous in a real sense.	Related but neither is prime.	No theoretical relationship.	No theoretical relationship.
'Complexity' is of -	'systems' which may comprise people.	'systems' which may comprise people.	'systems' and of people.	'people' who may conceptualise using systems' ideas.	'people', or 'myself' who might conceptualise using 'systems' ideas.
'Systems' are -	of a real world.	of a real world.	structures that may reflect a real world or help in the appreciation of conscious worlds.	abstract organising structures for our shared thoughts.	abstract organising structures for 'my own' peculiar thoughts.
Method of validating 'system' representations	Falsifiability or verifiability	Falsifiability or verifiability	Falsifiability or verifiability/ participative inquiry.	Participative inquiry.	None.

systemic realization of viewpoints represents the plurality of visions, and difficulties associated with the interrelations between interpretations.

Simplifying the debate to these contrasting positions raises an important issue, that evidently there are discontinuities between theoretical positions. We can detect an epistemological break.

5.5   A 'SECOND' SYSTEMS STRUGGLE: A 'FIRST' EPISTEMOLOGICAL BREAK

5.5.1   Introduction

In the previous section we considered how different the basic conception of the 'open system' metaphor is when viewed through different paradigmatic windows. Changing favor, from positivistic to interpretivistic theoretical underpinnings, will have a significant impact on the meaning and use of any abstract conception of 'system'. This rupture indicates an epistemological break characterized by legitimacies and limitations of each position. For example, if we theoretically explore the 'open system' metaphor then we will be able to outline some limitations associated with its positivistic application. This is the basis of a 'second' systems struggle, a 'first' epistemological break, that we will now briefly explore.

5.5.2   Unleashing the Open System Metaphor

The root metaphor 'open system', let us be reminded once again, implies that there are a number of constituents (elements and relationships), boundary, inputs, outputs, and feedback. There are also ideas of hierarchy, emergence, and many other support concepts.

The positivistic theoretical position leads to describing the world as if it were a complex of these 'open systems', both natural and social. For example, Laszlo's (1972) *Systems View of the World* is one of a world of systems. This proposition is obviously misconceived. Consider the idea of a boundary. In reality it is a nonentity. A boundary is the ultimate expression of systemic abstraction and abstraction is '...to do with, or existing in, thought or theory rather than matter' (*Oxford Dictionary of Current English*). It will not be surprising, therefore, to find that a main concern of traditional systems thinkers is an expansionary difficulty in boundary identification. Of course, we will go on searching for ever if the creature we are pursuing is simply something we have made up and then hypostatized (like Winnie the Pooh's search for a heffalump, Milne, 1926, Chapter 5). Neither should we be surprised with the mystical attitude of some traditional systems thinkers, who are faced with the dilemma of explaining in real terms the curious phenomena of emergence, a miraculous occurrence when real parts are brought together to synergistically form a real whole. We may snigger a little at these bold hard minded people who assume nothing more than vitalistic animism.

There is, however, a way forward if we make the advance of an epistemological break. Witness this below.

Since we have established that the world is not a complex of systems, the exercise of system identification in messy social contexts (qualitative or quantitative) becomes *all but* redundant. The *all but* qualification allows some room for breaking out of the traditional positivists' view. That is, a representation *is not all, but is one* viewpoint. We can extend this idea and arrive at Checkland's (1981) multiple perspective interpretivistic view. We might share with him the value of realizing this epistemological break. For example, in his Soft Systems Methodology, Checkland distinguishes 'real world' from 'systems' thinking. Through this we are released from an ontological realist bond to a world that apparently comprises systems. Ontology is given a back seat, while epistemology and particularly methodology become a main concern. The root metaphor 'open system' and indeed all other systemic metaphors can be employed as organizing structures that may promote understanding and debate.

5.5.3   Conclusion

This reasoning represents a 'second' systems struggle which, unlike the 'first' ontologically rooted one, is primarily epistemological. Like the 'first', however, there is evidence of the colonizing of the main entry points to discourse and an increasing domination of some of the main scientific outlets. Further, in the rising discourse we can witness significant discontinuities and reconceptualizations. Indeed, it is these that articulate the concepts, as we will now explore in the break from positivistic to interpretivistic systems thinking.

5.6   THE NEED FOR A SUBSTANTIVE SUBJECTIVIST SYSTEMS LANGUAGE AND CONCEPTS

5.6.1   Introduction

The need to explicitly consider a subjectivist language and concepts for systems thinking arose, in my own concerns, during the last stages of preparing the manuscript for Flood and Carson (1988). The text is largely introductory, dealing with the fundamental concepts of systems thinking and some applications in both natural and social domains. The following observations on my intellectual background are relevant here since they were decisive in determining the theoretical groundings on which the initial drafts of the manuscript in question were based.

My understanding of systems thinking as a science was revealed by the staff of a department which comprised engineers and a small number of social scientists, who drew upon the traditional methods of science and holism. This understanding was developed through research into the utility of quantitative (mathematical and statistical) models as aids to clinical decision making (Flood, 1985). It is hardly surprising then, that I confess to preparing the manuscript in classical positivistic style. There was little to sway me from this route. Indeed, awareness of other possibilities was restricted to a thin understanding of the works of a handful of systems oriented authors (i.e., Ackoff, Checkland, and Churchman). Virtually all other works I was aware of (the dominant discourse) supported or, more accurately, did not question the underpinning theory of the volume in preparation. The main challenge of systems writings gave the impression of a concern for a second dimension for science: the science of relations and holism (e.g., Klir, 1985) as compared to the science of reduction and refutation. These writings, together with the debates of the critics (e.g., Hoos, 1972; Lilienfeld, 1979), all shared the assumption that systems thinking needs 'to be/is' founded on paradigmatic tenets of functionalism.

At a late stage I felt compelled to undertake significant changes to the manuscript as a whole, in accordance with a personal recognition of the significance of interpretivism (for which I am indebted to a few of my informative UK colleagues). This amounted to my own epistemological break. Straight association with functionalist theory, which would be inferred from the text, was not an acceptable proposition after that break.

Undertaking the task of translation to imply plurality in meaning and nonobjectivity placed me in a unique position. The requirement was to eliminate the ambiguity that arises from use of the word 'system' both as a name for a part of 'the world' and as the name of an intellectual construct to understand or interpret 'the world' (see also Checkland, 1988b).

This section, then, is concerned with the genuine difficulties encountered when redrafting the manuscript and will document and discuss some of the necessary translations. All of this points to a clear epistemological break in systems thinking.

5.6.2   Translating a Manuscript

There were a number of necessary translations that occurred with great frequency, some occasionally and there were some which frustratingly did not fit the pattern for translation that emerged. This suggested a paucity of words, concepts, phrases and an under developed syntax for a subjectivist systems language.

The use and translation of 'system' is an obvious starting point. Table 5.3 documents a number of translations, where two theory based types emerge. Type A translations arose when 'system' was used in the context

Table 5.3

Translation of the word or concept 'system' from functionalist
to interpretive usage

WORD / CONCEPT	TRANSLATION
• system	TYPE A • 'system' • notional system • situation • thing • (use of commonly accepted labels, eg., dog, cat and so on TYPE B • representation • model • system of equations TYPE Z • (delete)

of reality, what is assumed to be out there, what is, ontologically. Type B translations arose when 'system' was used as a means of understanding and representing reality and finding ways to communicate this knowledge to fellow human beings. 'System' was used here epistemologically.

A third translation, Type Z, was in fact to remove the word 'system' altogether. This highlighted the general redundancy of the word in common language. Such thoughtless or contentless misuse has rendered any conception of 'system' effectively meaningless to society at large as argued earlier.

The translations documented in Table 5.3 were not adequate for all instances. A one-to-one translation broke down on occasion. This resulted in the need to change phrases and sentences rather than single words or concepts. A number of these are written out below, with a discussion following.

(1) 'This appears as a change in the nature of the system', was translated to, 'this, in 'real world' terms, appears to be a change in the nature of the situation'; and generally to sentences structured in the form, 'In systems terms,..., switching back to 'real world' thinking,...'

(2) 'Perceptions of what the system is doing', was translated to, 'perceptions of what might be going on in the situation.'

(3) 'Identifying systems from their environment', was translated to 'identifying systems from situations.'

(4) 'Systems have many variables', was translated to, 'situations can be represented as systems with many variables'.

Of course, the cogency of these translations may not be immediate outside the context from which they are drawn. Nevertheless, there are some important observations that can be made on these examples.

Case (1) draws attention to distinguishing the 'real world' from the systems thinking world. This was achieved by recognizing that 'switches' can be introduced in the text, transferring the reader's thinking between the two modes of thought. Such a 'switch' is given as the general example in Case (1). The commonality between this and the same distinction in Checkland's (1981) Soft Systems Methodology is obvious. The interpretive approach of the latter researcher apparently 'switches', backward and forward, between 'real world' thinking in Stages 1, 2, 5, 6, and 7 and systems thinking in Stages 3 and 4.

Case (2) involved recognition of plurality and *Weltanschauungen* or world-views. In this case, the rather concrete suggestion that there are systems out there (doing real things) was translated, so that such a categorical notion of what is (ontology) was eliminated.

The last two cases (3 and 4) are also Type A translations for the word or concept 'system'. A traditional notion of 'system' includes ideas of environment, elements, relationships, boundaries, and so on. In an identical way to the word or concept 'system', the use of these support concepts can and normally does suggest a realist ontology. In part to overcome this and in part to find distinct words for 'real world' thinking and its counterpart systems thinking, the 'translations' in Table 5.4 were chosen (all of Type A).

The use of the word or concept 'situation', in place of a realist inclined use of the word or concept 'system' (see Table 5.3), consequently led to the rejection of the word or concept 'environment' in terms of reality (as shown in Table 5.4). This is necessary because, in systems terms, the distinction between 'system' and 'environment' is achieved through the abstract concept 'boundary'. As is suggested in Table 5.4, translations for the concept 'boundary' proved to be problematic, indeed impossible, since there is no 'real world equivalent'. Thus, in terms of 'real world' thinking, notions of 'situation' and 'surroundings' were used (i.e., there is no clear cut structure) so that

Table 5.4

Translation of words or concepts that support notions of 'system' from functionalist to interpretivist usage

WORD / CONCEPT	TRANSLATION
• environment	• surroundings
• element	• component
• boundary	• (?)
• subsystem	• 'subsystem'

Table 5.5

Translation of the words or phrases or concepts relating to 'problem',
from functionalist to interpretivist usage

WORD / PHRASE / CONCEPT	TRANSLATION
• problem	TYPE A • problem situation • mess
	TYPE Z • difficulty
• problem context	TYPE A • situational context

• problem solution	TYPE C • 'problem solution'
	           • 'problem management'
	           • dis-ease reduction

there is (should be) plurality associated with both concepts. Translation of 'subsystem' not surprisingly proved to be problematic for the very same reasons. Additionally, to be consistent with the distinction between the 'real world' and the systems thinking world requires alternatives to the word or concept 'element' as well as other systemic terms and ideas not documented in Table 5.4.

The use of the word or concept 'problem' also warrants discussion here. Table 5.5 documents the most commonly used and relevant translations. For 'problem' a Type Z translation is shown, relating to ambiguity or misuse of the word or concept.

No more important in achieving clarity, but crucial in the context of theory, is the translation of the word or concept 'problem' to the phrase or concept 'problem situation'. This was carried out in accordance with Checkland's reasoning — that 'the problem' implies a concrete and tangible, singularly identifiable, part of reality. If only we can penetrate the fuzzy shell of the problem, then problem structure and solution can be identified — so suggests a functionalist's use of the word or concept. Checkland (1981) rejects such a view preferring interpretivist thinking, stating explicitly that we should consider 'problem situations' which can legitimately be considered from many viewpoints. Common perception, or a unitary view, is unlikely to be achieved in social contexts, yet it is meaningful to investigate such situations drawing upon rigourous interpretivist methodological principles, such as those emerging in the form of Soft Systems Methodology which helps to draw-out the many contrasting yet relevant viewpoints. As a consequence of this it is not surprising to find Type C translations in Table 5.5 (those pertaining to methodology). For example, 'problem solution' is an acceptable phrase or concept for so-called hard systems approaches, whereas 'dis-ease reduction' nests comfortably in an interpretivist framework of thought. Similarly, use of the phrase or concept 'problem context' (coined by Jackson and Keys, 1984) holds realist connotations that might be misleading. 'Situational context' was suggested as a translation.

There are other considerations. Plurality of perception emerges again and again as a central notion of interpretivist thinking. Pursuing this vein of thought, there were occasions when a seemingly trivial translation was required. This involved 'the' being translated to 'a/an'; 'the' relating to an unitary and 'a/an' to a plurality of interpretations. For example, 'the situational representation' may be translated to 'a situational representation' in the sense that there may be, in fact inevitably are, many acceptable ways of representing 'reality' (i.e., realities). Such translations may be Type A or B, or conceivably Z.

Many more examples could be presented. The purpose here, however, is not to provide an exhaustive list of translations. Nevertheless there are a number of peculiar examples that can usefully be presented in the context of this discussion (see Table 5.6).

Usage of the word or concept 'relevant', proposed by Checkland (1981), in systems writings helps in the development of ideas of plurality. In other examples of Table 5.6 there are two points to note.

First, the translation of 'management system' to 'management scheme' brings to our attention the use of the word or concept 'system' to describe a set of actions or objectives which are systematically or systemically ordered. This is to be expected, since these are the two adjectives of 'system'. Clearly, if we do not make clear which adjectival sense is being used, there is room for ambiguity and misinterpretation and the rich notion of 'system', in the systemic sense, suffers again. This is a Type Z difficulty.

The second point is fundamentally one of Type A. The difficulty of using labels such as 'communication system' and 'neurocybernetic system' will now be clear to the reader. Yet a translation to 'neurocybernetic situation' will gain little favour. In fact it is quite stupid. There is not a 'mess' in a 'soft' sense and indeed many, or most, would agree on the structure, processes,

Table 5.6

Further word or phrase or concept translation from
functionalist to interpretivist usage

WORD / PHRASE / CONCEPT	TRANSLATION
• ( )	• relevant
• management system	• management 'system'
	• management scheme
	• management complex
• communication system	• communication network
• neurocybernetic system	• neurocybernetic organisation
	• neurocybernetic structure and processes

and organization. Cybernetics as such deals with natural laws. A unitary view is virtually generally acceptable on a day-to-day basis. Nevertheless, with interpretive reasoning, the current argument rejects the use of the word or concept 'system' to describe any 'real world' things, stating clearly that it should be saved exclusively for systems thinking. The argument is that if we are able to agree upon the structure and process, and it is the notion of structure and process that makes the label 'neurocybernetic system' meaningful, then why not abandon the word or concept 'system' for what is essential to to our understanding, namely 'structure and process' (or perhaps 'organization' in some contexts). This saves the reader from the task of making inference and, in fact, adds meaning to an otherwise nonexpressive label.

5.6.3   Discussion

The point of this piece of the argument has been to show clearly and methodically that there is a need to develop a substantive subjectivist systems language. The inadequacy of this brief report is evident to me, yet the unique opportunity to translate a text with taken-as-given functionalist use of systems terminology, to one with subjectivist use, has uncovered certain regularities and uncertain irregularities in translation procedures. The latter, it is suggested, has come about due to a paucity of words or phrases or concepts available to the subjectivist thinker and also through a primitive understanding of syntax in this domain. Many of the words or concepts used in one–to–one translations have definitional origins in the works of Peter Checkland. In other cases there may well be criticisms concerning the loose usage of words or concepts. I accept that this is the case and can only point to the necessity of well-thought-out working definitions in so far as that is helpful and possible (although my refusal to include a Glossary in this book says something about my view on this matter).

In addition to the four types of translation presented above (Types A, B, and C, which relate to theory, and Type Z, which relates to general difficulties), there must surely be a Type D, thus conforming to four main debates in social theory (as presented by Burrell and Morgan, 1979). That the four types relate to ontology, epistemology, methodology and, with Type D, to theory of the nature of man is, with hindsight, obvious. It is important to note however that this structure was not drawn up as a means of support for the study. Type Z translations, although not theory based, are indeed important.

To conclude, despite the ontologically astounding nature of the discourse including Bertalanffy's and others' visions, promoting holism as opposed to reductionism, he and the ensuing researchers unwittingly adopted traditional tenets of functionalist thinking, which was dominant in the 1940s as   today.   The systems words or phrases or concepts that constitute the standard systems vocabulary thus evolved within that paradigm, evidenced not only historically, but also by inference from their language use.

In this section we have considered a systems language that would be necessary if a subjectivist oriented paradigm were adopted. Differences in the new language distinguish two different epistemological positions. This is evidence of a break that has occured, but it could be argued that this is not enough.

5.7   A 'THIRD' SYSTEMS STRUGGLE: A 'SECOND' EPISTEMOLOGICAL BREAK

5.7.1   Introduction

So far in this chapter we have: considered and disposed of the contentless everyday use of the term 'system', adequately portrayed the abstract richness (and disposed of abstract artificiality) of several systemic metaphor from both the natural and social sciences, exposed these to paradigmatic conceptualization and then, following this natural progression, have been able to meaningfully unfold the covers from what must be recognized in systems thinking as a 'first' epistemological break. These massive intellectual shifts in fact reflect resistance and battles that give rise to dominant positions, carried out in various ways such as by colonization of the points of access to the development of discursive formations.   In the following chapter we will be concerned with Interpretive Analytics and how this can aid us to critically deal with the result of colonization of discourse, that is liberation from inevitable domination. In Chapter 7 we will develop an adequate epistemology for systems practice through which liberated discourse(s) may be properly critiqued in an open and conciliatory way. Our understanding of 'system', however, has not yet been sufficiently developed for us to be able to rise to a proper liberation and critique. The purpose of the next section is to create such conditions by further developing issues of 'system' and 'complexity', focusing particularly on the latter.

5.7.2   Critical Systems Heuristics: Toward a Metaphysics of Design

5.7.2.1 Introduction

In 1983 Werner Ulrich published his outstanding book *Critical Heuristics of Social Planning*, which is only just now beginning to achieve the recognition in systems thinking that is deserved from such a master thought. In this work, Ulrich partially reconstructed Kant's philosophy and also dealt critically with the works of Popper and Habermas. As we will see later, this effort has influenced the working out of an adequate epistemology for systems practice presented in Chapter 7.

A part of Ulrich's discussion concerned the metaphysics of design, a step on the way toward a 'purposeful systems' paradigm. In this debate he stated that

> It has hardly been noticed ... that the system concept presupposes a metaphysical preconception of the nature of complexity. Without some previous understanding of the nature of complex social reality, the systems concept cannot help us to comprehend and manage this reality. (Ulrich, 1983, p. 319).

Ulrich's observations and the efforts of this chapter are in fact consistent. There are other interesting commonalities, in particular with the introduction to the section of his book that deals with application. Ulrich (1983, p. 317) dealt specifically with the concept of root metaphors as conceptualized by Pepper in his book *World Hypotheses* (Pepper, 1942). Ulrich pointed out that Pepper used the notion of root metaphor to designate basic analogies taken from common-sense experience. This can be likened to our earlier thoughts in Section 5.3 on 'Abstract Richness'. Further, it is explained that the structural characteristics of the root metaphor furnish paradigms with what is required for describing and explaining the 'complex real world'. It is argued by Ulrich through Pepper that the concept 'system' remains an empty abstraction so long as it is not linked to some root metaphor such as machine, biological organism, social group, or whichever. In fact, we have taken a different angle in this chapter by making out a case that it is paradigmatic conceptualization of the systems idea in terms of various metaphor that takes us from an abstract richness to paradigmatic contentfulness, but never mind because the essence of our positions are close enough.

Ulrich's following point is valuable. He noted that the question which needs our attention is not at all about whether we should rely on commonsense metaphor, *but whether we do so critically*. From this position it became Ulrich's task to offer planners an openly normative systems paradigm, so that they would not need to fall back on seemingly value-free, mechanistic, and organic paradigms of contemporary systems science. In fact, in this effort his main focus was on dealing with the positivistically oriented (and dominant) component of traditional systems science, rather than the interpretivistically oriented systems paradigm that was becoming a force in the U. K. at that time (although this is dealt with implicitly in his work as I shall soon highlight).

Ulrich's achievement was to point clearly and concisely for the first time in recent thinking, to a different epistemological position compared to any of those dealt with so far in this chapter. We can explore this as possibly a 'second' epistemological break. At least, this is how it might appear in my presentation, but we would only be re-establishing (in Ulrich's work, from Kant) a critical mode of thought that seems to have been lost in most of systems thinking since the rise of the discourse of General Systems Theory.

Within the theme of this chapter we are able to identify the necessary break that Ulrich wants us to introduce into contemporary systems thinking (in Chapter 7 we will develop the ideas relating to this break toward a complementarist account of an adequate epistemology for systems practice). The point will be made in the next section by summarizing and adding to Ulrich's (1983, p. 319–325) fictitious debate on the metaphysics of systems design, focusing on issues of complexity and dealing with the contrasting positions of H. A. Simon[1] and C. West Churchman.

5.7.2.2 Ulrich's comment

It is not surprising (for those familiar with the content of Note 1) that Ulrich makes the point that the tradition Simon subscribes to has built its enormous success on Caesar's old principle: *divide et impera!* which he translated into the language of systems science as, 'decompose and control'. This is an approach to complexity that reflects quite nicely the Type I and Type II positions on complexity derived earlier.

5.7.2.3 Social Systems Design

Distinct from the systemic-reductionist view of Simon is C. West Churchman's philosophy of Social Systems Design[2] (apart from the references to Churchman found at the back of the book, also see the *Festschrift* edition for Churchman in *Systems Practice*, Vol. 1, No. 4, with guest editor W. Ulrich). This is essentially a nonreductionist dialectical approach that guarantees recognition of subjectivity and a concern for social metaphysics in an understanding of rational design. It paves the way for sociological concerns such as false consciousness and effects of social material conditions (unlike the first epistemological break—see Chapter 7 for details).

An informative way of understanding these two positions at this stage is by contrasting their main characteristics (see Table 5.7 which otherwise appears in Ulrich, 1983, p. 321–323). This table is valuable in terms of our discussion because we can discover in it contrasting meanings of complexity

Table 5.7

Hypothetical discussion between H. A. Simon and C. W. Churchman

Position: Represented by:	'Sciences of the Artificial' H.A.Simon	'Philosophy of social systems Design' C.W.Churchman
Subjectivity is	avoided: excluded from the definition of objectivity; objectivity has no way to deal with the spirit of social systems	not avoided: must be included in the definition of objectivity; the designer must consider the spirit of individuals and whole systems in his design
Complexity is	hierarchical: complex systems are built up from hierarchies of sub-systems	not hierarchical: systems are complex because they cannot be described as hierarchies of components
Wholeness of systems (holism) is	denied except in a pragmatic sense: the whole is not more than the sum of the parts, though its analysis is not trivial; regarding complex systems as wholes does not help to explain them	critically considered: there are wholes that cannot be dealt with as sums of parts; regarding complex systems as wholes serves the critical purpose of reminding us of the limits of our understanding
Reducing complexity of systems to simple subsystems (reductionism) is	a source of knowledge: every system has components which are simpler systems; systems can be understood as black boxes, and the inquirers task is to make them transparent (reductionistic systems approach)	a source of irrelevance: what really matters are systems that are individuals; the inquirer's problem is to account for the individual aspects of systems (antireductionistic systems approach)
The purposeful character of systems (teleology) is	denied: ascribing purposes to social systems is a source of deception (teleological fallacy)	critically considered: ascribing purposes to social systems serves a necessary critical purpose against hidden value assumptions (teleological imagery is needed in addition to causal-analytic terms)
The decomposability principle is	accepted: near-decomposability of complex systems (the decomposability principle for artificial systems is applied to social systems)	rejected: design-nonseparability of the components of complex systems (the design-separability of components of artificial systems does not hold for social systems)
The description of systems must	focus on redundancy: by making use of the worlds redundancy, complex systems can be described simply (e.g., in terms of simple process descriptions standing for redundant state descriptions)	focus on uniqueness: every system has not only redundancy but also uniqueness; to the extent a system is unique, it is its own simplest description (description of uniqueness matters as much as description of redundancy)
The crucial design task to be solved is	problem decomposition: how to decompose a complex system into simple systems that are easy to be controlled? Or: how to design and control complex hierarchies? ('Divide et impera!' standpoint; control problem)	problem identification: how to describe unique systems and especially: how to identify the whole system on the one hand, the smallest system (individual) on the other? ('Ethics of whole systems' standpoint; boundary problem)
The designer's main tool is	objectivity: semantic precision of concepts, model building, causal-analytic explanation: mathematical analysis, empirical research, computer simulation, heuristic programming; scientific rigor, 'programmed decision making' (Science of the Artificial, 1969)	subjectivity: reflection on the sources of knowledge and deception: social practice, community, interest and commitment ideas, esp. the moral idea, affectivity, faith; ongoing debate and self-reflection, 'process of unfolding' (The Artificiality of Science, 1970)

as well as a variety of other systems concepts. These reflect different paradigmatic forces, underlining the argument of this chapter. We are particularly interested in the break that Table 5.7 begins to point to.

At first sight it might not be at all clear how Ulrich has advanced the work beyond Checkland. 'What is contained in the table surely amounts to nothing more than an interpretivistic vision for systems thinking?' After all, the main advance beyond Simon's work is in the recognition of subjectivity, 'Isn't it?'. Well, yes, this might be the case, but we need to take a very careful look at how Ulrich conceives of subjectivity. He says that subjectivity is 'reflection on the sources of knowledge *and deception'* (emphasis is mine). This will surely move us away from achieving a position of relativism in respect to people's subjective positions. With a notion of deception new concepts need to be introduced, such as false consciousness, which can be understood as freezing of people's *Weltanschauung*. This may occur in at least two interrelated ways. First, in the creation of forced visions (invisible to the dominated) about the value of work and other social and economic issues. Second, in terms of a super-science, or a dominant rationality, that shapes the way we treat 'the' external natural world, 'our' social world and 'my' internal world. This is a rationality that may dictate the formation of dominant discourse that ultimately may penetrate society and impose 'its' way on us, even to the extent of our sexuality as we have been informed (Foucault, 1979). These require a critical approach that has as a part of its discourse notions of deception, which Checkland apparently ignores.

In summary I suggest this. That while it is valid to state that Churchman did not properly come out with subjectivity in terms of theory (i.e., issues of ontology and epistemology—see Checkland's, 1988c, claim on this account), it is equally true that Checkland has never properly come out with subjectivity in terms of politically aware ideology (see also Mingers, 1984, debate on subjectivity). A main contribution in pointing to what I term a 'second' epistemological break, is recognition that we must aim to be critically reflective on both theoretical and ideological subjectivities, which will amount to our understanding of subjectivity. Now, if we reflect back on Table 5.7 we can understand much better, overall, how different the conceptions of complexity and other systemic concepts are through this 'new' epistemological position.

5.7.2.4 'Second' epistemological break

Whereas Simon's view aims to objectively explain and design whole unique social systems, Churchman's theory of complexity asks how we can design for social systems to become more whole and unique. As Ulrich explains, the crucial task is not in developing analytic tools such as simulation models (although these can be useful if critically employed), but rather to introduce dialectic tools to help planners *reflect* on their designs and enter into reasonable discourse with the affected. To this end Churchman (1979) presented a dialectical approach to the unfolding of the unavoidable conflict between systems planners who strive for systems rationality and the 'enemies' of any rationality, that relates to concerns of private and subjective rationality (see Ulrich, 1988b). Ulrich's point is, that no systems approach for handling real-world complexity should seriously be considered rational unless it allows for and encourages (self–)critical reflection of free citizens. This vision is forcing recognition of a 'second' epistemological break and provides the seed corn for an adequate epistemology for systems practice that will be fully worked out in Chapter 7.

5.7.3   Conclusion

At last we are beginning to get more than a sniff at the argument of this book. We have seen more clearly what the challenge is for inquiry: it is to *reestablish* a self-reflective, critically normative approach to practice by making sure that our concepts are properly understood in those terms (achieved in this chapter) and by working out an adequate epistemology for systems practice (achieved in Chapter 7).

5.8   CONCLUSION

At the beginning of this chapter I set out to fill in the details of the distinction between abstract and paradigmatic definitions of 'system'. This has been achieved by initially disposing of its everyday contentless use, showing abstract richness (and disposing of abstract artificiality) of systemic metaphors and by working out a diversity in paradigmatic contentfulness. All of this provides the vehicle by which we can argue in Foucaulvian terms that there are breaks and discontinuities in discourse relating to systems thinking. We have seen three in this chapter. These ruptures articulate and distinguish between discourses. This assumes and accepts resistance and struggles in discursive formations. Our aim for the next chapter is to operationalize the ideas of Interpretive Analytics for liberation of discourse, in particular from attacks based on untenable or impoverished epistemologies, as a necessary stage in the development of an unusually powerful critical approach to the liberation and critique of knowledges.

NOTES

(1) I have included this note to clearly explain some ideas that relate to Simon's position. It also helps to balance the argument of this book by detailing fundamental reckoning that supports traditional systems science.

Complexity and structural decomposition

Simon (1962, p. 468) refers to a system as complex when

> ...the whole is more than the sum of the parts, not in an ultimate, metaphyscial sense, but in the important pragmatic sense that, given the properties of the parts and the laws of their interaction, it is not a trivial matter to infer the properties of the whole.

An application of systemic decomposition in the natural sciences which necessarily related to this position (Flood *et al.*, 1988) will help us to contrast a traditional view on complexity with a critical view, and help us to understand the importance of the idea of a further epistemological break. The following key features related to Simon's work surfaced.

The essential ideas can be found in a discussion on levels of organization and reduction, where Bunge (1977) noted that the concepts of level and hierarchy are central issues for modeling (in biology). If we wish to represent complex biological processes in order to analyze them in terms of levels (i.e., decomposition for manageability and validation) it is essential that a systemic approach be taken.

Although the study of complexity is of a systemic nature from this position, the desire to reduce complex representations into sets of smaller and more manageable units runs the risk of neglecting a most important systemic phenomenon, that of emergence. Partitioning models across richly interactive faces will inevitably give rise to a loss in properties (i.e., error).

Using Nearly Completely Decomposable Matrix Theory (NCDMT), complex representations may be analyzed by structural decomposition. In some cases, however, it must be accepted that a model is found to be nondecomposable. The NCDMT technique has been developed for stochastic 'finite complex systems' and is one that brings out the main points concerning complexity from this position. We will critically discuss this 'class of system' (i.e., the way 'system' is understood in advance of working out the technique like ideas).

'Finite Complex Systems' (FCS)

It can be argued from Simon's position that mathematics has been used successfully for modeling either small or infinitely large 'systems', with analytical mathematics being used to analyze each 'part' together with the interactions between parts. Typically, a small number of significant factors and a large number of insignificant factors appear initially as complex, but on investigation hidden simplicity is found. This type of discovery is typical of 17th, 18th, and 19th century sciences (Klir, 1985).

For infinitely large 'systems', where both the number of 'parts' (or 'subsystems') which make up the 'system' and the interaction between the 'parts' is very large, such that the variables might be said to exhibit a high level of random behaviour, continuity of the functions can be assumed. Then statistical mechanics or, through careful aggregation of the variables involved, classical mathematics may be employed successfully in analysis (it is claimed).

Following this position, an intermediate class of 'system' may also be encountered. These are much too rich and complex for explicit solutions to be calculated and not complex or homogeneous enough to be able to assume the continuities required for aggregation of variables or the use of techniques that work effectively on a large degree of randomness. Such 'systems' of intermediate complexity are commonly referred to as FCSs.

Weaver (1968) described three classes of 'system'; organized simplicity, organized complexity, and disorganized complexity. FCS equates to 'systems' of organized complexity. Klir (1985) claims to have identified some of the wide range of the class organized complexity (or FCS):

> ...instances of systems with organized complexity are abundant, particularly in the life, behavioural, social and environmental sciences as well as in applied fields such as modern technology or medicine.

Because of this apparent abundance, Klir, Simon, Courtois, and others set about developing technique-ideas for powerful analysis, such as structural decomposition.

Analysis of FCS representations by structural decomposition

An important theoretical contribution to the study and analysis of FCS is structural decomposition. This is particularly useful for empiricist or structuralist validation of mathematical models, where the validity of sub-representations may be sought, for example, as required by a validation methodology applied by Flood *et al.* (1986) to a large-scale simulation model of fluid volume maintenance in man. Some ideas on this theme are presented below.

The extent and discipline of structural decomposition, or the disconnectability of model elements, has been rigorously studied (Albin and Gottinger, 1983; Simon and Ando, 1961). Their work concerned the analysis of large dynamic mathematical models in terms of nearly completely decomposable matrices. It was claimed that mathematical models may be viewed as composite systems of terms representing interactions of the variables within each subsystem and terms representing interactions between subsystems. Researchers concluded that, over a relatively short period, the first group of terms dominated the behavior of the model and hence the subsystems can be studied approximately independently of other subsystems. Over a relatively long period of time the second group of terms dominated the behavior of the model. (The term 'approximately independent' is interpreted as a weak interaction or link, as opposed to the strong interactions which dominate model behavior.)

Such properties would have important implications for validation by decomposition. Typically, decomposition of models must be undertaken using functional rather than relational criteria. The above quoted paper of Flood and co-workers, for example, considered validation at five levels (see Figure 5.5) where the first two are clearly based on functional criteria. For beneath the surface theoretical validation, this may be acceptable. For on the surface empirical validation, particularly using model emulation, appropriate relational decomposition is essential so that the two groups of terms and their modes of domination, which exist at the whole model level, are reflected in the analysis of subsystems. Failure to achieve this will, in terms of this theory, invalidate empirical observations on the validity of the subsystems.

A logical extension of the domination properties for weakly coupled sub-systems is that their short-term behavior and relative

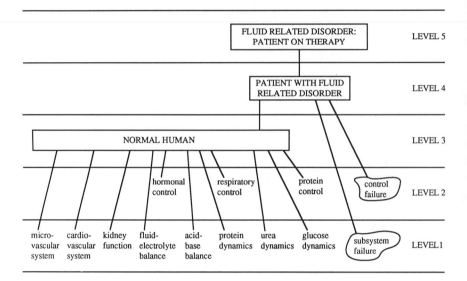

Five levels for validating a complex model of fluid-electrolyte dynamics in man

Figure 5.5

equilibrium values can be evaluated in isolation, that is, as if the model were completely decomposable. Since subsystem equilibrium is approximately preserved in the long-term, the long-term behavior and validity of the whole structure can be evaluated by a macroscopic model. Each subsystem's relative equilibrium state only needs to be represented in an aggregated way with a manageable number of variables. This may help in achieving a parsimonious representation, depending on modeling purpose, while also promoting validation of complex models over longer periods of time, without repeating lengthy simulations.

These ideas can be extended. Courtois (1985) stated that in a multilevel model where subsystems at each level are themselves nearly decomposable, analysis and validation proceeds level by level, starting from the lowest level where the interactions are strongest.

Mathematical representation of a stochastic FCS

A stochastic FCS can be represented by a state transition matrix. Analysis presents a real difficulty in manipulation of the matrix and involves computational complexity in both space and time.   Decomposition of the matrix reduces computational complexity. Consider a matrix Q (a model) that can be rearranged to the form Q^* after appropriate permutation of rows and columns:

$$Q^* = \begin{bmatrix} Q_1^* & & & \\ & \bullet & & \\ & & Q_i^* & \\ & & & \bullet \\ & & & & Q_n^* \end{bmatrix} \tag{5.1}$$

where Q_1^* to Q_n^* are square submatrices and the remaining elements (not displayed) are all zero. The matrix is said to be completely decomposable. In reality, a matrix representing a FCS will not be completely decomposable, but after row and column permutation it may be possible to form the major elements into submatrices along the diagonal as shown for Q^*. The minor elements can then be separated in a matrix C. This yields:

$$Q = Q^* + \varepsilon.C \tag{5.2}$$

where ε is a very small real number and C is a new arbitrary matrix (not arbitrary in total since the sum of each row equals zero) of the same dimension as Q^*. The matrix Q represents a model S which is nearly completely decomposable. The submatrices of Q^* on the diagonal represent the nearly decomposed subsystems of S. From the matrix C an error bound can be calculated. Errors are caused primarily by the fact that the weak couplings between subsystems are ignored when the short-term relative behavior of the subsystems are evaluated in isolation.

Simon-Ando theorems justify the use of a procedure of variable aggregation to approximate the inverse and steady-state eigenvector of the nearly completely decomposable stochastic matrix. In fact, both the Simon-Ando (1961) and the subsequent Ando-Fischer (1963) existence theorems aim at proving that whatever standard of accuracy is required from such approximations, there always exists a sufficient degree of near-complete decomposability such that an aggregation procedure would meet this standard.

Courtois (1977) concentrated on the approximation of the eigen system; he showed that the process of aggregation yields an approximate accuracy of ε, being the maximum degree of coupling between the aggregates. Courtois and Semal (Courtois, 1977; Courtois and Semal, 1975) have also shown that a procedure that makes use of eigen characteristics of the aggregation matrix and the steady-state vectors of the aggregate yields an accuracy of ε^2.

(2) An isolationist stance would deny that the two approaches, of Churchman and Simon, were theoretically commensurable. In a spirit of complementarism, however, Churchman (1968a, Chapter 14) argued that either position becomes absurd if taken as absolute and that both are needed for adequate rational thinking (according to context we might add).

CHAPTER 6

ON 'SYSTEM': HISTORIES AND PROGRESSIONS OF SYSTEMS THINKING (STRAND 3)

Discovering differing conceptions on the history and progress of systems thinking. Liberating discourse, an example and some ideas on legitimacies and limitations. The need for a broad theory of legitimacies and limitations

6.1   INTRODUCTION

The question concerning the necessity of this chapter must arise since it is often stated that, universally, systems thinking is recognized as coming together 40 to 50 years ago. I shall contend that this view can be fundamentally challenged, as would be expected considering that a Foucaulvian notion of the development of knowledge underpins the reasoning of this thesis. Accordingly we shall reject the idea of one history and progression in systems thinking.

My aim and justification for an historical analysis follows the gist of Carr's (1964, p. 30) message from his Trevelyan lectures at Cambridge: that '...history is a constructive outlook over the past and present ... between the events of the past and progressively emerging future ends.'

Thus, history and progress of systems thinking and emerging new trends, such as Critical Systems Thinking and our studies on Liberating Systems Theory, could be considered to be part of the same dialogue. Carr's view, however, does not make the Foucaulvian power break of introducing the notion of many past histories of knowledge, but in essence does link in an idea of critique ('constructive outlook') and that the past can contribute to the 'progressively emerging' future ends: but we must not stretch Carr's rationale too far.

The point of this chapter, if there is a single residual, is to show that a liberating rationale over knowledge can be achieved. Then we will be in a position to ask of our achievement: 'Given a diversity of freed knowledges, how can we deal with them in terms of legitimacies and limitations?' This can only be brought about by developing an adequate epistemology, which is worked out in the following chapter. For now, in preparation, we are going to review a number of ideas on the history and progress of systems thinking, consider briefly what these would mean in respect to knowledge and then we will set about a Foucaulvian study. We will see how the methodological principles of Foucault discussed in Chapter 3 can be effected through an application to the now largely refuted and suppressed General Systems Theory.

6.2   VIEWS ON THE HISTORY AND PROGRESS OF SYSTEMS THINKING

6.2.1   Introduction

If we were to take a general survey of social theory with a particular focus on how history (in particular of knowledge) has been treated as a discipline, then we could justifiably argue that there are at least four approaches with contrasting views. These will be outlined in a short comparative appraisal below and assessed in terms such as complementarity or contradiction. This section was first published by Flood and Gregory (1990).

6.2.2   Ideas on the Nature of the History and Progress of Knowledge

The four main approaches I have chosen to present are as follows:

(1) Linear sequential — the notion of a single trajectory on which there is just one direction that is aligned to time (a two-dimensional theory). In this case, then, ideas are generated and tested and tangible knowledge is accrued. The scientific method of observation as traditionally conceived would be appropriate for these incremental and chronological expositions. With this view the history of knowledge is evidently characterized as cumulative as 'the jigsaw' becomes ever more complete.

(2) Structuralism — the superficial notion of a single trajectory is not deemed to be sufficiently rich, or able to explain the cumulative nature of knowledge. Complex systemic scientific models are therefore developed, offering explanations which are understood by the workings of feedback cycles. These last aspects of the models are internal, while the whole model itself is aligned to the direction of time (they are three and four dimensional). In this way model output, in terms of knowledge, is unidirectional, incremental, and of chronological expositions. This can easily be supported by traditional scientific methods that include investigations for that which is beneath the observable surface. The analogy of a jigsaw construction also holds for this case.

(3) World-viewism — is a position that rejects the notion of unidirectional model output as not being sufficiently rich to be able to explain contrasting and even contradictory knowledges. An alternative model of how world-views come about is proposed (Kuhn, 1970, 1977). This is a repetitive general cycle, having periods of normal science where exposure leads to the uncovering of anomalies in theories by certain groups, whereupon periods of extraordinary science give rise to new views that explain the old anomalies (plus, apparently, all other phenomena that the replaced theory was able to deal with). Another period of settled normal science follows and so on. In this case, then, it is the world-view that changes and with it what amounts to differing knowledges. The notion of contrasting perspectives on 'the same world' is anti-incremental, anti-cumulative although it is clearly chronological.

The main area of study of world-viewism has been the results of positivistic scientific methods, although the explanation about how different positions emerge is interpretivistic. In other words, there is an interpretivistic model of the history of knowledge, yet the knowledges to which world-viewism relates and was constructed to explain are positivistic in their assumptions.

(4) Genealogy — the notion of world-viewism is rejected since it (a) takes a macroview ascribing ownership of knowledge to communities and (b) it neglects to properly take on board the notion of power. A straight introduction of notions of power into world-viewism would simply lead to issues of sovereignty. This would not be acceptable with genealogy (as discussed in Chapter 3, but also see Foucault, 1979, 1980) where microanalysis is proposed, that is, the forces of power are applied at a microlevel, the impact of which works upward forming networks and clusters of knowledge. Thus there is the notion of discursive formations, or statements in the form of networks, that cut across sentences and other written discourse. These discursive formations are dynamic and are shaped by power relations applied at the microlevel and evidence of them may be found in communities but must be explained methodologically by working upwards from the microlevel.

Generalizing from these four approaches, we can identify a number of issues that broadly feature in ideas of history and progress of knowledge. The ones that I reckon important are: teleology or finalism or terminalism (the issue of end points); origin or emergence (the issue of start points); descent (the record); originator (who or what was responsible for the origins); mode of progression (what dynamics are involved); ownership of knowledge; agent of change; literary versus nonliterary influences; and metaphors to explain progress. A record contrasting these ideas is given in Table 6.1 relating to the four approaches. The essence of and differences between each approach are evident in this summary.

We are now in a position to undertake a review of a number of proposals about history and progress in systems thinking, according to researchers in the systems field.

6.2.3 Approaches to the History and Progress of Systems Thinking
6.2.3.1 Introduction

In this brief review we will be considering a number of historically oriented approaches to systems thinking through the windows of the four general ideas described and discussed above.

Table 6.1

Contrasting four ideas on the history and progress of knowledge

GENERALISED ISSUE	FOUR IDEAS ON HISTORY AND PROGRESS OF KNOWLEDGE			
	LINEAR	STRUCTURALIST	WORLD–VIEWISM	GENEALOGY
FINALISM	Assumed	Assumed	Rejected	Rejected
ORIGIN	Unitary	Unitary	Plurality	Plurality
DESCENT	Determinate	Determinate	Intended	Accidental
MODE OF PROGRESSION	Cumulative	Cumulative	Change in world view forced by anomalies	Historical succession of discursive formations as a matter of contests and struggles over systems of rules
OWNERSHIP	Sequentialists -elites	Structuralists -elites	Sovereign -elite communities	*Ideally* all
AGENT OF CHANGE	Causal and *natural*	Holistic and *natural*	Forcing of an extranormal science and *culture*	Colonisation of mechanisms of *power*
DOMINANT METAPHOR USEFUL FOR EXPLAINING THEORY	*Black-box* (input-observation; output-knowledge) with feedback control of verifiability or falsifiability	*Organic* (deep generative mechanisms) with feedback control of falsifiability	*Culture* communities in peace and conflict	*Power* continual contests and struggles between and in living networks
STATUS	Objective, positivistic	Objective, positivistic	Subjective, interpretivistic	Critical

6.2.3.2 Review

Checkland states that '...clearly it is not possible to write objective history. As Popper points out the least we can do is to write history which is consistent with a particular point of view.' (Checkland, 1981, p. 23) This strongly suggests a world-view approach, yet his argument is augmented by two tables depicting the linear chronological structure which, accordingly is 'inherent in the history of science'. Further, Checkland perceives science as having evolved through two main phases — Greek Science and the so-called Scientific Revolution. The latter is shown to be dependent on the former, drawing on it for rules by which we conduct scientific enquiry. He describes this approach as '...a sketch of the development of science which enables us to understand the nature of systems thinking as being complementary to scientific thinking.' (Checkland, 1981, p. 23). Science is perceived as a 'cultural invention' (Checkland, 1981, p. 23) stemming from a unique religious, social, and economic climate. It is also depicted as rational and all pervading and as providing '...testable knowledge of the way the natural world works.' (Checkland, 1981, p. 24).

Besides presenting both a world-view and a linear chronological analysis of the history of science and systems thinking, Checkland's writings also lean toward historical structuralism in that scientific knowledge is cumulative where each new philosopher builds on knowledge from a variety of previous philosophers (see Checkland, 1981, p. 55). The accrual of knowledge can be explained by a model of science based on three major characteristics and it is this model of reductionism, repeatability, and refutation that Checkland believes systems science transcends.

Checkland's understanding of the history of science is summarized as

...a method of enquiring, or learning, which offers us, at any moment of time a picture of our understanding of the world's reality which consists of certain conjectures, established in reductionist repeatable experiments, which have not yet been demolished. (Checkland, 1981, p. 57).

There are others who, like Checkland, have drawn upon several of the approaches identified in the previous section. In Flood (1988a) I expressed the view that systems emerged through one world-view struggle, yet was now in the midst of a second world-view struggle. This process involved reconceptualization of old concepts, as the fundamental tenets of the interpretive paradigm were more widely adopted. This was epitomized in Flood (1988b, discussed in Chapter 5), where a call for a new language to aid this second world-view struggle was made and some tentative ideas were offered. Yet, in Flood and Carson (1988, Chapter 1) an historical structuralist approach was offered, in the form of four interlinked development cycles put together to explain how and to some extent when systems theory and practice emerged. All of this work is now better understood in the argument of this book.

The world-view approach has also been proposed by Dando and Bennett (1981), who specifically applied Kuhn's model of scientific advance to Operational Research (OR) which, during the 1970s and 1980s, was considered by several prominent members of its community to be in a state of crisis. Indeed, Ackoff (1979) went so far as to state that *The future of OR is past* — a statement which he backed by his effective withdrawal from the OR community. In our complementarist scheme worked out in the next chapter, the methods of OR are given a practically useful position.

Dando and Bennett were concerned to show what evidence existed to support the claim that OR was in a crisis, or that extraordinary science was being undertaken by the practitioners of OR. They chose to study two periods separated by a ten year interval (i.e., 1968 and 1978) and undertook a comparative analysis of the types of OR articles published. They concluded that the Kuhnian model of science, as characterized by scientific revolutions, could effectively be applied to investigate possible transformations occurring within the OR paradigm. By then comparing articles from 1963 to those of 1973 (i.e., having four markers, 1963, 1968, 1973, 1978), they argued that

> ...in the 15 years from 1963 to 1978, the OR community has shifted from a widespread feeling of certainty about its role and optimism about its future, to a state in which significant sections are experiencing and expressing considerable uncertainty and pessimism. (Dando and Bennett, 1981, p. 23).

In another worthwhile paper *The structure of the systems paradigm*, Cornock (1978) made a credible effort to get within the incoherent whole which, Cornock believed, is systems science. The aim was to provide the lay person with a general model of linked concepts which portray the entirety of the science. This model, not surprisingly following the title, is structuralist and provides the reader with a representation of the current state of the science, although the underlying processes and transformations which ultimately led to that particular configuration are not displayed. Cornock proposed that, with concepts in general and the model in particular, knowledge of a situation/problem/system can be gained and thus the science developed from systems ideas might progress. Retrospective analysis, however, was not undertaken.

Van Gigch and Stolliday (1980), the last of our cases, reviewed the 'epistemological foundations of the systems paradigm'. The co-workers constructed an historical structural view of science and systems science. They describe a model of the development of systems science which, it was proposed, provides the context within which their required analysis of the systems paradigm could take place. They conceptualize the history and development of science as punctuated by a bitter divorce ('the divorce of faith from reason...') which occurred at the end/collapse of the the medieval world and by the seduction of men by reason (Van Gigch and Stolliday, 1980, p. 41). Furthermore, they expressly address the problems of human sciences which initially adopted the traditional scientific method. Through the difficulties experienced by these human sciences they see the science of systems emerging.

The model proposed by Van Gigch and Stolliday is one of paradigms and thus is similar in conception to that of Kuhn's world-view approach.

Their analysis, however, is less concerned with the processes than the structure and the interconnections between the perceived paradigms. In the reviews above we have clearly seen three of the four approaches that we are interested in, implicitly and occasionally explicitly drawn upon. Many of the issues earlier detailed are evident in these writings. To conclude, we shall now briefly summarize some observations and thus outline a way forward for our studies.

6.2.3.4 Conclusion

We have seen that a number of researchers have found utility in adopting several approaches to study history and progress of systems science, on occasions at once. This must raise the question whether there are inherent contradictions in these works, after all the linear sequential approach assumes cumulative knowledge whereas world-viewism assumes nothing of the sort (see Table 6.1). A general survey of this suggests that contradiction may not be prominent and that, by subsumptional or other means, 'versions' of plurality may have been achieved. A complementarist reconstruction of these ideas might prove to be interesting research.

One feature of the above review is, however, absolutely clear. Only in the vaguest of manners is any notion of power introduced (with the exception of Dando and Bennett who stress the role of extra-disciplinary influences on the development of Operational Research) and in no case is Foucault's work touched upon. The lack of attention paid to the forces of power shows some naivity. One hardly has to search far to find relevant evidence, (e.g., any of Foucault's later works). Foucault's notion of genealogy considers descent (origin) and emergence of concepts through an archaeological framework. Emergence in particular momentary manifestations arises because of domination at local discursivity levels imposed by nondiscursive subjugators. Thus there are forces holding together discursive formations. A situation of conflict leads to subjugation and thus to resistance and relations of power. Historical succession of discursive formations becomes a matter of contests and struggles over systems of rules or interpretations. This is quite typical of competing theoretical and methodological endeavours in systems thinking and constitutes the basic reasoning for our continuing investigations.

6.3   ABANDON GENERAL SYSTEMS THEORY? AN INTERPRETIVE ANALYTICAL CRITIQUE

6.3.1   Introduction

As we have already discovered, there are various views about how and why theories, or knowledges, come into and slip away from the community of reason. Some believe that each phase is a natural linear or generative progression, while others believe that new world-views emerge according to their ability to deal with anomalies of another extant one. There is, in my opinion, a more helpful way of explaining the phenomena of the emergence of theories or knowledges in Foucaulvian Interpretive Analytics. In order to be meaningfully researched, such inquiry needs to take account of five methodological principles. All of this is dealt with in detail in Chapter 3, but now we will accept Foucault's

> ...invitation to researchers and analysts to study power in terms of its mechanisms, techniques and procedures at its point of application, in its exercise or practice and (will) dispense with the juridicial-political theory of sovereignty which has exercised a conceptual dominance over analysis of power. (Smart, 1985, p. 84).

In order to give an example, in particular of the fourth and fifth methodological principles, I shall be carrying out a critique of General Systems Theory, since this apparently has been discredited (remember, the fourth principle is that analysis of power should proceed upward from a microlevel and seek to reveal how mechanisms of power have been colonized, and the fifth that the exercise of power is accompanied or paralleled by the production of apparatuses of knowledge).

With General Systems Theory we have an opposing discourse, not against the dominant rationality of positivistic thought (a high-level generalized dominant discourse that consumed the ontological break of General Systems Theory), rather as a challenging discourse within the boundaries of the positivistic rationality. The historical *a prioris* of positivism legitimated invisibly, quietly and absorbingly what could be thought and accepted as true or valid. The challenge of General Systems Theory was intra-paradigmatic, challenging discourses (and knowledges) of the same rationality. Certainly the discontinuities represented disorder but they were hardly revolutionary as is the case with inter-paradigmatic discontinuities and breaks. The intra-paradigmatic suppression of General Systems Theory was achieved effectively through domination, where colonization of the mechanisms of power in the very fabric of society was not successfully achieved. I would argue that this is a clear case of power producing (or suppressing in our case) knowledge, rather than being a case of the peculiar force of the better argument (i.e., this supports Foucault's rather than Habermas' notion of power). The *strategic skills* of the General Systems Theorists must have been in part faulted. Systems thinking fell foul, even at this early stage, to the peculiar attraction of conceptual reflexivity and the notion of a finite and closed set of concepts that could be used to explain everything. The colonies in place remained bound against this simplifying concept. The strength of the systems argument also became its main enemy under positivistic thought. This was a theoretical fault. Further, things have not been aided by the messing about with the main institutions, or organizations, of the systems movement as we will briefly consider below.

The term General Systems Theory disappeared from the name of the flagship organization of the systems movement over thirty years ago. Almost as soon as it was established, the 'Society for the Advancement of General Systems Theory' became the 'Society for General Systems Research.' The term 'General' has now disappeared altogether, with the change of name in 1988 to the International Society for Systems Sciences.

I intend to approach some points as to why this might be the case and why the notion of General Systems Theory has been largely subjugated by the systems and extracommunities. The emphasis is philosophical and will consider:

(a) whether the notion of General Systems Theory could be resurrected (considered in this chapter) and
(b) whether and how it would be beneficial for the movement to do so (considered in the next chapter).

The study will be working through adversarial arguments and so will be dealing with what General Systems Theory has been accused of constituting. By largely refuting the main criticisms of nonreflective positivists, neo-positivists and interpretivists, I shall establish a basis from which the notions of General Systems Theory can be reconsidered.

Our discussion will begin with a review of conceptions of General Systems Theory. I will suggest that while the common conceptualization contains admissible flaws in terms of the adequate epistemology of the next chapter, the notion of General Systems Theory has to date been criticized and summarily dismissed on the basis of clearly refutable criteria. Such attacks will be examined therefore in terms of a review of the mechanisms which prompted the historic apostasy. This section was first published by Flood and Robinson (1990).

6.3.2   What Is Meant by General Systems Theory?

General Systems Theory suffers, in a way, from a surfeit of definition. Here we will discuss some of the most common views of what General Systems Theory is thought or said to be. I am not claiming to know just what General Systems Theory is, nor am I weighting any of the views presented.

The name most commonly linked to General Systems Theory is that of Ludwig von Bertalanffy (see Bertalanffy, 1968). He attempted to develop a set of theoretical concepts based on simplified mathematics of 'systems'. He claimed this advance could culminate in a unification of the sciences.

Central to this set of concepts was a belief in isomorphisms. Theorists reckoned that the importance of isomorphisms would be shown through the realization that the same laws would find expression in different and apparently unrelated fields. On this foundation General Systems Theory would then serve as an important regulative device in science. It would make possible the transfer of simplified conceptual models from one field to another and lead to parsimony in scientific research. At the same time by formulating exact criteria, General Systems Theory would guard against superficial analogies which are useless in science and harmful in their practical consequences.

Boulding (1956) went further in establishing a teleology of General Systems Theory, giving it a definition and an objective. He perceived General Systems Theory as, '...a body of systematic theoretical constructs discussing the general relationships of the empirical world. This, then, would be the quest of General Systems Theory'. (Boulding, 1956, p. 11).

Further, Boulding predicted that General Systems Theory would develop something like a spectrum of theories — a system of systems which may perform the function of a gestalt in theoretical construction. Such gestalts, it was argued, have been of value in directing research.

General Systems Theory in Boulding's (1956, p. 12) conceptualization is clearly teleological and predicts a theoretical output: 'It is one of the main objectives of General Systems Theory to develop these 'generalized ears' and by developing a framework of general theory to enable one specialist to catch relevant communication from others.'

Later Boulding (1956, p. 13) hints at the development of a philosophic framework by defining a further objective for systems theorists:

> If the interdisciplinary movement is not to lose that sense of form and structure which is the discipline involved in various separate disciplines then it should develop a structure of its own. This I conceive to be the great task of General Systems Theory.

A structural development for General Systems Theory was suggested by Boulding among others. One approach would be to look over the empirical universe and pick out certain general phenomena and to seek to build up general theoretical models relevant to these phenomena. This would be a 'GENERAL General Systems Theory'.

A second approach would be to arrange the empirical fields in a hierarchy of complexity in terms of an organization of their basic individual or unit of behavior, and try to develop a level of abstraction appropriate to each. This would be a 'SPECIFIC General Systems Theory'.

These approaches actually suggest two different things. Respectively, General Systems Theory as a 'Generalized Theory of Systems' and General Systems Theory as a 'Theory of Generalized Systems'.

For many others, General Systems Theory begins with a philosophical, almost metaphysical emphasis. To Downing Bowler (1981), it represents:

(a) the quest for relational universals that are true for systems in general and universals that emerge at new levels of complexity; and

(b) a model of the whole of existence as the interaction of entropic and negentropic processes.

This strategic importance of General Systems Theory, its appeal and ambition, rests in this conceptualization as fundamentally a description of relationships that may be represented by mathematics or other symbolic methods.

6.3.3   Common Areas of Criticism

Although a number of the principles of General Systems Theory outlined may well require rethinking in terms of an adequate epistemology for systems practice outlined in the next chapter, it is peculiar to find that the spirit of the propositions are held in such obvious contempt by the systems community as well as critics from outside. This we will address below. Before looking at more complex defenses of the concept from philosophical and paradigmatic standpoints, we will begin with a brief résumé of areas of criticism of the notion of General Systems Theory.

First, it has been suggested that General Systems Theory suffers at the hand of criticisms launched from a position that is shared by many so-called 'general theories' (Jones 1978), in that they are too vague, hard to prove, disprove, or use in any practical or convincing way he suggests.

Jones gives Freud's theory of psychoanalysis and Marxian economic theories as examples: while it is possible to use such general theories to formulate specific, testable predictions, an outcome contrary to the prediction does not really shake the theory. Jones (1978, p. 144) explains, 'This is because both reality and theory are rich enough to allow for constant reinterpretation'.

Real world practitioners, however, commonly prefer more rigorous guidelines. It has often been said that General Systems Theory failed to bear the fruits it offered. In this respect we must decide whether such criticism pertains to the theory or the practice. Good theories have been rejected in favor of poor data in the past. As a heuristic, or possible gestalt, we might argue that General Systems Theory may still have something to offer.

Second, it can be argued that it is clear that it was the practical offshoots of the notions originally heralded as the forbearers of a General Systems Theory which took precedence. There is evidence that this is true of Information Theory, Cybernetic principles, Organization Theory, Control Theory and perhaps even Management Science (Boulding, 1956). Specific development of practical methodology was emphasized in these and other related spheres.

It has been further suggested that the pragmatic emphasis left these exemplary theories, together with the possibility of a meta General Systems Theory, philosophically immature. In this respect, General Systems Theory as a concept appeared ephemeral and insubstantive. This view has been perpetuated but 'How many so-called systems scientists could give a satisfactory answer to even a casual enquiry as to 'What is General Systems Theory?' 'How many could specify with sureity how the everyday business of systems science differs from the longer term teleology prescribed to General Systems Theory?'

Last, it has been assumed that the development of General Systems Theory required that the torch be taken up by other disciplines. This has not obviously occurred. In fact, many other disciplines have taken General Systems Theory rather as a platform from which to snipe at subsidiary systems activities.

We will now concentrate upon the philosophical criticisms levelled at General Systems Theory.

6.3.4   Reviewing the Philosophical Criticisms
6.3.4.1 Introduction

We will now survey three philosophical attempts to dismiss the concept of a General Systems Theory; attempts by (a) nonreflective positivists, (b) neo–positivists, and (c) interpretivists.

These three positions may also be said to reflect paradigmatic implications for the systems movement (discussed in Chapters 5 and 7).

6.3.4.2 The positivist attack

Peter Caws suggested in 1967, that attack and criticism from the positivists is possibly attributable to the unwillingness of the Society for General Systems Research to dignify a mere working hypothesis with the label theory. The tone reflects paradigmatic connotations concerning the legitimization of a notion of a General Systems Theory.

We may follow Ayer's (1971) criticisms of the positivist adoption of conclusive verifiability as a criterion for significance. Before looking at the propositions of General Systems Theory it is helpful to look at other more obvious general laws. These may take a broadly empirical form such that 'all men are mortal' or that 'arsenic is poisonous'.

The very nature of these propositions, however, dictates that their truth cannot be established with certainty by any finite series of observations. This has been acknowledged by General Systems Theory. Naturally it is impossible to describe all systems, hence General Systems Theory proposes to deal with a typical example in each class. A phenotypic system is likely to omit, of course, certain aspects found in the genotypic system, although a task of General Systems Theory was to recognize this and construct a theory that is a logically consistent set of propositions concerning a wide variety of systems models.

The positivists, in pursuing their own argument, must acknowledge that if such general propositions of law are designed to cover an infinite number of cases, then it must be admitted that they cannot, even in principle, be verified conclusively. In adopting conclusive verifiability as our criteria for significance, the positivist is logically obliged to treat any general propositions of law in the same fashion as they treat the statements of the metaphysician. This is clearly a most impractical position and in the face of this difficulty, some positivists have adopted the heroic course of saying that these general propositions are indeed pieces of nonsense, albeit essentially important pieces of nonsense.

Introduction of the term 'important' is simply an attempt to hedge and marks a recognition that the positivist's view of any general proposition is philosophically paradoxical, without in any way attempting to deal with the paradox. The contention is then that no general proposition, apart from a tautology, can possibly be anything more than a probable hypothesis. Conclusive verifiability as a criterion for significance cannot make a distinction between the concept of a General Systems Theory against other clearly practical general propositions.

6.3.4.3 The neo-positivist attack

The root of the neo-positivist criticism lies in a conceptualization and an ascribed importance of isomorphism. While we should acknowledge that this is one of the areas requiring reconceptualization and one we will be returning to shortly, diverting the neo-positivist attack is still quite straightforward.

An important facet of von Bertalanffy's conception of General Systems Theory rests on the idea of isomorphism. Indeed, the isomorphism found in general systems principles is of a more or less well developed General Systems Theory.

On the basis of the existence of isomorphism across disciplines, General Systems Theory could be expected to play useful roles in the meaningful transfer of models from one field to another, while weeding out the meaningless similarities. Von Bertalanffy has been criticized in this respect for not specifying the criteria by which General Systems Theory will distinguish the meaningful from the meaningless similarities.

Again, by taking up criticisms that General Systems Theory fails to distinguish between meaningful and meaningless statements, neo-positivists have made an arguably inappropriate assumption which questions the status of General Systems Theory as a scientific theory (i.e., in terms of neo-positivist tenets). General Systems Theory in this respect is not a scientific proposition by the criteria of falsificationism which defines scientific statements as falsifiable in principle. Since this is not necessarily the case, logically principles of General Systems Theory must move into the area of philosophical statements.

In pursuing the falsificationists' argument, according to De Vries and Hezerwijk (1978), Popper has been credited with showing the impossibility of the neo-positivists efforts to demarcate sense from nonsense and hence the meaningful from meaningless in philosophy. He attributes their attempt to a naturalistic fallacy.

A separation of meaningful and meaningless should or would be coterminous with the distinction between science and metaphysics. Popper has satisfactorily shown that the difference between science and metaphysics is not of a naturalistic character. Instead, there are conventions stipulating norms that may enable us to come nearer the goal of science (and in this respect General Systems Theory), that is, explanation. This goal is of course a normative convention not given by nature as argued in detail in the next chapter.

Once again the proposition of a General Systems Theory supports a refutation on these grounds in that the strategic importance of General Systems Theory, its appeal and ambition, rests in a conceptualization as fundamentally a description of relationships. It is recognized that definitions other than Bertalanffy's could be constructed leading to another kind of General Systems Theory. For example, Miller's (1978) classification of generalization suggests that there are at least two kinds, those pertaining to uniformities across a given class and those pertaining to different classes.

6.3.4.4 The interpretive attack

From within the systems movement, attack has been made by interpretivists who are paradigmatically unable to accept concepts of nomic isomorphism, in particular for social contexts.

General Systems Theory rests easier by far within the context of a natural science paradigm. It has not been seen to struggle in the natural sciences in the same way as elsewhere. This may be partially explained by the empirical emphasis in natural sciences, together with the benefits that a general theory development offers in this area (see Troncale, 1986).

Serious problems arose with General Systems Theory in the attempt to transfer general models into the social sciences. In the social sciences the difficulties may begin even in attempts at identification of a 'system', which interpretivists only acknowledge as a concept that may be used as an organizing structure or conceptual tool for putting together our thoughts, perhaps to aid in real world intervention. It is impossible in this area, interpretivists argue, to recognize any concept of nomic law-like isomorphism. Perhaps, once more, there is a misrepresentation of the spirit of General Systems Theory?

General Systems Theory has been previously conceptualized as referring to ontological matters of fact, so-called real systems in a real world. We have, in this context, established that no general proposition referring to a so-called matter of fact can ever be shown to be necessarily and universally true. It can, at best (and I mean at best), be a probable hypothesis. This is true of all propositions which pretend to a factual content.

Although that argument failed to dispose of the possibility of a General Systems Theory in the factual natural science paradigm, it appears that the criteria of that argument persist in the interpretive paradigm despite the condition that anything other than subjectively objectified facts have no status in what was termed, in the last chapter, a 'second' systems struggle.

Furthermore, interpretivists and social scientists are really only able to theoretically reject the notion of nomic isomorphism. In a General Systems Theory description of a 'system', it is the business of the related methodology to demonstrate that phenotypes are representatives of real systems evidenced in empirical data. Since we have dismissed the naive argument that General Systems Theory is only able to handle real systems evidenced in natural science, then why should it not be extended into perceptual or communicative systems? An awareness that there might be such concepts as issue-based contextual, rather than nomic, isomorphisms might prompt interesting research?

6.3.5   Discussion

The reasons for the above resistance should be clear by now. Principally, it was felt that the vehemence with which General Systems Theory has been denied by systems thinkers required some reconsideration.

It is concerning to observe that everyday systems thinkers who use concepts relating to 'open system' (such as inputs, outputs, feedback, homeostasis, etc.) still find themselves unable to seriously contemplate the possibility of a General Systems Theory. This is, I suggest, partly explainable as the resulting side effects of some of the functionalist philosophical arguments described above. Positivism, for example, largely precludes that statements can ever become logically certain, a conclusion that must be accepted by every consistent empiricist. Ironically, this may be thought to involve the positivist in skepticism. Now, many systems thinkers go so far as to shrink away from general theory concepts: examples easily spring to mind, Ackoff (1963), Naughton (1979), and Lilienfeld (1979). This does not have to be the case. Just because the validity of a proposition cannot be logically guaranteed in no way entails that it is irrational for us to believe it. What is irrational is to look for a guarantee where none can be forthcoming and to demand certainty where probability or interpretation is all that is achievable.

Some comparisons which may seem logical by the tenets of General Systems Theory will evidently prove to be pointless and futile in the long run (see the ideas on legitimacies and limitations in the next chapter). Yet much of science is based on analogical principles and isomorphic assumptions. With the interpretive paradigm we would acknowledge that 'system' is not a concrete thing but an abstract concept that constitutes particular relationships that can be actualized in a number of ways.

Further, we could accept the view put forward by Foucault and others that theories may be thought of as some kind of structured whole. While it is commonly accepted that theories, as structured wholes, may themselves be thought of as general 'systems', it has ironically escaped notice that concepts of a General Systems Theory in the interpretive paradigm may have some role to play.

Surely the development of General Systems Theory was not intended to end with the last full stop of von Bertalanffy or any other relevant theorist? The 'genius of Bertalanffy', suggests Battista (1977), does not depend on the validity of the classical systems theory he devised, but rather that he was attempting to devise an altogether new kind of theory. It would not be in the spirit of Bertalanffy to attempt to develop a theory that could integrate all of science, or to accept his version of General Systems Theory as the singular or final form, any more than it would be in the spirit of Freud's attempt to develop a general theory of psychology to accept the concept id as the final unequivocable version. In other words, why should we carve out a total universal and closed vision of any theory and then go about refuting it once and for all? The claim, for example, that General Systems Theory has the potential to unite science has been interpreted in many ways. Does unification of science refer to a reduction to a common language, a synthesis of concepts or a form of encyclopaedic theory among disciplines? In essence, our main concern should not be so much with defining and refuting or establishing theories, but rather dealing critically with the kinds of assumptions that we might make through the use of the theories.

In this context we may lastly return to Ayer (1971), who emphasized a point which appears to have relevance to General Systems Theory within the wider systems movement, namely, that the most pressing matter is not so much universals of science, but rather the unity of philosophy with science. Ayer (1971) stated that

> With regard to the relationship of philosophy and the empirical sciences, we have remarked that philosophy does not in any way compete with the sciences. It does not make any speculative assertions which could conflict with the speculative assertions of science.... Of course, it is impossible by 'merely' philosophizing to determine the validity of a coherent system of scientific propositions. The function of the philosopher is 'merely' to elucidate the theory by defining the symbols which occur in it...science is blind without philosophy.

General Systems Theory has survived a variety of attacks on its conceptual and practical validity and still appears to offer some potential to become a philosophy with associated methodology for the systems movement. It is part of our intellectual legacy and high time it was given some respect.

6.4   CONCLUSION

The aim of this chapter was to complete our study relating to the many issues that arise under the heading 'system'. In the previous chapter we broke away from the natural tendency for systems thinking to slip into a blind conceptual reflexivity, and then considered abstract richness of 'system' and diversity in constituting varying paradigmatic conceptions of that abstract idea. This does not mean to a critically oriented thinker that any one conception must be declared superior or automatically redundant and useless. What does seem to be the case, however, is that any one may apparently emerge as victor or the defeated because of the strong force of isolationist thinking. It is important, then, for us to look behind the prison doors. Foucault's Interpretive Analytics at least offers us methodological principles that acknowledge the dynamics of localized forces of power and that colonization of the mechanisms of knowledge are to be held responsible for this subjugation. In this chapter we have drawn upon Foucault's principles, in particular the fourth and fifth described earlier in Chapter 3, to challenge the refutation of a General Systems Theory. This did not reflect any preconceived isolationist position that such a theory was superior, rather the aim was to challenge the forces of domination and subjugation. The ideological intent with this liberating rationale will be made explicit in the following chapter when developing an adequate epistemology for systems practice.

In this second section of the argument of the book, we have considered a critique of systems-based knowledge in terms of articulation and release. In Section 3, following, we will turn our attention to the reasoning that leads to our conception of limitations and legitimacies. Then we will have put together a theory and unity for liberation and critique, standing boldly against universals.

SECTION 3 OF ARGUMENT

- SPECIFIC -

'LIBERATING SYSTEMS' THEORY ('LS'T)

A critique of knowledges: legitimacies and limitations: against universals

CHAPTER 7

ON 'INQUIRY': SYSTEMS 'PROBLEM SOLVING' (STRAND 4)

Establishing a complementarist vision and three rationalities. A critique of the three rationalities in terms of legitimacies and limitations

7.1 INTRODUCTION

In previous chapters we have been concerned with abstract richness and paradigmatic interpretations of systemic concepts, particularly focusing on 'system' and 'complexity'. In the last chapter emphasis was placed on histories and progressions in systems thinking, but of course this too was centered on issues relating to systemic concepts as they are articulated by discontinuities in discourse. In fact, up to now, we have dealt with liberating 'systems theory' (L'ST'), trying to work out a position where the full potential of systems thinking can be clearly understood and not masked by self-misunderstanding or self-grandeur.

Perhaps in this set task this book has served to bring to the surface important issues relating to self-reflection within the discipline, and has left a lot of hard work yet to be done. Nevertheless, given some success in showing that intellectual liberation in systems thinking is worthwhile, we can meaningfully pursue issues of 'liberating systems' theory ('LS'T), that is, systems theory for liberation and emancipation of individuals, races, genders, workers, and whoever else may be disadvantaged or in need of more equal opportunities and self-determination. These are issues involving inquiry.

In this chapter we will direct our attention to matters of inquiry. I shall be putting together another general framework that encompasses a full range of paradigmatic concerns, therefore including ideology, theory (epistemology and ontology), methodology, and method. We will be concerned with the impact of our understanding of knowledge-constitutive interests and how this leads to a complementarist argument for inquiry. Having developed that position against a number of other scenarios, we will then work out in detail the basis of an adequate epistemology for systems practice. You will not be left simply with an indicator about a perceived as necessary epistemological break, nor just a scent and whiff of what it might be like. Rather, the fundamental ideas of a carefully reasoned systems and sociological epistemology will be proposed, that is essentially in agreement with a complementarist approach to inquiry. Then the last part of the argument of this book will be in place, which reflects back over conceptual anti-reflexity, abstract richness, paradigmatic contentfulness, and histories and progressions in systems thinking. In other words, we will have achieved a liberating rationale for systems thinking as such, while then making adequate use of systems ideas for liberation of the human condition.

7.2   GENERAL FRAMEWORK ON INQUIRY

7.2.1   Introduction

The framework presented in this chapter was originally constructed (see Flood, 1989a, b) to promote and add consistency and comprehensibility to a study that I was undertaking concerning scenarios for the future of systems 'problem solving' (discussed a little later). The investigation was a development of the work carried out by Jackson (1987a), who in turn was interested in some original work by Reed (1985).

The study referred to above elaborated on Jackson's four strategies for the future of Management Science, coming up with six scenarios for the future of systems 'problem solving'. These came under four principles: pragmatism, complementarism (renamed from pluralism) , imperialism, and isolationism.   We have already brushed against two of these, complementarism and isolationism,[1] when reflecting in Chapter 4 on the necessary conditions for conceptual reflexivity to hold (which in fact was not possible if you recall).   Let us now briefly look at each set of principles arising from the six scenarios, or styles of inquiry (a more detailed exposition follows in the next section).   Then we will be in a position to begin to comprehend the general framework as such.

7.2.2   Four Principles, Six Styles

The four principles named above usefully break down into six styles of inquiry. For reasons that will become evident, isolationism will be split into two approaches, theoretical and methodological isolationism; and ideas relating to imperialism also split into two, methodological imperialism by annexation and methodological imperialism by subsumption. With these four we shall contrast pragmatism and complementarism. Each will be briefly sketched out below insofar as it is necessary to achieve an initial understanding of the general framework.

I have defined *pragmatism* as atheoretical (being aware of the philosophical position of pragmatism that is different from my conception). The approach involves evaluation of assertions solely by way of practical consequences without reference to theory.   On the other hand *complementarism* is theoretically based. Its most important feature is theoretical commensurability at a meta-level (i.e., drawing upon meta-reasoning) which associates methodology with context, and is therefore characterized by methodological incommensurability.

CLASS	STYLES OF INQUIRY [marked by *]	
1	pragmatism *	
2	complementarism *	
3	isolationism	methodological isolationism * theoretical isolationism *
4	imperialism	imperialism by annexation * imperialism by subsumption *

Four principles and six styles of inquiry for systems 'problem solving'

Figure 7.1

Isolationism splits into two distinct approaches: theoretical and methodological isolationism. *Theoretical isolationism* obviously makes reference to theoretical groundings. It differs from complementarism because it rejects theoretical commensurablility. In this approach a range of methodologies may be used as defined from one theoretical world-viewpoint. Methodological isolationism merely gives preference to a single approach. There are two forms of imperialism. First, where a methodology is built onto by part annexation from other methodologies; and second, when outside methodological approaches are subsumed within one isolated approach. These ideas are summarized in Figure 7.1.

7.2.3   The General Framework

To build some substance into the general framework, eight observations were made on each of the six styles (i.e., there are six styles as defined by the issues relating to these observations).   These split evenly into observations on theory and on methodology, eight questions in all.   The following was assessed (some bracketted explanations from Midgley, 1989b).

(a) Is the approach theoretically/methodologically referential (i.e., are theory and/or methodology specifically referred to)?

   For theory — are ontology and epistemology explicitly recognized?

   For methodology — are strategic and constitutive rules adhered to (see Petrie, 1968; Naughton, 1977; Checkland, 1981; Flood and Carson, 1988)?

(b) Is theoretical/methodological commensurability assumed in the approach (i.e., are a variety of theories and/or methodologies considered to be complementary)?

For theory or methodology — is there a standard by which differing theoretical paradigms or methodologies can be assessed or operated between?

(c) Is inter-theoretical/methodological 'partitioning' accepted or carried out through the approach (i.e., is it considered acceptable for two or more theories and/or methodologies to be 'sectioned' and 'recombined' into new forms when appropriate)?

For theory — are there definable theoretical paradigms recognized or actively worked between?

For methodology — are methodological boundaries recognised and adhered to?

(d) Is intra-theoretical/methodological partitioning accepted or carried out through the approach (i.e., is it considered acceptable to take out just part of a theory or methodology for use in particular contexts)?

For theory — within definable theoretical paradigms, are separate schools of thought recognized, or actively worked between?

For methodology — are distinct methodologies disassembled and used in separation?

The findings of this survey are summarized in Table 7.1 and are briefly discussed below under the titles of the six styles of inquiry.

7.2.4   Comments on the Six Styles
7.2.4.1 Pragmatism

The most striking feature about the pragmatic approach is that no apparent reference is made to inferable underlying theory or methodological rules. The main emphasis is on intra-methodological partitioning; (i.e., using parts and techniques in an heuristic, trial and error fashion). The use of a single whole methodology is not inconsistent, although somewhat unlikely with this approach. There are no explicit considerations of either theoretical or methodological commensurability, nevertheless, superficially the pragmatist is assuming measures by the same standard.

7.2.4.2 Complementarism

No two approaches contrast so starkly as pragmatism and complementarism. In fact, the only areas of overlap are somewhat dubious anyway. These are inter-methodological partitioning which the pragmatist could in principle undertake, and theoretical commensurablility which is

Table 7.1
Archaeology of (systems) inquiry

style or 'strategy' > observation ⌄	pragmatism	comple-mentarism	theoretical isolationalism	methodological isolationism	methodological imperialism (annexation)	methodological imperialism (subsumption)
1. Theoretically referential	NO	YES	YES	YES	YES	YES
2. Theoretical commensurability	not explicitly considered, but superficially YES	at a level of meta-reasoning YES.	NO	NO	NO	NO
3. Inter-theoretical partitioning	NO	YES	YES	YES	YES	YES
4. Intra-theoretical partitioning	NO	YES	within bounds of the isolated theory YES	in the sense that part of a theoretical paradigm is given precedence YES.	in the sense that part of a theoretical paradigm is given precedence YES.	in the sense that part of a theoretical paradigm is given precedence YES.
5. Methodologically referential	NO	YES	YES	YES, although reductionist analysis may bring in refinements.	YES, although the rules may change when annexation occurs.	YES, although reductionist analysis may bring in refinements.
6. Methodological commensurability	not explicitly considered, but superficially YES.	NO	YES	NO	NO	in the sense that outside methodologies are seen as special cases YES.
7. Intermethodological partitioning	not necessarily, unlikely, but consistent with the approach YES.	YES	YES	in the sense that one methodology is isolated from an irrelevant external mass YES.	NO	YES
8. Intramethodological partitioning	YES	NO	NO	NO	YES	NO

widely contrasting even in their 'agreement'. In terms of recognizing complementarism, the key observations are methodological incommensurability and theoretical commensurability (at a meta-level of reasoning). Equally important, however, is inter- and intra-theoretical partitioning, which might pave the way for context and methodology to be linked.

7.2.4.3 Theoretical isolationism

Reference to theory is made, although only the tenets of one paradigm are accepted, while all others are objected to (i.e., there is theoretical incommensurability). Another label for this is a world-view approach. In this case differing methodological approaches are accepted, there is methodological commensurability but each is considered to work only from one world-viewpoint. In other words, certain contexts demand only a subset of concepts from the adopted paradigm. Concepts from an 'inferior' paradigm may deal with these certain contexts but for other contexts their 'inferiority' is shown in the form of anomalies. The vital difference is the methodological commensurability of theoretical isolationism, which then pairs with theoretical incommensurability.

7.2.4.4 Methodological isolationism

There is one very important distinction between methodological and theoretical isolationism and that concerns methodological commensurability. In this case, a single methodology is isolated within some paradigm, to which users remain loyal by exclusion of all other methodologies. The key methodology may itself require minor modifications following reductionist developmental analysis.

7.2.4.5 Methodological imperialism (by subsumption)

In this approach a methodology is adopted that may call upon other methodologies at a specific point in order to act as submethodologies to deal with specific matters. For example, if the 'what' had been decided upon through use of a mother methodology, a 'how' methodology may then be drawn into the process. In terms of observations in Table 7.1 there is great similarity and no outright contradiction between this approach and theoretical isolationism. The main differences are that in theoretical isolationism different methodologies are used according to favoured principles, whereas subsumption means that one methodology is used although different methodologies may be called upon to help out.

7.2.4.6 Methodological imperialism (by annexation)

Whereas subsumption suggests a facilitating or mother methodology that guides and directs the use of other inferior methodologies in restricted cases, annexation is a proposition that parts of other methodologies may be attached, perhaps as a front end, in order to deal with specific matters of inquiry. This is seen to strengthen the methodological approach within a theoretical framework and so this imperialism, alongside subsumption, is clearly a form of advanced isolationism.

7.2.5   Conclusion

In this section I have presented and made some basic observations on an archaeology of inquiry, with the aim of promoting consistency and comprehensibility in the following study of six scenarios for the future of systems 'problem solving'. From this archaeology, the logic of any one of the styles can be assessed. The table also acts as an awareness map so that we may critically review our activities in terms of other potential practical bases. There are, however, some contentious issues to be considered for each style, and merits and demerits need to be assessed for each one. These will be aired and dealt with below.

7.3   SIX SCENARIOS FOR THE FUTURE OF SYSTEMS 'PROBLEM SOLVING'

7.3.1   Introduction

Since the disastrous attempts to apply systems engineering in social contexts in California in the 1960s, which were based on the assumption that the techniques and methods that overcame complex engineering problems, especially in aerospace, could surely help to resolve the rather simpler difficulties of transportation and housing for example (the naivity of this view has been successfully argued by Hoos, 1972), and following several other hard-hitting criticisms of systems application and theory (see Lilienfeld, 1979, for example), the systems community has been attempting to reestablish its credibility. These efforts are by no means unidirectional, but there is an underlying theme which concerns an adjustment of method where human beings constitute an important element in a situation of interest. Systems Engineering (for instance, Jenkins, 1969), Operations Research (for instance, Daellenbach *et al.*, 1983), and Systems Analysis (for instance, Atthill, 1975) have all, more recently, exhibited some sympathy toward the human element. For others these partial involvements are not satisfactory and subjectivity associated with the thinking-being-man becomes of paramount importance. As Jackson (1982) has clearly shown us, the works of Ackoff, Churchman, and Checkland exemplify this soft school of thought (as opposed to the hard traditional approaches mentioned above). Vigorous debates at conferences, symposia and in the scientific literature are symptoms of underlying conflict between the two main schools, each perceived to be vying to attain a pinnacle position with an emerging dominant discourse for systems thinking and practice. To complicate the issue further, the 1980s have seen the emergence of a new and powerful argument of Critical Systems Thinking (e.g., Ulrich, 1983, 1988a; Jackson, 1985a; Oliga, 1988; Flood, 1989c, and the thesis of this volume) which recognizes both the utility of the systemic metaphor, the innate subjectivity of human interpretation, but additionally recognizes the need to manage conflict and coercion. To satisfy the last requirement requires a genuine appreciation of the systems epistemological ideal, as we shall find out later on in this chapter.

For the novice seeking a satisfactory way to penetrate the fundamentals of systems 'problem solving' this state of affairs is difficult and somewhat off-putting. For the long-serving generals and sergeants of the systems movement the debate has become tedious, leading largely to disinterest in other positions but with occasional necessary resurfacing in order to defend a trench or launch an attack on an enemy's position. Debates in this area have been dominated for the last fifteen or so years with issues relating to the merits and worth of hard versus soft ideas, these being essentially paradigmatic. 'Is hard a subset of soft?' 'Is soft a subset of hard?' 'Are hard and soft distinct?' To the exclusion of most other activities, this isolationism has led to reductionist analysis of particular parts of methodologies, a sometimes necessary and fruitful, if wholly insular, way of developing these theoretical models for investigation, representation, and intervention (for example, and running the risk of being accused of picking out one methodology for scrutiny which is not my intention, the *Journal of Applied Systems Analysis* shows this tendency for Soft Systems Methodology; see Rhodes, 1985 and Woodburn, 1985 as two cases at hand).

So, the question arises for the systems 'problem solver' — 'Is this our lot?' The answer is — 'Not necessarily'. Thankfully such outdated debates now face and certainly should be replaced by the following higher-level argument. The reverse view of isolationism and reductionist analysis is complementarity and holistic synthesis. Contrasting with complementarism are a number of correlative views with different principles, as found in the archaeology presented above. We will consider these in detail immediately after the following overview.

Possibilities for a pragmatic approach have been discussed in depth (Flood and Carson, 1988; Ellis and Flood, 1987). The essence of this anti-philosophy is the evaluation of assertions solely by way of practical consequences, without informed reference to theory. This seems an easy way out and, as argued below, is a rather frail proposition for a rigorous systems practice.

The common understanding of imperialism is the policy of extending a country's influence by acquiring dependencies, or through trade, diplomacy, and so on (*Oxford Dictionary of Current English*). Applying this idea to systems methodologies suggests extension of a methodology by annexation from other methodologies. In recent times one strand of the call for correlativity between methodologies has been precisely this. For example, to deal with the difficulties of multiple viewpoints, we might be told to build on a soft front-end to a hard methodology. This seems too good to be true and, as argued later, is rather simplistic.

A second and more credible form of methodological imperialism is to remain in isolation but to draw in methodologies to deal with sub-difficulties. With this position, when the 'what' in a problem situation has been dealt with (what should be done) it may be necessary to use a 'how' methodology (how should we do it). In this way whole methodologies are *subsumed* within a facilitating methodology.

Methodological isolationism, in its pure form (imperialism offers advanced forms), is nothing more than the use of one favourite or known methodology for all problem contexts. Theoretical isolationism is distinctly different in that many methodologies may be drawn upon according to context, yet their application is carried out wholly in accordance with the fundamental tenets of the isolated theory.

A complementarist way forward is a powerful call for correlativity. The aim here is to investigate situational complexity in addition to analysing how various systems methodologies deal with different aspects of complexity. It is then possible to link methodology to situational context via meta-reasoning and thus to direct the systems 'problem solver' toward an appropriate methodological approach. There are some unresolved difficulties associated with this approach that will be explored in due course.

The aim of this section, then, is to investigate six possible ways forward for systems 'problem solving'. Complementarism, a critical approach, emerges from this discursive study as offering promising ways forward. This conclusion is drawn only after careful exploration of the relationship between theory (ontology and epistemology) and methodology with the aim of uncovering two things simultaneously: (a) to find an approach which offers prospects for the long-term survival and success of systems 'problem solving' in practice and (b) which does this without incorporating theoretical contradictions.

We shall now look in detail at the six approaches in turn. To start, I have dealt with the nontheory-based pragmatism which, as a consequence of its lack of worked out theoretical foundations, offers a relatively easy terrain to explore. The remaining studies deal with theory based approaches and are naturally debated in continuum.

7.3.2   Pragmatic Approaches

Tomlinson (1987) and Naughton (1979) have expressed the pragmatic approach in 'hard' and 'soft' terms respectively, and Jackson (1987a) has considered these. An overview of the main ideas of pragmatism can be found in Flood and Carson (1988) and Ellis and Flood (1987) which are developed below.

The pragmatist remains optimistic about correlativity between hard and soft approaches, but does not make reference to underlying theory (thus the optimism is hardly critically challenged). While this reference is not made, however, the pragmatist will be blindly assuming the rationality of a dominant discourse. This will be working invisibly, quietly, and absorbingly on their practical efforts. The approach can be clearly explained below by comparing and contrasting it with the fundamentally different theoretically based approaches.

We can appreciate two views of systems 'problem solving'. One view is systems as a coherent theory about how to work with people and 'manage problems'. Such a theory would explain what kinds of situation are commendable to what kinds of 'solution' with what kinds of client (we will lump all theory-based approaches into this category for now). It would tell you how to work when involved in a systems study, which amounts to an epistemology (difficulties associated with such approaches will be discussed below). On the other hand there is the pragmatist's view that systems is a craft. The practitioners have some command over a 'bunch of tools' which they use and find out about, more or less by trial and error, until one works. They have no theory of what would work when or why. Of course there is a theory which can be inferred, emanating from the dominant view of the world implicit in the tools and language used, but practitioners do not make it coherent or rigourous. In essence this is a systems technology.

The pragmatist may be seen as someone who has a systems tool bag in which all methodologies and techniques are contained. This kit is then used in an analogous way to cathedral building of old. The craftsmen were able to build complex structures using their own tool kit, but had no idea why the thing stood up, why a beam fixed one way cracked, but fixed another way did not. They only knew how to do it from the practice of trial and error (Hamwee, 1986).

This argument is summarized in Figure 7.2, where the left-hand side refers to the theory based systems approaches and the right-hand side refers to pragmatic systems technology. In terms of constitutive and strategic methodological rules (Naughton, 1977) there is no unidimensional methodological trajectory in the technology version. The methodological trajectory would transcend definable theoretical spaces, apparently without making reference to these deep foundations. Such practitioners link the tools (which could be techniques or methodological components) that are appropriate to distinct stages of 'problem solving' activities in a thought-to-be phased and controlled manner (according to experience). The

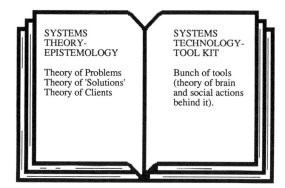

Theory based and pragmatic ideas about systems practice
Figure 7.2

requirements are a knowledge base acquired through learning by practice, and a creative flair. The more experience, the more complete the utilization of the tool bag becomes.

Such a correlative philosophy has been promoted by Warfield (1984) with Interactive Management. A system of management decision making approaches is proposed as a response to a perceived impoverishment in any single approach. This reflects the view that complexities of interdependence come in many contexts. The ideas are, however, pragmatic. If an intervention is deemed to be successful then the factors of that situation are noted and when they are encountered again (or in a similar form) intervention will follow the same course, using the same whole methodologies (i.e., there are main stages in Interactive Management, but at each stage there is pragmatic choice between approaches; see Warfield, 1984). This rather weak heuristic approach contrasts most strongly with the deep reasoning behind the theoretically based complementarist approach.

There are at least two types of pragmatist that we should look out for. The first is the strategist who makes explicit the desire for a tool kit approach (e.g., Naughton, 1979), the second is the *unwitting* pragmatist who pursues such an approach because it is the first furrow that is stumbled into.

Of course, this approach cannot pass without scrutiny. Difficulties associated with systems technology arise because of the lack of reference to theory. In particular, managers and consultants put priority on keeping clients happy. In other words a preconceived, prestructured appreciation of 'a problem' effectively gives rise to a predetermined 'solution', since other factors which might have been uncovered are neglected because they do not conform to the prestructured view. Related to this is the notion that managers cannot afford to 'get it wrong' or be seen to fail. This argument could be extended to incorporate the concern that the pragmatic approach leads to the maintenance and increase of power of elites.

In an interesting survey *The Economist* (February 13, 1988) showed that 'people are rightly skeptical about management consultancy'. The practicing pragmatist could well be a synonym for the management consultant according to the message of this article. Criticism does not always fall on the consultant however. The firm is often to blame. Witness this extract.

> In harsher practice, a firm will often call in consultants because it does not know what to do next; because it is fashionable; or to get a seal of approval for an already planned course of action. The worst case of all is the calling in of consultants for reasons of internal office politics: to strengthen one faction's case for a strategy, or even to provide a pretext for sacking particular managers. (*The Economist*, Survey: Management Consultancy, February 13, 1988, p. 6–7).

This transmits the message of the previous paragraph in harsher terms. Even in a situation where the trial and error process is not constrained there are severe criticisms. The question of unfortunate social consequences arises. Heuristic *in vivo* experimentation on social situations runs the danger that unthought-of and unacceptable levels of damage and distress might occur.

Mattesich (1978) epitomizes this anti-pragmatist view. At the outset of his book he banishes the general notion of pragmatism:

> Too many of us are satisfied with the pragmatic criterion that science is true because it works. Works for how long? Until Mother Earth has become uninhabitable thanks to this working? How can we be sure that the expedient of today is not the impedient of tomorrow? Could the pragmatic answer not become the death certificate of science and mankind alike? Indeed, truth and knowledge deserve a firmer foundation than short-run usefulness. (Mattesich, 1978, p. 4).

A case for practice being based on sound theoretical principles does therefore emerge and provides a springboard for the following discussions. So let us turn to the theory-based approaches.[1]

7.3.3   Isolationist Approaches

Isolationist approaches are theoretically referential. Theoretical isolationism is the case where, at a deep level, clear ontological and epistemological beliefs are held, are consistently subscribed to and, in fact, protected against extra-paradigmatic 'enemies' (i.e., other beliefs are presumed wholly invalid). In addition to this theoretical isolationism, further restrictions are set and adhered to by methodological isolationists, namely through the isolation of a single methodology which is used in all cases — the 'house methodology' as some commercial consultancies would have it.

Methodological isolationism is also static in the sense that reductionist type analysis may bring about changes but they are, at least after the early developmental stages, somewhat limited changes, more like refinements.

There seems to be little benefit pursuing the methodological isolationist route. The world of 'problem solving' is far too rich and various to allow us to be content with this simple option. Theoretical isolationism is, however, much more promising. Our restriction is merely paradigmatic. Working within a clearly stated normative framework is not obviously problematic — after all the generally well received world-view, or *Weltanschauung*, philosophy is substantively based on the same notion. This correlative debate, however, can easily be confused and/or conflated with the complementarist one. These two therefore need to be articulated in proximity. This will prove to be vehicular in terms of the main conclusions of this section. Before we reach that decisive point let us first think through the imperialist approaches.

7.3.4   Imperialist Approaches

The main difference between imperialism and pragmatism is in the adoption of a core theory (in the former) which is built upon by drawing on ideas or methodologies from other persuasions which, in some way, appear to offer ways of overcoming outstanding anomalies or difficulties. The core theory is based upon fundamental tenets that the protagonist will neither negotiate nor endanger. An imperialist will draw upon ideas from other approaches, but sees these approaches as restricted and explainable in their (the imperialists') own terms.

Imperialism by annexation can be seen as 'advanced isolationism'. Because new approaches emerge some isolationists, feeling dissonance about their approach because of anomalies which may exist, consequently respond by developing their own approaches. A more cynical view is that annexationists are rapacious in their research, tracking down the 'titbits' and drawing upon them, while discarding the (so-perceived) offal.

Imperialism by subsumption is a thoroughly different approach and one that does seem to offer some promise. The main commonality with annexation concerns the adoption of a core theory that the protagonist will neither negotiate nor endanger. This apparently is satisfactorily achieved because certain contexts are deemed to be special cases that can be dealt with by drawing upon a limited number of concepts from the adopted theory, and special case methodologies associated with these. Only the facilitating methodology, however, is accepted as sufficiently rich to work within the variety of possible contexts and must on all occasions drive the inquiry.

One of our concerns in this section is to consider whether the ideas of such a strategy are theoretically sound. The answer here is rather obvious since a set of coherent fundamental tenets forms the foundations of imperialism and these will not be sacrificed. If new ideas or methodologies are appended to or incorporated within the preferred approach, then they are suitably molded so as not to incur contradiction as a cost. Thus far it seems that theoretical contradiction is an exclusive weakness of the pragmatist.

Our second concern is with the prospects imperialism offers for the future of systems 'problem solving'. Here we find some fundamental difficulties and worries. Take for example Beer (1967) who, according to Jackson (1987a), 'sets out the imperialist manifesto for organizational cybernetics'. A critical analysis of his later work (see Flood and Jackson, 1988) showed its eminence in the functionalist paradigm but raised some penetrating questions from thinkers of the interpretive paradigm. For example, Checkland (1980) asked 'Are organizations machines?' and 'Can they not legitimately be seen from many other viewpoints?' (cf. Morgan, 1986 and his multiple metaphors as ways of perceiving organizations, and Section 5.3.3 above).

Ultimately imperialism, or advanced isolationism, must fail on the same reckoning as pure isolationism in terms of complementarity (i.e., *complete* domination is unlikely because of paradigmatic conflicts). Consequently Jackson (1987a) concluded that imperialism is unlikely to come about as a result of natural developments since attempts to convert adherents of other persuasions will usually be fruitless and are unlikely to help in the achievement of total domination (imperialism of course being expansionary). Although the lack of learning and conversation between competing groups is to some extent overcome, the real benefits of this openness in terms of satisfactory conciliation are minimal because of the narrow view of situational context that is taken. We will now, therefore, explore approaches which, at least in their aim, attempt to draw a variety of methodological approaches together to deal separately with different contexts in a genuinely open and conciliatory fashion.

7.3.5   Complementarist Approaches

In their seminal paper *Towards a system of systems methodologies*, Jackson and Keys (1984) were engaged in the development of a two-dimensional grid into which system types may be 'classified'. They then

	Unitary	Pluralist	Coercive
Mechanical	M—U	M—P	M—C
Systemic	S—U	S—P	S—C

A complementarist vision of methodology choice

Figure 7.3

considered a range of methodologies and how these related to the grid. Accordingly, the difficult question of knowing 'which methodology should be used when' was raised. Jackson (1987a) claims that this is a pluralist (we use the term complementarist) way forward, so let us investigate this assertion.

For the first dimension of the grid a distinction is made between 'systems' that are perceived to be simple or complex. The work of Ackoff (1974) and the expressions 'machine age' (mechanical) and 'systems age' (systemic) were drawn upon. The essence of those expressions in the context of types of 'system' is highlighted in Figure 7.3. The second dimension of the grid reflects the nature of the decision makers (or 'participants'), in particular considering the degree of consensus among them. The dimension ranges from unitary consensus at one extreme, to pluralist dissensus at the other extreme; and to coercion in later developments (Jackson, 1987a). This unitary-pluralist-coercive dimension does highlight the political awareness (as distinctly different from political motivation) of the original authors. What is interesting is that this 'system of systems methodologies' can show, within the politically aware structure, how the range of systemic metaphors discussed in Chapter 5 may be brought in to help understand that methodologies have inherent assumptions about the nature of social reality. This analysis has been explicitly dealt with elsewhere (Flood and Jackson, 1991a) but some main observations are interjected in the discussion below.

The two dimensions of 'system' and 'participants' therefore suggests mechanical-unitary (M-U), systemic-unitary (S-U), mechanical-pluralist (M-P), systemic-pluralist (S-P), mechanical-coercive (M-C), and systemic-coercive (S-C) problem contexts (using Jackson and Keys' terminology).

To assess the usefulness of the grid for practitioners, it is necessary to consider how appropriately the regions reflect a range of systems based methodologies, at least initially theoretically. To achieve this a representative sample of methodologies will be considered. This task was duly undertaken in the second part of Jackson and Keys' paper, which is appraised below.

Classical Operations Research (OR as exemplified in Daellenbach *et al.*, 1983) is reflected by mechanical-unitary problem contexts, since this approach can only effectively be used when there is general agreement about the attainability of the system goals. Systems Analysis and Systems Engineering, for example those of the RAND Corporation and M'Pherson (1980, 1981) respectively, were dealt with.

This classification seems appropriate because Systems Engineering and Systems Analysis are dependent on achieving compromise given multiple and conflicting objectives (i.e., they assume a unitary context). Furthermore, the kind of models developed are much more typical of Ackoff's machine age. The evidence is that their advocates are strongly in favor of consensus (e.g., with group utility functions, Keeney and Raiffa, 1976). Some contention may arise with this classification. The systems engineer may perceive that (s)he is working in the systems age. The situations dealt with are filled with people, open, have purposeful parts, are partially observable, and cannot be tackled with anything other than a holistic approach (also recognized by Oliga, 1986, 1988). Similar arguments could be made of Operations Research and Systems Analysis. Although it is true that such hard methodologists think this, they must be criticized for contradicting themselves by attempting to model soft situations mathematically in true unitary fashion, and thus ignore the difficulty of inherent subjectivity of mankind. Other related work, such as early Ackoff and Churchman (see Churchman *et al.*, 1957), did at least attempt to deal with plurality of viewpoints in order to promote straightforward Operations Research Studies. It is unfortunate that their progressive thinking has been largely ignored in Operations Research in a desire to treat everything mechanically. Recalling our discussions of Chapter 5, an important metaphor guiding these systems approaches is the organization as a machine.

Cybernetics is thought to constitute systemic-unitary regions. Beer's work (Beer, 1979, 1981, 1985; Espejo, 1979, 1987; Espejo and Harnden, 1989, and also see the special issue on the Viable Systems Model in *Systems Practice*, Vol. 3, No. 3) examines the application of a well tried and tested control unit to organizations (i.e., based on the neurocybernetic structure and processes and representing the brain of man). Jackson and Keys concluded that Beer's work was indeed suited to systemic contexts and that its successful use depended upon there being full agreement about the goals of the situation. We could also add in Warfield's (1976, 1984) Interactive Management here, since it has been designed as an aid to resolving complex problems and issues, and is relevant when complexity of organizations, or parts thereof, stem from increasing interdependence. It holds a cybernetic view to the development of society and is explicitly a means-end approach. The developers of Interactive Management want an effective society through efficient and effective mobilization of interactive resources. The notions of complexity resulting from interdependence and means-end suggest that this reflects and is reflected by the systemic-unitary region. General Systems Theory also has strong cybernetic tendencies. Two important metaphors underpinning the cybernetic-based approaches are those of the organization as an organism (management cybernetics) or as a brain (organizational cybernetics).

SAST (Strategic Assumption Surfacing and Testing) was associated with the mechanical-pluralist context (see for example, Mason and Mitroff, 1981). The developers claim it is useful in systemic situations, but Jackson and Keys quite rightly observed that the approach ignores systemic characteristics, offering a powerful approach to resolving conflicting issues or pluralism. Mason and Mitroff state that once the conflict has been resolved, the 'problem' can then be dealt with using traditional methods of Management Science.

The works of Ackoff (1981; see the *Festschrift* in *Systems Practice*, Vol. 3, No. 2) and Checkland (1981) typically constitute the systemic-pluralist region. Ackoff advocates Interactive Planning, with three operating principles of participation, continuity, and holism. Appropriate use allows full consideration of factors relating to and between, 'subsystems', 'the system itself' and 'the wider system'. An idealized future is created or designed into which the current problems dissolve and further problems emerge, thus requiring a continuous planning approach. Systemicity and pluralism are therefore apparently the main kinds of issue dealt with.

In Checkland's methodology, relevant viewpoints are developed in an attempt to promote mutual understanding and meaningful debate. The CATWOE mnemonic (Customers, Actors, Transformation, *Weltanschauung*, Owner and Environmental constraints) and the stage where comparison is made with formal and other systems models, among other aspects of the methodology, point to a high degree of awareness of pluralism and the need to deal with systems age phenomena. An important (although multivarious) metaphor underpinning these pluralist approaches is that of the organization as a culture.

The remaining regions of the grid arose from Jackson's (1987b) work, extending the 'system of systems methodologies' to include a coercive element on the participants dimension. The mechanical-coercive region is characterized by significant differences in *interests*, values, and beliefs that lead to *conflict* where different groups seek to use whatever *power* they may have to import their favored strategy upon others (the emphasized words relate to a dimension of the political metaphor presented in Chapter 5). Only

Ulrich's (1983) Critical Systems Heuristics has been recognized as constituting this region, dealing with issues such as what interests are being served by a proposed system design and how a genuine debate can be organized between those involved in the system design and those who have to live with consequences of the design.

The systemic-coercive region additionally reflects issues of complexity so that, unlike the mechanical counterpart, the true sources of power of various participants is hidden. Jackson has noted that no systems methodology currently bases itself upon the assumptions that problem contexts are systemic and coercive. In Flood and Jackson (1991a) we project that a methodology based upon such assumptions would have to consider:

(a) various sources of power in organizations,
(b) the organization's culture and the way this determines what changes are feasible and
(c) the mobilization of bias in an organization.

Important metaphors reflecting issues of these regions and pointing out what should be tackled by useful methodologies for coercive contexts, are those of culture, politics, and prisons.

By viewing only the important metaphors from this discussion we can see how closely the original conception of complexity of Flood (1987b), discussed in some detail in Chapter 5, resembles the two dimensions of the grid under discussion. There, we saw complexity essentially splitting into metaphors of natural sciences ('systems dimension') and social sciences ('participants dimension'). The 'system of systems methodologies' argues for a critical handling of these images of social reality. This convergence of ideas from very different sources is encouraging and highlights some broad general agreement about the types of situation we have to deal with in systems 'problem solving'. This is an agreement that will survive the following hard-hitting critical analysis on a 'system of systems methodologies' in terms of complementarism.

Several fundamental difficulties apparently arise with the complementarist approach. For instance, the reasoning of Checkland, one of the authors in question, would reject the idea of problem contexts suggesting that there could be no assumed structure to a 'problem situation'. Ignoring this difficulty from soft systems thinking, the hard thinkers would be confronted by the difficult task of identifying the problem contexts correctly and the inevitable attempts at 'pigeon holing' would be difficult. Most fundamental of all, however, is that both hard and soft systems people believe their approaches are better suited to 'solving' the same sort of problem situation (a difficulty arising from theoretically isolationist stances). This essentially theoretical difficulty is reflecting possibly irreconcilable paradigms which cannot be overcome simply with some 'system of systems methodologies'.

In fact the most pressing difficulty seems to lie with the unitary-pluralist-coercive dimension and the underlying theory, or paradigm, that each categorization is associated with (or derivable from). Because of the difficulties posed by paradigm incommensurability (discussed by Jackson, 1987a) it is hard to deny the force (not necessarily desirability) of the isolationist argument since it gives rise to a tendency for divergences into separate paradigms and distinct methodologies and methods therein. Based on this, one argument against the complementarist approach might be that such a development for systems 'problem solving' is impossible because convergence is inconceivable (i.e., beyond imperialism or the superficial theory empty pragmatic approach). This, however, is not well explained at the methodological level where Jackson and Key's argument lies.

Looking beyond each categorization, a theory can be inferred and it is at this level that a coherent epistemology for systems thinking would have to be found. Yet at this theoretical level there are associated views of 'what is' (ontology). Functionalist systems scientists, for example, confuse/conflate the notion of system (and the concepts thereof — elements, relationships, boundaries and so on) with reality in a literal sense (i.e., what is *is* systems). As we have discovered, an interpretivist's view is very different from this, drawing upon systemic concepts for reasoning and organizing our thoughts (e.g., using the concept notional system). The ideas of Jackson and Keys (1984) could be misinterpreted as ignoring possible ontological incompatibilities, asking us to accept their ideas at a methodological level.

Another tack is to explicitly consider language. Each view of 'what is' historically develops a suitable vocabulary, as with the concepts of any discourse. So functionalists talk about 'systems out there' whereas interpretivists talk about 'situations and our means of appreciation' (we discussed this in Chapter 5). Now, taking into account the methodological propositions under discussion, and for current purposes considering each of the diffuse regions as categorizations or isolated boxes (M-U, M-P, S-U, ...), we can consider the possibility of conversation between workers from different isolated environments. Critics will say, 'How can this be done without any one thinker needing to change the use of language (terminology)?' The doubt arises because any discussion would inevitably refer us to issues of theory (ontology and epistemology). Whichever set of terms were adopted there would be, for some, an unacceptable inferable theory. We could skilfully ask, 'Is this not paradigm incommensurability?'

One of our aims is to have an argument that is watertight (epistemologically valid) and yet the complementarist view insists that we have methodologies and paradigms as they are, using the language unaltered (since commensurability would demand that). 'Surely, only the isolationist notion of paradigm incommensurability is epistemologically tenable?'

But there is a further difficulty here because isolationist positivistically based approaches in social science have been shown to be epistemologically untenable (see this in detail later in this chapter), since they set out to be objective and yet both the means and ends of the approach can be shown to be value-laden. So the question arises, how can complementarists incorporate positivistic approaches without introducing epistemological contradiction into their scheme of things?

In order that the viability of the complementarist position is maintained, the argument against the positivistic approaches has to be accommodated for and an objective condition has to be accepted. But the paradigm is epistemologically untenable and cannot be allowed to remain in the complementarist scheme of things. This cuts out positivistic approaches and that surely goes against the spirit of openness and conciliation, the essence of complementarism and a central requirement to be accomplished with this view. It could be argued that a complementarist should not discard any approach on the grounds of theoretical concerns, otherwise they are routing it and saying that it is invalid, and that means paradigm incommensurability.

One possible implication of this is the impossible task of developing a coherent epistemology derived from complementarist methodological thinking, when there is apparently ontological and epistemological contradiction.

The twist in the tale, critics might say (although I would not be one of them), is that Jackson and Key's approach must be taking a pragmatist's *view of methodology*. Of the latter approach, I have previously argued, 'bits of this and bits of that' (techniques, methodologies and so on) are pieced together because they seem to work — thus inevitably leading to theoretical neglection and contradiction. 'Do we not see this style adopted by Jackson and Keys at a methodological level?' I hear the voices of dissent say.

What appears to emerge here is a tension/contradiction between: (a) wanting to theoretically guide methodology choice (not be a pragmatist) and (b) wanting choice to be possible and therefore not conceding to the force of paradigm incommensurability at the theoretical level. If, therefore, we want to theoretically guide method choice in a complementarist way we would have to deal with the problem of paradigm incommensurability which Jackson and Keys have done only partially and implicitly?

Consequently, a misconceived but not wholly unexpected criticism is that with this complementarist approach we are restrained from making theoretical reference by an argument that holds us at a methodological level, yet at the theoretical level we apparently find contradiction. I shall leave this argument for now since enough doubt has been cast for us to want to consider further the possibilities of an isolationist approach, in particular interpretive isolationism.

7.3.6   Pursuing an Isolationist Approach

7.3.6.1 Introduction

Let us leave the tack that our ultimate aim is to identify guiding insights which are methodologically directive when confronted with situations where context may be defined according to certain attributes of complexity. On this account, enough fraught evidence has emerged to at least justify pursuing the argument for some form of isolationist approach.

Perhaps we as prospectors can identify some criteria by which to judge the merits and demerits of the available systems methods in order that a *single* approach (methodological isolationism) can be identified which, therefore, we can adopt, analyse and develop (through theory and practice) in reductionist fashion? Then the holistic debate, which appears to be entangled within a complex theoretical web, might be satisfactorily left alone.

What follows below is an attempt to uncover some validation criteria that would allow us to distinguish between, and select from, the multivarious systems 'problem solving' methodologies that are available. This achieved, we could claim to have satisfactorily concluded the debate of this section.

7.3.6.2 Validation criteria

A validation procedure is thus required — one which offers neutral rules and logic. Suitable neutrality may be found in the scales of measurement. In a form of Kantian thinking, our reasoning may then proceed with principles of judgement according to unvarying laws (logic and rules). Measurement prescribes the extent of space and time and like those, is intuitive and is positioned as the basis of the empirical. It is of our sensibility and contributes to empirically reflected intuition or perception of objects. The rules of measurement detail permissible manipulations of space and time representations when empirical-intuitive contact is made (Flood and Carson, 1988, Chapter 4). All mathematical and statistical manipulations are permissible for ratio measurements, whereas, there are effectively no such useful manipulations for nominal measurements. Whichever theoretical creed is held, we cannot deny this form of sensibility in our reasoning. It is a simple argument as follows. Familiarity with technologically developed instruments of measurement is widespread in our society. To some, the notion that a questionnaire is an instrument of measurement for the social scientist is less familiar. But even the 'least scientific' approaches (although not necessarily least rigorous), such as those of the interpretive reasoners, are dependent on conceptions of measurement. Nominal measurement abounds in interpretive fields of inquiry as certain manifestations of reality undergo labeling, measured by the most ancient of all instruments, the mind and mind processes (in cooperation with our sensuous being, but not neglecting the transcendental). To deny that measurement is of any importance in social contexts is to deny the possibility of extramind contact and the role of our senses.

In situations where such a unitary view is not attainable, we might expect questions such as, 'What would be the overall effect of new power stations?' rather than the typical systems engineer's question 'What is the best new power station design?', although the two questions here may differ in boundary conception and/or the level of anxiety held for environmental morality (systemic use, see Ulrich, 1988b). These are efficacious questions rather than ones of efficiency and effectiveness.

Let us now consider messy situations, where issues manifest primarily in terms of psychological and/or cultural and/or political complexity. Such a use of measurement and numbers (as opposed to numerals and symbols) as that discussed above for technology becomes problematic, where observability is partial, or insufficient for explanation (i.e., what lies behind the observation), or when situational behavior is apparently changed by the measurement procedure (as exemplified in the classical case of the Hawthorne studies, Roethlisberger and Dickson, 1939). This leads to vehement objection by some parties. In such cases, it could be argued, only nominal measurement through action research is acceptable.

Now, it appears that finding a valid methodological isolationist stance is a difficult task. Hard systems approaches which attempt to apply quantitative analysis to soft situations have come under severe attack. To optimize, select the best (satisfice), or chase objectives (deemed as wholly inappropriate by the soft school in messy situations) does require comparative methods such as system worth based on, for example, normalized utility functions (as described by Keeney and Raiffa, 1976).

The case is that both hard and soft protagonists believe (and are certain they can justify that) the approaches/methods they adopt/develop are better suited to the same sort of problem situations (or problems, depending on the theoretical stance). This makes it impossible to identify the method for such situations through some predefined neutral criteria, since this would only be possible if other related *a priori* knowledge or theory were universally the same – which they are not. Placing a neutral framework on epistemologically 'biased' theory and then pursuing reasoning will only lead to controversy and 'talking over each other's head'. Such controversy is exemplified by the dispute between the early Wittgenstein protagonists who hold the views presented in *Tractatus* (Wittgenstein, 1922) and the later Wittgenstein protagonists who hold the views presented in *Philosophical Investigations* (Wittgenstein, 1953).

Pursuing empirical solutions such as the validity of methodological approaches is thus fruitless. For example, the hard school (favoring observational methods) might prefer validation by numbers which show improvements in the problem, whereas, the soft school (drawing upon interpretivistic reasoning) might say that, at best, if the dis-ease in a problem situation has been reduced then methodological success could be claimed. This attempt to determine validity would encounter the very same difficulty that it was trying to resolve — epistemological bias.

In essence, from an isolationist stance, we are unable to break away from theoretical incommensurability (i.e., there cannot be measures of the same standard between paradigms). There are no such validation criteria on which isolationists can justify the choice of any one approach.

The next two sections, while taking on board the notion that we cannot select between methodologies according only to their related paradigmatic principles, work toward understanding everything from just one theoretical viewpoint.

7.3.6.3 Theory implied through language

I now have to rescind the all encompassing image that I may have constructed concerning the utility of measurement. I do not revoke the notion of measurement as at least partially intuitive and lying *a priori* as the basis of the empirical. It is this very notion which defines clearly that concepts of measurement do hold utility when used in certain and permissible contexts. But what of the metaphysical — morality, politics, aesthetics, and religion — all of which must concern the systems practitioner (as argued by Ulrich, 1988a). These issues are more clearly of consciousness and amenable only to critical reason, as conceived as long ago as 1787 by Kant (see Kant, 1934). Not only is there epistemological bias to contend with, but there is also a metaphysical component. These together (and with the inferable ontology and view of the nature of man, Burrell and Morgan, 1979) constitute the fundamentals of paradigms (of course, even when the researcher chooses to ignore their relevance, i.e., as with pragmatists as they have been defined for our purposes). This extends to the use of language where, to some extent theory can be inferred from the use of words and concepts (argued in detail elsewhere).

Kuhn (1970) stresses that there is no possibility for neutral language or concepts and it is therefore impossible to verify competing paradigms (which in the current argument can be seen to underlie competing methods). Kuhn says that scientific knowledge, like language, is intrinsically the common property of a group or nothing at all. Nature and language are learned together and in this way there is tacit knowledge (Kuhn, 1970, p. 200–204).

The significance of this for me arose when redrafting a manuscript that reflected by inference functionalist thinking, but which I preferred to reflect a subjective outlook (as discussed at length in Chapter 5).

In that analysis it became clear that the translations fell into four distinct paradigmatic groups: epistemological, ontological, methodological, and views on the nature of man. Thus the integrated relationship between paradigm/theory and language clearly emerges and the notion that such concepts underlie world-viewpoints gains clarity — reminiscent of the writings of *Weltanschauungen* philosophers (such as Feyerabend, Hanson, Sneed, Stagmiller, Toulmin; which is discussed by Suppe, 1974). Evidently there has to be paradigm incommensurability?

7.3.6.4 World-viewpoints: The answer to the riddle?

World-viewpoints are most typically associated with *Weltanschauung* philosophers. In Sigmund Freud's view

> ...a *Weltanschauung* is an intellectual construction which solves all the problems of our existence uniformly on the basis of one overriding hypothesis, which accordingly, leaves no question unanswered and in which everything that interests us finds its fixed place....Possession of a *Weltanschauung* of this kind is among the ideal wishes of human beings. (Freud, 1973, p. 193)

Might this extremely appealing notion (one I have fended off on many occasions) be dangerous in the way that it promotes 'merely' a blinding influence? Kuhn has some further ideas that might settle our concern about this world-viewism.

Kuhn's idea that nature and language are learned together and that therefore knowledge is tacit, led him to uncover the most novel idea of *The Structure of Scientific Revolutions* — that paradigms are shared examples. 'Is it with this notion of world-viewpoints that the key to the utility of the Jackson and Keys framework can be found?' What has been presented as a theoretical riddle, testing our ingenuity in divining an answer, may have, as many riddles do, a rather obvious solution. With the solution that follows,

'Can we put to rest the nagging doubt that a methodology–context linked approach is destined to have inherent theoretical contradictions?'

The example that Kuhn presented, which might provide the obvious solution, compared the position of an Einsteinian theorist to that of a Newtonian theorist. But let us first remind ourselves of Kuhn's main thesis. He proposed that science does not accumulate knowledge. Rather, given an unresolvable anomaly scientists search for a new theory which explains that anomaly as well as all other phenomena that have previously been explained by the replaced theory. The new theory, it is proposed, offers a new and different view of the world. Knowledge does not accrue in an additive fashion (see also world-viewism in Chapter 6).

Now, Newton's theory and equations defined space as necessarily flat, homogeneous, isotropic, and unaffected by the presence of matter. In this world, motion of planets and engineers' mechanics are all explainable. But the anomalies arising in fast motion led to an Einsteinian scientific revolution where the flat matrix of space was replaced with a new world-view of a curved matrix of space. Attempts to derive Newton's equations from Einstein's did not fail in the sense that Einstein's equations could be manipulated to represent the same dynamics of slow motion, but did fail to prove the curved matrix view of space. Or as Kuhn put it 'Both are looking at the same world and what they look at has not changed. But in some areas they see different things and they see them in different relations to each other.' (Kuhn, 1970, p. 150)[2]. It could be claimed that such a revolutionary change has taken place for systems thinking, with the growing recognition of interpretive thinking. With this understanding of nature has also come a new language: the use of the terms 'problem situation' and 'notional system' in place of 'problem' and 'system', two examples discussed in Chapter 5, are deemed to be necessary for messy situations. But this does not exclude the use (with an interpretive view) of the last two terms in unitary situations, in technological design for instance. The soft school has no difficulty in describing such aspects of the world using Systems Engineering terminology — because they work even through an interpretivistic perspective.

To take the example further, we may assume that a particular and explanatory nonlinear relationship in a model can be represented as linear if our concern is with small perturbations only (i.e., small deviations from a normal state). Nonlinearity can in a handful of restricted cases be represented with the much easier to handle linear form. Similarly in the restricted case of slow motion, a flat matrix of space may be used to represent the world. Thus the unitary and pluralist dimension of Jackson and Key's (1984) approach are entirely acceptable to the isolationist interpretive thinkers with their (the interpretive) world-view — a world-view (paradigm) that apparently irons out the anomalies of the hard approaches discussed earlier (e.g., the Californian experience).

There is, then, no theoretical contradiction in adopting a correlative approach for the interpretive thinker who sees and understands complexity textures of the real world according to structures that offer some form of comprehension (models and language). This may also be true for the functionalist thinker, however, according to their world-view position they will have to tolerate epistemological anomalies which abound when positivistic assumptions are made in social contexts.

This argument also throws some light on the viewpoints of two British professors — Checkland (clearly interpretivist) and M'Pherson (clearly functionalist). Checkland (1981), seeking to find a suitable methodology for soft 'problem solving', argued that hard systems thinking is a subset of soft systems thinking. Oliga, in the context of the thesis of this section, expresses this notion well — 'As such, hard systems thinking reduces to a special case of soft systems thinking, appropriate only in those problem situations where the presumption of consensus is unquestionable.' (Oliga, 1988, p. 105). I once found this notion appealing (Flood and Carson, 1988), but now prefer to impose some clarification on the sense. If this is interpreted in the cumulative sense then I have to reject the notion. If we can bend the notion slightly so we understand that the hard approaches are inherently part of the interpretive view and can help in particular situations and since I feel that this is what Checkland meant, then I attribute to him this rather important point. That Checkland has adopted an imperialistic subsumptional (advanced isolationist) approach is at least consistent with this general view.

M'Pherson (1974) on the other hand claims that soft systems thinking is a subset of hard systems thinking which, in terms of an interpretive argument, is a weak observation since the claim clings on to a dated theory riddled with anomalies. In Kuhn's explanation such stubbornness occurs when old theories are replaced by new, but with Foucault we would understand it better as resilience to counter a developing and challenging discourse.

We must not, however, hand over the prize to the interpretivists so easily, since similar observations could be made by those interested in emancipatory methods (i.e., the interpretive view encounters a genuine difficulty in dealing with coercion and conflict).

In Section 7.5 we will finally put these issues to bed in terms of legitimacies and limitations by showing the epistemological untenability and/or impoverishment of isolationist approaches alongside the adequacy of

Table 7.2

Legitimation of complementarism, pragmatism and isolationism

	LEGITIMATION	IMPLICATION
COMPLEMENTARISM	Immanent legitimacy *and* limitations.	Reason how to "do it" but always remain critical.
PRAGMATISM	Anything goes, everything is legitimate.	If it seems good "do it".
ISOLATIONISM	Totalising legitimacy	"Do it" this way.

complementarism. For now, Table 7.2 summarizes the ideas of what constitutes legitimation for the three main scenarios of complementarism, pragmatism, and isolationism (all forms).

7.3.7 Summary

To summarize, the Jackson and Keys framework could be used within the world-view of a functionalist, an interpretivist, or an emancipatory theorist (i.e., from inside any paradigm it would seem equally convincing). Yet the critical position of the argument of this book, if interpreted through isolationism or world-viewism, would suggest that a larger number of anomalies are apparent with functionalism over the other two paradigms because objectivity is assumed; and a larger number of anomalies are apparent with functionalism and interpretivism over an emancipatory approach because a regulative view of society is assumed (i.e. without progressive change). Isolationism offers a competitive, 'closed' and an impoverished mode of thought. World-viewism has several theoretically oriented scenarios, each one neglecting to recognize that no single position has or is ever likely to explain everything. The complementarist scenario recognizes that a reason underlying the development of various methodologies and theories is that phenomena are so complex, that we can only begin to enrich our comprehension by diversifying rather than converging our thinking. The complementarist position is a powerful argument that offers us critically oriented guidance in this direction, but also demands us to completely rethink epistemology for systems thinking and particularly for systems practice.[3,4]

7.4   THE NEED FOR A NEW EPISTEMOLOGY

The previous section was inconclusive. The attempted decisive investigation broached issues in terms of method, methodology, theory, and ideology. All sorts of penetrating questions were asked and doubt cast on all of the six scenarios. The two approaches which emerged as most likely were complementarism and imperialism by subsumption. Essentially,

however, the debate is between complementarism and isolationism
(imperialist approaches are only advanced isolationism). One reason put
forward to explain the difficulties of complementarism as presented by
Jackson and Keys (1984), was that they pitched their argument at a
methodological level, but the most testing questions arose as
epistemological ones. There are good reasons, therefore, to want to develop
an adequate complementarist epistemology. Furthermore, since an
interpretivist form of isolationism came across as the most difficult of all to
budge, an exacting epistemological inquiry into this would be welcomed and
informative. Through the development of an adequate epistemology we will
find that complementarism shows its comprehensive strengths, and
isolationism of even the most resilient form finally gives way to this, no
longer being able to stand as a credible or desirable alternative.

The hidden epistemology behind the methodological concerns of Jackson
and Keys (1984), that offers us the basis on which to develop this adequate
epistemology, is that of Habermas (1971a, in particular), as Jackson (1985a,
1987a and 1987b) makes clear. In Chapter 3 Habermas' complementarist
position was presented at length, as part of the process 'liberate and
critique', and does not need to be recounted here. Our main aim must be to
establish clearly the epistemological debate not fully explored in the
scientific literature up to this time.

The task of the next section, then, is to develop the complementarist
vision by developing an adequate epistemology based on Habermas' notion
of knowledge-constitutive interests and issues of limitations and
legitimacies. The following section is a joint argument first published in
Systems Practice by Flood and Ulrich (1990).

7.5   TOWARD AN ADEQUATE EPISTEMOLOGY FOR
         SYSTEMS PRACTICE

7.5.1   Introduction

The systems view has often been misunderstood to 'embrace all in its
outlook'. Now it is certainly true that comprehensiveness is in fact an ideal
of systems thinking, but from an epistemological point of view this ideal is in
need of careful qualification. If epistemology is 'reflection on the gaining and
disseminating of knowledge and on the validity of that knowledge', then the
epistemological ideal of classical comprehensive rationalism would require
systems thinkers 'to know everything and know it is valid'. This is evidently
impossible. Such an ideal does not even have a regulative function for
systems thinking because it tells us absolutely nothing about how to deal
with our inescapable lack of comprehensive knowledge and understanding.

The call, as will be understood more clearly later, is for a switch in emphasis from *systems science* to *systems rationality*: systems science referring to a conventional understanding of what systems scientists do (explained among other things in Flood and Carson's, 1988, eclectic work) and systems rationality referring to a critical (Kantian) rather than an untenable pre-Kantian understanding of rationality. More specifically, by systems science we mean any effort to employ a systemic outlook in doing basic or applied science according to the conventional ideals of nonreflective positivistic empirical-analytical rationality (objective data, testable hypotheses, valid modeling, and so on), whereas by systems rationality we mean an ideal that may orient applied inquiry toward a critically rational social practice in the face of incomplete knowledge and understanding.

We will consider the following proposal, that an appropriate epistemological ideal for systems thinkers is not the systems-scientific ideal but must be sought through the critical idea of systems rationality, by giving back to the systems idea its originally critical sense (as forwarded by Immanuel Kant and reconstructed by Ulrich, 1983). Unfortunately and as argued throughout this book, the critical intent of the systems idea has been almost completely lost in contemporary systems science. This historical reflection today translates into what has been designated in this thesis a call for a 'second' epistemological break toward a critical approach in systems thinking. The 'first' epistemological break in our understanding is marked by Checkland's (e.g., 1981) moving away from instrumental control of positivist approaches toward mutual understanding through interpretivistic systems thinking, and is characterized by a routing attack on modern systems science. Consequences of interpretivism are that systems thinking must free itself from dominance by scientism with its roots in ontological realism.

The 'second' epistemological break does not deny importance in the achievements of the 'first', but should be seen as more than an advancement on that line of thinking. Consequences of this critically normative systems thinking are that the two knowledge-constitutive interests in instrumental control (positivism) and in mutual understanding (interpretivism) need to be complemented (and reflected upon) in terms of an emancipatory interest in Enlightenment, and liberation of people from domination by people or machines by false consciousness or by whatever conditions that prevent people from truly realizing their potential as individuals.

We will find, therefore, that such a 'truly' critical systems thinking cannot merely reflect against a backboard of a systems epistemological ideal as sketched out earlier in terms of just systems rationality. Further issues of sociological epistemology are equally important. In fact, this is an exceptional point which demands that we find a way of pursuing and somehow bringing these together (i.e., sociological and systems epistemologies) through an epistemological ideal of critical rationality. Witness a first attempt at this below.

We wish to develop an expression of an adequate epistemological ideal for social inquiry. This we shall do by linking our difficulty with the 'problem of metaphysics'. We must therefore propose to introduce the difficulty in question as one that is equivalent to the 'classical philosophical problem of (inevitable) metaphysics'.

Metaphysics[5] refers to our theories (conceptions or understandings) of social reality which always go beyond that which the empirical (the phenomenal surface reality that we can observe) apparently tells us. But we need to continually remind ourselves that the difficulty in question is not only (or even primarily) one of theoretical explanation (via concepts and understanding) but is also (or rather) one of taking into account and justifying the normative assumptions flowing into our theories of social reality. These normative assumptions concern, for example, political issues such as assumptions about the 'right' distribution of power, but may be complicated by the possibility of false consciousness and effects of material conditions. These are likely to produce genuine conflicts of world-views and interests and may lead to coercive conditions.

Ulrich (1983) has suggested that we use the term social metaphysics (finding Kant's metaphysics of experience inadequate to social inquiry in terms of social theory and systems practice) in order to help us appreciate these very relevant concerns. Social metaphysics can be explained as the totality of relative *a priori* judgements that flow into social theories or designs but cannot be validated either empirically or logically.

Now this is helpful because we can clearly see the need for a critical approach, in the precise sense of being politically conscious or self-reflective, distinguished by an openly declared emancipatory interest in an equal distribution of power and chances to satisfy personal needs and in liberating people from dominance by other people (as argued in this book in terms of discursive and nondiscursive practices). Our understanding of subjectivity (stated at the end of Chapter 5) dictates this ideal, since subjectivity is conceived as theoretically anti-positivistic and ideologically emancipatory (thus, for the constructivist minded reader, political consciousness is a necessary and logical inclusion). So, we now need only one small conceptual step to realize the earlier stated desire that our concern with sociological epistemology must also deal with systems rationality. In other words we must propose a dialectical approach to the problem of practical discourse. This should occur between those claiming the whole systems rationality of some design (i.e., of its normative implications) and those bearing witness to the life-practical irrationality of the designs in question. Hegelian (or Churchmanian) dialectics, working in an adversarial mode, is complementary to our desire for practical discourse between 'a rationality' and 'an irrationality'. This leads to our adequate epistemological ideal for social inquiry.

At last we have some regulative and methodologically directive ideas. Let us not be mistaken, however, by concluding that critique should be distinguished from other main areas of social theory (i.e., positivism and interpretivism). Being critical is not a quality of a certain position or approach, rather it is the quality of remaining self-reflective with respect to particular and all positions or approaches. This tells us that every conceivable approach to systems thinking can be dealt with by a critical handling of its inevitable limitations, the quintessence of a complementarist position.

In these systems and sociological terms we will conclude over the course of this section that:

(a) *nonreflective positivistic approaches*, by denying the relevance of social metaphysics, inevitably deny subjectivity and the notion of 'whole systems rationality' and are epistemologically untenable (hence the need for a first epistemological break);

(b) *nonreflective interpretivistic approaches*, despite recognizing the inevitability of social metaphysics and in this way moving toward an adequate epistemological ideal for social inquiry, side-step sociological issues of critical significance such as effects of material conditions and the possibility of false consciousness, and therefore have an impoverished epistemology (hence the need for a 'second' epistemological break);

(c) critical, or *self-reflective*, ideas amount to an adequate epistemological ideal for social inquiry in terms of systems rationality, sociological epistemology, and systems practice.

We will therefore be considering the legitimacies and limitations of these three contrasting conceptions of rationality.

7.5.2 Contrasting Conceptions of Rationality: Legitimacies and Limitations

7.5.2.1 Introduction

Over the years there have been many attempts at reasoning out rational approaches to inquiry. Of particular interest in the social sciences and somewhat belatedly in systems thinking, are three rationalities:

positivistic, interpretivistic, and emancipatory theories. In one interesting critique of these three types of science Fay (1975) uncovered some reasoning as to the limitations of positivistic and interpretivistic rationalities, and suggested why an emancipatory approach might be legitimate where the other two are not (in fact it is fair to say that in this work Fay's emancipatory ideas conflated radical with critical). There has been vigorous debate in social theory along these lines. This is a serious matter because it then becomes too easy to slip into an unwanted adversarial mode of reasoning such as: emancipatory approaches are legitimate while instrumental control represents an inferior kind of inquiry. This would simply reintroduce old prejudices such as the humanities against the natural sciences, with a value continuum marked bad on the right positivistic side and good on the left emancipatory side. What we require is an approach to systems practice which makes plain the idea that we are dealing with complementary concepts of rationality, each of which has its place and is legitimate so long as we respect its limitations (see Ulrich's, 1988a, research program and the preceding argument in this book). This is an extremely important point that should stay with us throughout the following discussion lest we slip into a competitive rather than critical mode of thinking.

We can now look carefully at three sciences/rationalities in order that we may expose some limitations and assess the legitimacies, and think about the epistemological breaks which might be proffered in respect to each type. The rationalities are nonreflective positivism, nonreflective interpretivism, and emancipatory (the last defining both a meta-theoretical framework through which all rationalities may be dealt with and the fundamental ideas for emancipatory theories as such). Toward the end of this chapter we shall summarize our findings on limitations and legitimacies in tabular form, which helps to highlight the contrasting interests of the three types of science/rationality.

7.5.2.2 On positivistic science/rationality

A positivistic approach to science offers a traditional rationality that we can critically examine in various contexts, but in particular in our application domain we can legitimately ask — 'Why should we pursue a traditional social science and what would be the consequence of this?'

Brian Fay (1975), somewhat along the lines of Habermas (1971a, 1971b), proposed on behalf of traditional social scientists the following reasoning. The natural sciences have very effectively provided mankind with knowledge with which the natural environment can be controlled making it more hospitable and productive. We might be inclined to conclude from Fay's account that it would be a reasonable suggestion to apply the same epistemological (of truth, neutrality and objective knowledge) and methodological ideas in social contexts, discarding the notion of our needs and values in order to give us the requisite power for objectively based social control, thus making for a more certain and rewarding social environment.

If this idea of a social science sounds appealing (it does not in our or Fay's judgment), then surely we must find out how we can have a social systems science. 'How can the ideas of reductionism be translated into those of holism?' The answer is simple. Generally, traditional scientific investigation promotes the identification of causal laws between variables according to observational properties. By building these into a 'system' of causal laws in a clearly specified (holistic) way we might begin to understand how phenomena are related so that by manipulation of input or internal variables, or by changing structure as defined by model parameters, future scenarios can be generated (along with a whole host of descriptive, predictive and explanatory investigations). For example, through this, feedforward control can be imposed in order to avoid undesirable future ends by steering toward what is perceived as more desirable. This would presumably make way for an optimal social environment (i.e., in this strategic means-end fashion it is possible to identify one best way to maximize, or at worst satisfice). Thus there would be '...universally recognisable decisive solutions to particular problems.' (Fay, 1975).

Now, the question of theory-neutrality and value-freedom over means and ends must surface here. It is argued by scientists of the positivistic persuasion that objective and neutral decisions can be realized by determining the most efficient means to an end. 'But what of ends?' Traditional science cannot inform us of what teleological goals we *ought* to be pursuing since it is fact-based. It is not possible to have neutral social goals. If we are informed of a *should* approach then we will at least know that it is value-laden. Perhaps, then, the idea of means-end might be considered respectively as fact-value and so the scientific approach might play an important role in determining an efficient means to a subjectively based end? But, we might ask, 'Efficient in terms of what?' 'Who is to say that we should maximize in terms of money, manpower, time or happiness or what?' as Fay questioned. We see again that what is required to be neutral is actually value-riddled.

Simply referring the choice of efficiency criteria to the definition of ends and then hoping that once ends have been selected decisions on means can be value-neutral, will not deal with the difficulties of value judgments.

This is so because the underlying means-end dichotomy is epistemologically untenable. Counter to what the eminent German sociologist Max Weber (1949) assumed in his decisionistic model of the relation of science (theory) to politics (practice), decisions on means cannot be kept free of normative implications by referring all value judgments to the choice of ends; for what matters is not the value judgments that an inquirer consciously makes (or not) but the life-practical consequences of his/her propositions (regardless of whether they concern means or ends) for those affected.

It is true that Weber's intent originally was a self-critical one: he found it necessary to avow that decisions on the adequacy of ends cannot be justified scientifically, but ultimately remain matters of personal faith. Weber was willing to pay this price because he hoped it would make accessible to scientific justification the selection of appropriate means for given ends. Once ends are chosen, he argued, decisions on means can be kept value-neutral because they only need to refer to relationships of cause-effect. What Weber apparently did not consider is that in a context of applied science, propositions regarding means have not only instrumental but also life-practical consequences; and these cannot be justified *vis-a-vis* those affected by reference to theoretical-instrumental knowledge of cause-effect (relating to the surface) relations, but only by demonstrating their normative acceptability to all concerned citizens. Weber's and his followers' error was to conceive of (applied) social science in non-life-practical terms. The implication of this for our ideal of practical reason (normative acceptability) is that it is reduced to instrumental reason (feasibility). This approach cannot therefore yield what it claims, namely an immunization of propositions on means against value judgments. Rather, it immunizes such propositions against the critical efforts of practical reason. We must conclude that any social science and likewise any social systems science, that adopts the means-end scheme is in great danger of succumbing to positivism.[6]

So we have reasoned the following.

(a) Traditional social science claims objectivity: means to end ≡ fact to fact.

(b) Ends *are* value-laden, so: means to end ≡ fact to value.

(c) Criteria of efficiency are also value-laden, so: means to end ≡ value to value.

Therefore a positivistic science claims an objective epistemology, which we have proven above is untenable.

A powerful argument against a positivistically oriented hard approach to systems 'problem solving' in social contexts that would be based on such theoretical premises as outlined above, has been proposed by Checkland (e.g., 1981). He shows through practical considerations that the 'designation of objectives (i.e., ends) is itself problematic.' Notably, however, Checkland misses the opportunity to highlight the ideological implications of this positivism.[7] Ideological considerations are important and concern us with issues relating to order and change, a central aspect of our attitude toward 'problem solving' in social situations that must be explicitly addressed.

Positivistically oriented traditional science,[8] according to its advocates, can tell us of the laws of social being according only to empirical relationships as derived by scientific experts. Once that structure has been identified, traditional science will go on to explain how it functions, but will never ask what value implications it has and how to assess them, for such questioning is beyond the traditional scientific ideal of objectivity (see again Weber, 1949). But this way of avoiding value judgments often has paradoxical consequences: by not questioning structure and its function with respect to its value content, traditional science implicitly accepts its being there as if it were necessarily and naturally that way. Proposals are therefore made in terms of continued existence. Dominant-submissive social relations tend to be accepted by positivist social science as natural and unchallengable. Hence positivism is as a rule conservative, reconciling people to any social order that is being investigated. Systems methodologies that hold a positivistic rationality advocate instrumental reason in telling us how to do things, the *ought* having been 'sold-out' to empirically based scientific findings of what is (according only to surface observation or beneath the surface theory).

We proposed at the outset that it is necessary for us to 'look through' our systems (scientific) models to uncover normative assumptions that are inherent in them. If this is done then these assumptions could, *in principle*, be subject to critical reflection. This, of course, cannot be achieved with a nonreflective positivistic view of the assumptions.

In summary, on nonreflective positivistic rationality in social contexts, we note that:

(a) it does not lead to objectivity;
(b) it is expert driven;
(c) the systems epistemological ideal will always be ignored;
(d) what is claimed is epistemologically untenable;
(e) what is said is ideologically conservative; and therefore
(f) what would be achieved is maintenance or strengthening of power relations.

If the positivistic view of science must be abandoned in social contexts and we have shown that it must on epistemological grounds and believe that it should on ideological grounds, then the question will arise whether there are alternative views (or rationalities) and if so then — 'What can be determined about them epistemologically and ideologically?' 'What is legitimate and what limitations are there?'

As argued above, in recent systems thinking there have been two alternative views — broadly speaking, the introduction of interpretivism or of critical thinking. These will be considered in the next two sections respectively.

7.5.2.3 On interpretivistic science/rationality

We will now consider interpretivistic science and its strengths and weaknesses (along the same lines as the prior discussion on positivism) as a systems and a sociological epistemology and what ideological thinking is inherent in the tenets of the theory. We found Fay's (1975)[9] framework of ideas useful here.

Interpretive social theory is concerned with situations as defined through action concepts (hence the need for an interpretive systems language, as discussed in Chapter 5). Understanding cannot simply arise from observation and theory (surface and beneath the surface material analyses of the traditional positivistic scientific approach) since the human actor will have reasons, or intentions, that lie behind each action (these are not material). For example, slapping someone on the back might be interpreted as either a friendly or a hostile action, or kneeling in the street could be interpreted as religious or an inebriated act. Observation is not enough to properly appreciate these actions. Deeper understanding is necessary, for example, from the above two situations we could begin by saying, well we need at least intentional and conventional action concepts. But how can we progress beyond the descriptive/observational (surface) approach to realize an explanation for actions? Surely it is nonsense to search for material generative mechanisms that lie beneath a material surface?

The interpretivist moves completely away from issues of materialism and introduces the idea that a specific action concept can only be transparent in the context of a certain set of *social rules*. It is in terms of these that an actor can be said to be doing some particular thing. Beyond an observation, we are told, is a *set* of social rules, a *social practice*, that can be drawn upon to explain the action.

There is also a third nonmaterial deeper layer that the interpretivist introduces, that of constitutive meaning. This is the least accessible layer to the actors, for as a social practice lies behind an observation, a constitutive meaning lies behind the social practice. It is in terms of these meanings that people speak and act. In order that these meanings can be more fully appreciated, it is necessary for an actor to adopt a contrasting constitutive meaning and thus 'take a look' at their own world-view from 'the outside'. In this, admittedly difficult, way it is possible to 'get a handle' on one's own reality.

An interpretivist social theorist is not, therefore, concerned with privileging views by asking questions such as — 'What is the correct action in a certain social context (typical of what a scientistic view would be)?' Rather than asking what is appropriate, an interpretivist thinker would pose the question — 'What makes it appropriate (surely a key question also to ask a systems practitioner about designs)?' A constitutive meaning, then, is equivalent to a world-view or *Weltanschauung* that reflects a cultural conception of human needs and purposes.

Table 7.3

Three layers of interpretive analysis: action concepts, social practice and constitutive meaning

'1st LEVEL' CONVENTIONAL AND INTENTIONAL ACTIONS	'2nd LEVEL' SOCIAL PRACTICE	'3rd LEVEL' CONSTITUTIVE MEANING
What is done	Set of negotiated rules that explain what is done.	Fundamental assumptions that underly what is done and make it meaningful.
Implicit reference to social practice	Implicit reference to constitutive meaning.	Fundamental *a priori* assumptions.
EXAMPLE: FAMILY		
Embracing	Generally understood rules reffered to by the concept family which define embracing, e.g., to embrace involves some perceived emotional exchange of love and affection.	The family unit is something that has a particularly important role in our lives and within society.[1]
EXAMPLE: MARKET PLACE[2]		
Buying and selling	Generally understood rules referred to by the concept market place which define buying and selling, e.g., to buy involves exchanging my money for someone elses' goods.	It is right to exchange goods and services to maximise one's own resources; open compeition is fundamentally important.[3]

1. In large sections of Western society two men embracing would come across as natural if they were family and strange if they were merely friends. 2. Adapted and tabulated from Fay (1975). 3. There are other possible constitutive meanings for the concept market place.

Interpretivistic rationality can more easily be seen as systemic in outlook because it helps us to see people's lives as a whole by uncovering subjective meaningfulness (i.e., conceptual interactiveness) of the social rules (i.e., the social practice) in terms of an *a priori* constitutive meaning. To elucidate and summarize this we have developed two examples and presented them in tabular form (see Table 7.3).

There are clearly advantages to such a theory. For instance, the ideas should increase the possibilities for communication by accepting subjectivity and by making dialogue possible where previously only suspicion and distrust 'filled the air'. Interpretivistic rationality does this by opening up one's own situation to others (and *vice versa*) and by encouraging mutual understanding about what is being done and why it is being done. 'Truth' is approached as communication increases and, in an ideal world, a 'valid' systems intervention would require full participation of those involved and affected.

A penetrating critic might however say — 'Well these ideas are all well and good as far as they go, but what of *material conditions*?' 'It seems that with your subjective idealism you have forgotten to deal with the effects of material conditions!' (see for example, Jackson, 1982; Rosenhead, 1984).

Now, we should have some sympathy with this critic, but should also have some concern about how such matters might be dealt with. It is tempting to claim that there is a missing fourth layer (i.e., what material conditions underlie constitutive meanings and what is the history of these?). This argument might continue; material conditions do inevitably affect social life since social structure will adapt to changes in the natural and/or technological environment. And so, following on, the social communicative world of the interpretivist is not all, it cannot be independent of the physical stage on which the actions are performed.

An understandable concern with such a rationality is that it is apt to produce confusion about the nature of the social reality (the material conditions) in question. The danger is that such a rationality sets a tightrope to walk, with a substantial danger of toppling into the positivistic trap of hypostatizing (relating to an underlying substance as distinct from an interpretation or idea) material social conditions as if there were some kind of science that could have access to a social reality of concern. This is in distinction to other types of inquiry that content themselves with considering interpretations and ideas only. It makes no sense to distinguish, say, an emancipatory as opposed to less critical kinds of inquiry in terms of ontological realism versus idealism.

The relevant distinction here must be an epistemological one, for the issue of interest is — 'What are the epistemological requirements that interpretive science does not meet but which are indispensable for adequately dealing with material conditions?' Our answer is that the crucial difference is whether or not an inquirer accepts the proposition that rational justification always implies claims to both theoretical and practical rationality. Both a realist and an idealist can adopt a critical stance with respect to this crucial issue. Following Kant, however, critical (or 'problematic' as Kant says) idealism is a much better position to depart from because realism tends to hypostatize the real world and hence to succumb to a fundamental objectivist illusion. Since we have no direct access to reality we cannot know reality in all its pristine clarity. All reality is real to us only through our minds and all knowledge that we can have is perspective-bound and therefore selective. It is dependent on our world-views, values, interests and so on. Ulrich (1983, p.185), referring to Korzybski (1985), explains that the fundamental and indispensable message of critical idealism is that all our knowledge is in terms of maps and we should never confuse the map with objective reality.

A critical idealist will know to avoid the danger of hypostatizing social material conditions because it is accepted that there are no social realities *a priori* to constitutive meanings. To the critical idealist it is the other way round: human intentionality is constitutive of the perception and experience of phenomena such as power, unequal distribution of resources, social stratification, discrimination etc., just as it is constitutive of (subjectively) rational action.[10] Critical idealists distinguish themselves from subjectivist idealists by accepting that 'out there' are some hard factual conditions that do not exist in the mind only. It is incorrect, however, for interpretivists to make accusations of positivism and hypostatization. Critical theorists depart from the assumption that we might gain some truly positivist direct objective access to scientifically describing those conditions. We can describe maps of social material reality and, the analogy suggests, a good map will lay open the perspective and scale it uses; but we do not distinguish ourselves from interpretive inquirers by claiming some more direct access to a material social world. From a critical point of view, we can only claim to provide adequate maps of our (or a defined client's or participants') social reality.

This type of analysis must involve what Fay (1975) terms quasi-causal accounts of the way certain material conditions give rise to forms of action. 'Quasi', we must argue, because the 'causes' in question are the subjective acts of human intentionality — human motives, purposes etc., including impulses and desires not controlled by the human will — rather than the nomological laws ruling the physical world. In other words the social communicative world of the interpretivist (of mutual understanding) does of course depend upon material social conditions (and should be critically recognized as such), but these conditions have a quasi-causal rather than a strictly causal importance. They condition our subjective perception of social reality (and of possible improvement) and hence can become obstacles to mutual understanding in need of critical reflection. This is the point rather than the assumption that (of course) social reality or social practice is never independent of physical reality.

There is also a further meta-complication. Interpretivistic rationality assumes that if only we could break out of our world-view our actions could be clearly seen for what they are, as perceptions of actions on certain *a priori* constitutive meanings. Yet this ignores the possibility of coercive forces working against the potential for emancipation that an interpretivistic view apparently offers, forces which may be designed to freeze the dominant constitutive meaning (freeze emancipation) by claiming, through nontransparent false means, that the situation is good or necessarily as it is. This is the case of false consciousness built on lies, propaganda, half-truths, and so on.

Perhaps interpretivistic inquiry does indeed offer hermeneutic scientists the means for uncovering false consciousness, for example, in respect to a historian's possibly faulty (nonauthentic) interpretation of historical documents. But it seems that the art of hermeneutics, thus understood, still clings to an ideal of objectivity that is unacceptable to applied inquirers. Hermeneutic inquiry, to the extent that it succeeds in decoding the authentic message of its subject, might claim to be objective; applied inquiry however never can. For us, there is no hermeneutic (interpretivist) 'royal way' to seizing social reality objectively (much less to redesigning it), simply because there is no such thing as the objective authentic interpretation of social reality as such. As Ulrich (1983, p. 64) has written,

> ...there is only one way in which we can claim 'objectivity' — in the general sense of freedom from hidden presuppositions — for our empirical basis of rational discourse: namely, by acknowledging, in each case, the knowledge-constitutive interests on which the validity and meaning of 'facts' depend. *To claim objectivity for one's knowledge by referring to the objectivity of one's empirical basis is an impossible undertaking; but to pursue the ideal of objectivity in the sense of emancipating oneself and others from the objectivist illusion is an indispensable idea.*

Our conclusion must be that for the applied sciences, the ideal of objectivity translates into what Habermas (1971a) has called the emancipatory interest of the critical sciences.

The translation basically reads like this. Mutual understanding (or more generally speaking, as a hermeneutic scientist would probably prefer to say, *authentic* understanding) is a necessary but not a sufficient ideal condition for critical applied science. Authentic understanding of each other's subjective intents is all right in that it allows rationally motivated discourse, but it does not secure by itself the right standards of value being applied. Authentic understanding will take the message it believes to have understood authentically as providing the right standard, 'But what about ethically reprehensible implications of the message?' Clearly, following the understanding yielded by authentic interpretation leaves little room for discrimination, so that every viewpoint must be accepted as equally valid — otherwise, the interpretation is no longer authentic. This poses a major difficulty in terms of ways forward in practical situations since there is no critical means of directing decision-making.

This last exact point can be directed at interpretivistically oriented systems practitioners such as P. B. Checkland (1981) and Soft Systems Methodology (SSM), which he largely developed. Throughout the methodological process, as SSM has been defined, we are encouraged to work out ideal systems views that are relevant to participants of a problem situation, but there is no indication as to what might be chosen as most relevant and on what basis this choice should be made; save for the 'constraints that must be met' as defined by 'the unique norms, values and roles of the problem situation' (i.e., cultural feasibility as Checkland defines it). Fuenmayor (1985) has shown, on behalf of the soft systemists, what an onto-epistemology for such a methodology would look like and in this has shown such a theory leads to a position of relativism. With this there are no guidelines for choice, (like the old tale of the donkey who could not make a choice between two equal-length straws and consequently died of starvation). There are no criteria by which we can realize a process of decision making without explicitly introducing/accepting, for example, ideological matters that may well have a direct association with any so-called facilitator of the choice process (proceeding from an understanding process that interpretivism has much to contribute to).

Following another line, in an ideological sense interpretivistic science is implicitly conservative since the only possible way of explaining social tensions is in terms of imperfect communication between involved and affected actors. This accordingly can only be corrected at the communicative level through the promise of enhanced communication which cannot be promoted by clearing up misunderstandings with the view that the natural flow of discourse and order can be reestablished. The point is that a lack of authentic understanding is always involved in situations of coercion but mutual understanding alone cannot secure emancipation; critical reflection on the norms implied in that which is authentically understood can ('critical reflection' meaning to examine the justifications of conflicting norms with respect to their generalizability thus distinguishing rational from merely factual consensus emanating from practical discourse — see Ulrich, 1983, p. 144–147).

In summary, on nonreflective interpretivistic rationality in social contexts we note that:

(a) it promotes the notion of subjectivity;
(b) there are no explicit directives in the theory that aim to prevent the approach from being expert driven;
(c) by recognizing social communicative action it takes one of several necessary steps for reaching out toward the systems epistemological ideal;
(d) it would be epistemologically tenable in its own sociological terms if full participation was facilitated; however
(e) because false consciousness and the effects of material conditions are not dealt with critically, the rationality is clearly epistemologically impoverished and may well lead to ideological conservatism; and therefore
(f) there is nothing in the rationality that helps to prevent the maintenance of power relations.

Presumably and since earlier we noted that only positive criticisms would emerge that would contribute to the development of the interpretive line of thinking, we can expect there to be an alternative sociological theory that takes on board some of the lessons drawn out above. This is the case and the theory comes under the broad heading of critique.

7.5.2.4 On critical science/rationality

We noted earlier that a truly critical systems approach must satisfy the two following requirements:

(a) it must reach out toward the systems epistemological ideal in terms of 'systems rationality' and
(b) it must be consistent with the sociological emancipatory spirit of critique as such.

I propose that the two requirements, far from being mutually exclusive, ultimately imply each other. Whoever takes seriously the *systems epistemological ideal* cannot help but conclude that beyond the positivistic (objectivist) and the interpretivistic (hermeneutic) ideals of science, the emancipatory force of critical self-reflection is necessary — critical self-reflection, that is, on the gap that will always separate the practice of inquiry from those ideals. Similarly, whoever takes seriously the ideal of critical science — emancipation from hidden presuppositions — will have to conclude that they cannot easily dispense of what Kant termed the unavoidable transcendental idea of a totality of conditions molding their knowledge and understanding (i.e., the systems idea).

This becomes apparent if we consider the danger that a one-sided pursuit of either requirement poses to the inquirer. The systems epistemological ideal — a critically motivated quest for comprehensiveness — in practice too easily lends itself to uncritical claims of comprehensive rationality, neglecting the fact that we never know and understand 'the whole system' (the totality of relevant conditions). On the other hand, the ideal of critique just as well lends itself to an uncritical absolutism of one's critical standpoint, for it is an impossible imperative to permanently question all one's presuppositions, including one's standards of critique; but presupposition-free critique is impossible. It seems that the two requirements mutually complement each other in a useful way: 'Think systems, but don't ever assume to grasp the whole!' implies the system's inquirer's need for critical self-reflection and 'Think critically, but don't ever allow your standards of critique to become absolute!' implies the critical scientist's need to think beyond his particular standpoint and to look for comprehensiveness in his understanding.

Ulrich's (1983) program of a Critical Systems Heuristics[11] builds on the assumption that the two requirements are both indispensable and mutually interdependent (neither can be practiced without the other) for a truly critical systems approach. A wealth of powerful ideas on the notion of a critically understood systems epistemological ideal are contained in this program. Basically, Ulrich suggests that the key to a critical understanding of the systems idea can be found in the works of Immanuel Kant. Ulrich's modern day reconstruction of Kant's ideas is what I have termed in this book a 'second' epistemological break for modern systems inquiry. Systems thinking, as understood through Kant's writings, refers to the totality of relevant conditions on which theoretical or practical judgements depend, including basic metaphysical, ethical, political and ideological *a priori* judgments. For those systems thinkers who argue that the holistic concept is of no practical significance and who are denying Kant's position, we must point out that such a systems concept offers us a critical ideal of reason, (i.e., we must reflect heuristically on the unavoidable incomprehensiveness and selectivity in every systems definition). *Reflection*, that is, on the normative content of the *a priori* 'whole systems' judgments flowing into our systems designs. And heuristic in that it does not attempt to ground critical reflection theoretically, but to provide a method by which presuppositions and their inevitable partiality can be kept constantly under review (Jackson, 1985b).

Ulrich's work demands that we carefully reflect upon the epistemological ideal of holistic thinking, but its critical effort is directed at the practical goal of understanding why social reality is the way it is, exactly and of improving it. Both goals will require us to deal with the effects of material conditions and false consciousness that were recognized earlier as additional to the three layers of interpretivism.

Let us now consider some critical objections that may (and perhaps need) to be raised against such a programme. For instance, it has ben argued by Jackson (1985b, p.880), that Ulrich's Critical Systems Heuristics neglects the importance of material conditions because

> ...it is critical in terms of the idealism of Kant, Hegel and Churchman, but is not critical in terms of the historical materialism of Marx and the Frankfurt School of Sociologists.

In terms of our argument above, we must indeed appreciate the material conditions that shape our perception of social reality (just as our world-views are constitutive of our perceptions of material conditions). Jackson (1985b) noted that Ulrich's style of critical analysis would help to point to such material conditions but could not help in the examination and explanation of the nature and development of those conditions (the possibility of Jackson slipping into hypostatizing material social conditions cannot be excluded according to the formulation of his words). Ulrich would reply that critical heuristics and critical theory pursue different, perhaps complementary, ends and that neither can replace the other. Habermas, for example, pursues a difficult theoretical purpose and Ulrich a likewise difficult practical (heuristic) purpose; it makes little sense to dismiss either one by raising the charge of missing the other's difficulty.

Regarding the charge of idealism, it is important to understand the critical significance of Kantian idealism. Kant conceived of his idealism in terms of problematic or critical idealism, in distinction to the solipsist's extreme subjective idealism. Kant's point is not of course that the world exists only in the mind, but rather that all our knowledge of the real world is in terms of maps and 'the map is not the territory' (after Korzybski, 1958). That is to say all our knowledge is perspective bound, selective, or (in Kant's terms) phenomenal only; not even the most comprehensive systems approach nor any kind of objective theory will ever be able to change this understanding. The critical idealist, unlike the realist, will always be reminded that all knowledge and understanding of the real world is in terms of phenomenal maps only and that a good map ought to lay open its perspective and scale, its selectivity and purposes and should never allow itself to be taken for the territory.

Given this understanding of the basic message of critical idealism, we find it to be an indispensable part of a critical systems approach. Although in sympathy with Jackson's critical intentions, it is not possible to identify a truly critical or radical approach in terms of ontological realism vs idealism, as Jackson's argument implies. Nor can it be identified in terms of ideological radicalism vs idealism, whatever those labels may be taken to mean specifically. The point in trying to be critical is not adopting the one or the other ontological, epistemological, theoretical, or ideological position but rather to keep reflecting on the limitations and value implications of one's position in every specific context of application, whatever that position may be.

There also remains the question, raised by Jackson (1985b), 'Why should the powerful bother to take account of the views and interests of those affected but not involved?' Of course, no methodology, not even a truly critical systems approach, can by itself make the powerful less powerful; but this is no different from even the most radically materialist social theory. A more relevant point is this. As a rule, the powerful are interested in concealing, rather than laying open, their access to power (strategic action) instead of achieving won consensus (rational communicative action). They seek to conceal their specific private interests behind some facade of common interest, of generally acceptable norms or objective necessities. A critical approach, although it cannot force the powerful to take account of the less powerful, can at least unveil this facade of rationality and objectivity which is so characteristic of the strategic action of powerful vested interests in present-day 'interest-group liberalism' (Lowi, 1969).

Critical Systems Heuristics, more than any methodology or theory before, specifically addresses this issue with its unique tool of the polemical employment of boundary judgments (or whole system judgments); it pays careful and explicit attention not to presuppose that those in control of decision power are willing to take account of the views and interests of those affected, but only that they are interested in making their own views and interests appear to be defendable on rational grounds.

Let us now start to summarize our position. A critical theory is (at least partly) rooted in the felt needs and sufferings of individuals and groups of people and therefore the interpretive approach of understanding people from their own view is fundamentally important. This is not enough, however, since we have already recognized that social action (as expressed through action concepts, etc.) may be shaped by the effects of material conditions and by the possibility of false consciousness.

We need to work toward both the systems and sociological dimensions of a critical theory. It is therefore important for a critical approach to tie its knowledge claims to the ability to satisfy human purposes and desires and thus validity of the theory must primarily be judged in terms of its potential in bringing about practical application and emancipation. It is therefore important to build in a facility whereby practical judgements can be constantly reflected upon in transparent nonexpert terms and their partiality revealed by everyday accounts of the nature of social experience in ordinary language. Only in this way can we conceive of a theory that might be translatable into practice so that those involved and those affected can share in the heuristic and critical approach to design and decision making.

Drawing this section to a close, we need to understand that notions of inevitable convergence, or absolutisms, should be avoided in critical studies. For instance, it is anti-critical to expect that we can work toward a view with which 'we all feel comfortable' (a bounded idea promoted by several eminent systems thinkers) be it with the outputs of methodological activities or indeed the methodological approach itself! Contrary to this we propose that we should remain uncomfortable. A truly critical approach must be open to emancipation from itself and even to calls of abolishment, as must the output of methodological activities. As we take our theories to the practical world of men and women, we must equally allow those practical people to bring their worlds to our systems intervention.

The proposal is that these ideas form the basis of a truly critical systems thinking of which in summary we note that:

(a) it promotes subjectivity;

(b) it is explicit about preventing the approach from being expert driven;

(c) it reaches out toward the systems epistemological ideal by accepting the critical idealism of Kant, Hegel, and Churchman and Marx's critical ideas of historical materialism;

(d) it is epistemologically tenable in both systemic and sociological terms;

(e) it is explicitly ideologically emancipatory; and therefore

(f) it promotes emancipation from all repressive conditions.

7.5.3   Conclusion

At the outset the call was for a switch in emphasis from 'systems science' — the use of systems ideas in traditional scientific practice — to 'systems rationality' — a critical understanding of rationality. It was suggested that a truly critical systems thinking cannot just reflect against a backboard of a systems epistemological ideal in terms of systems rationality. The proposal we made suggested integrating sociological and systems epistemologies through an epistemological ideal of critical rationality. This could only be achieved by dealing with the difficulties of social metaphysics — the totality of relevant *a priori* judgements that flow into social theories or systems designs but cannot be validated either empirically or logically: and by addressing normative assumptions that may be complicated by the possibility of false consciousness and effects of material conditions. Three rationalities were considered in the context of these issues and aspirations: positivistic, interpretivistic, and critical.

Of nonreflective positivistic approaches we considered the unappealing idea of directly transferring ideas from the natural sciences to promote objective and neutral power for social control. This was easily shown to be epistemologically untenable because there cannot be theory-neutrality or value-freedom with the notion of means-end, so we must ask 'What should be done?' and 'How should it be done?' (normative assumptions flowing into these questions are emphasized by the use of 'should').

Also, since positivistic approaches adopt traditional scientific rationality, then we expect similar conclusions to arise like: what is discovered is naturally and inevitably that way, which highlights the inherent conservative ideology of positivism.

Of nonreflective interpretivistic approaches we found that the empirical (surface) and structuralist (beneath the surface) approaches were replaced with ideas relating to action concepts. Actions can be thought of as defined surface events, but these are made meaningful only if two nonmaterial deeper layers are introduced. Social rules are the second layer, in terms of which actors can be said to be doing some particular thing. A third deeper layer is of constitutive meaning that lies behind the social practice and makes the actions and rules meaningful. This does promote mutual understanding, but can be shown to be epistemologically impoverished because interpretive science does not adequately deal with effects of, say, material conditions. The critical idealists distinguish themselves from subjective idealism (interpretivism) by accepting that 'out there' are some hard factual conditions that do not exist in the mind only. The critical idealist, however, does not expect to achieve direct access to those conditions, separating themselves from interpretive inquirers by claiming to provide adequate maps of our social reality. Interpretivist epistemology is equally impoverished because the notion of freezing constitutive meaning (freezing emancipation) through nontransparent false means (i.e., false consciousness) is not explicitly dealt with.

Also, interpretivist science is implicitly conservative since the explanation of social tensions in terms of imperfect communication can only lead to correction at the communicative level through the promise of enhanced communication. We have argued that correction cannot be promoted merely by clearing up misunderstandings with the view that the natural flow of discourse and order can be reestablished. The point is that a lack of authentic understanding is in many cases involved in situations of coercion, but mutual understanding alone cannot secure emancipation; critical reflection on the norms implied in that which is authentically understood can.

In Ulrich's view *a critical solution to the problem of practical reason* is the most urgent of all, for other kinds of inquiry have already developed methodological frameworks that work fairly well in (systems) practice: the experimental or scientific method works well for the purpose of securing instrumental rationality (it becomes scientistic in a derogative sense if its limitation to instrumental action is forgotten); the humanities have their hermeneutic method for securing communicative rationality and mutual understanding; but the applied disciplines, amongst them systems practice, have not satisfied the quest for some kind of critically comprehensive

Table 7.4

Summary of findings on a search toward an adequate epistemology
for systems practice

	POSITIVISM	INTERPRETIVISM	CRITIQUE
ASSUMED VIEW OF THE NATURE OF SOCIAL REALITY	Objective	Subjective	Subjective
KEY ACTOR(S) IN METHODOLOGICAL ACTIVITIES	Expert (elitist)	No explicit directives that prevent expert domination (potentially elitist).	All involved or affected (democratic).
THE SYSTEMS EPISTEMOLOGICAL IDEAL	Ignored or neglected.	It takes one of several steps that can be achieved by recognising subjectivity of man and the importance of the social communicative world.	It reaches-out in terms of critical idealism of Kant, Hegel and Churchman *and* Marx's Historical Materialism.
EPISTEMOLOGICAL VALIDITY FOR SOCIAL INQUIRY	Untenable	Impoverished	Tenable and adequate.
IDEOLOGICAL STATUS	Conservative	Conservative	Emancipatory
MEANS OF DEALING WITH POWER RELATIONS	Maintenance or strengthening.	Accepts	Attempts to emancipate, in particular by dealing with effects of material conditions and false consciousness.

Table 7.5

Three rationalities contrasted in terms of their theoretical,
ideological and practical premises

PARADIGM	THEORETICAL PREMISES	IDEOLOGICAL PREMISES	PRACTICAL PREMISES
TRADITIONAL SYSTEMS	Positivistic	Declared as neutral, but of technocratic control, i.e., it is conservative.	Design and engineering methodology, applied systematically, developed heuristically from practice.
SOFT SYSTEMS	Interpretivistic	Declared as neutral, but practiced in the confines of maintenance of social order, i.e., it is conservative.	A plurality of soft systems methodologies, applied systemically, developed heuristically from practice with (some) reference to the theoretical premises.
CRITICAL SYSTEMS	Accepts the neccesity of interpretive categories in social science, but only in relation to ideological premises, i.e., the 'social turn' (it is critical).	Actions are quasi-caused by social conditions that must be understood in order to prevent domination and subjugation, i.e., it is emancipatory.	Practioners must seek and discover quasi-casual and functional laws of social behaviour in particular social contexts - methodology is thus linked to context through their theoretical and ideological assumptions, systemically or systematically according to context.

rationality and have not established an intersubjectively reproducible way of ensuring rational practical discourse on disputed (because of conflict) norms of action.

In my own view developing such an emancipatory rationality for systems practice is vital. Equally important, however, is the accompanying idea of complementarity between the three sciences or rationalities which we have discussed (i.e., complementarism, the sixth and the only acceptable scenario for the future of systems 'problem solving', discussed at length earlier in this chapter), that can be developed in terms of legitimacies and limitations as set out in this section. The aim is to ensure that diversity is accepted as a strength rather than fragmentation as a weakness in systems-based 'problem-solving' by drawing upon approaches of various rationalities. The argument of this section is summarized in Table 7.4 and Table 7.5.

7.6   CONCLUSION

In this chapter we have assessed six scenarios for the future of systems 'problem-solving'. Each scenario has been considered from many

angles. One by one, each possible way forward was shown to present some
genuine difficulties. Eventually we were able to boil the argument down to a
residual of complementarism v. isolationism. They were shown to be highly
problematic at a methodological level and so it was necessary to develop a
new epistemological debate for systems thinking. In these terms, even the
forces of interpretivistic isolationism could not stand the test, coming across
as impoverished. Admittedly, interpretivistic systems thinking has made a
necessary step toward an adequate epistemology by introducing the idea of
subjective thinking, but this seems to have neglected to recognize that the
theory of such a paradigm must be explicitly concerned with its own
ideological context. In the last section of this chapter we have seen the
penalty that has to be paid with such impoverished thought and have
subsequently worked toward an adequate epistemology for systems practice
through critically oriented thinking.

NOTES

(1)   An alternative introduction by Flood and Jackson (1989) is
      reproduced in this note.

> There are many important avenues of current systems
> thinking such as Systems Engineering, Cybernetics, System
> Dynamics, General Systems Theory, Soft Systems Thinking and
> Critical Systems Thinking. This necessary *diversity* should be
> seen as a *strength* of the systems movement rather than the
> poorly thought out criticism that this is a fragmentation and a
> weakness. The *proper* theorizing of the relationships among the
> tendencies that make up the systems movement is certainly one
> of the most important challenges that the systems community
> faces for the remainder of this century. Its future growth and
> prosperity as a unified body of scholars and practitioners, and
> the realization of its potential for massively increased influence
> in the affairs of organizations and societies, critically depend
> upon the resolution of this difficulty.
>
> At present, two possible 'theoretical resolutions' to the
> difficulty seem to be on offer—neither yet wholly developed and
> neither free from internal inconsistencies.
>
> The first of these is roughly a 'Kuhnian' position, which sees
> the recent history of systems thinking in terms of the
> replacement of the old 'hard' paradigm (Systems Engineering,
> General Systems Theory, Cybernetics, and so on) with a new

and vigorous 'soft' paradigm. The 'hard' paradigm, unable to deal with the 'anomalies' arising when it is applied in complex, human-centered, organizational, and societal situations, has given way to a soft 'paradigm,' which both preserves the achievements of the hard in its specialized domain of application and extends the area of successful operation of systems ideas to the behavioral and social arena. When this story is told from the soft systems perspective, the progress of systems thought tends to stop at this point. From a critical point of view, however, it could be argued that the difficulties with which soft systems practitioners currently wrestle in attempting to apply their approach to situations characterized by unequal relations of power, contradiction, and so on are yet new 'anomalies' that will eventually lead to the dominance of the newly emerging critical systems paradigm—one that accepts the utility of each approach, but only after self-reflective and critical examination.

For those who reject the notion that hard and 'cybernetic' approaches are simply special cases of the soft and that critical systems thinking is simply a soft approach coupled with a 'loony left' ideology, the second possible resolution of the difficulty of interrelationships may seem preferable. This is the complementarist position, which seeks to recognize the complementary strengths of the different systems tendencies and to align each of them with the sort of problem situation for which it should, in theory, provide the most suitable approach. Thus it is argued that the difficulties of 'logical ordering' which are the concern of hard approaches are best seen as different in kind from the difficulties pursued by Soft System Thinkers, and likewise with the difficulties of communication, control, and organizing which lie within the domain of Cybernetics. The question remains for complementarism that once it accepts the existence of wholly different systems approaches resting upon apparently irreconcilable presuppositions (inhabiting different paradigms), 'How can 'contradictions' of the paradigm incommensurability be overcome?' Without privileging any of the competing positions, how can a meta-theory be realized which respects the relative strengths and weaknesses of each and oversees their 'correct' employment by systems practitioners?

(2) A comical, if not wholly outrageous illustration comes from the script of the film *Sleeper* written by Woody Allen and Marshall Brickman. The story is that Miles Monro is awoken from cryogenic preservation two hundred years on (in the year 2173). The first dialogue presented below is between a male doctor (I shall call Dr. M.) and a female Doctor (Dr. F.) shortly after Miles' reawakening.

Dr. F.   "He has fully recovered...except for a few minor kinks."

Dr. M.   "Has he asked for anything special?"

Dr. F.   "Yes, this morning for breakfast he requested something called wheatgerm, organic honey, and tiger's milk."

Dr. M.   (Chuckle) "Oh yes, those are the charmed substances that some years ago were felt to contain life-preserving properties."

Dr. F.   "You mean that there was no deep fat, no steak or cream pies or ... hot fudge?"

Dr. M.   "Those were thought to be unhealthy, precisely the opposite to what we now know to be true."

Dr. F.   "Incredible."

And in dialogue a little later.

Dr. M.   "Now here, smoke this and be sure you get the smoke deep into your lungs."

Miles   "I don't smoke."

Dr. M.   "Its tobacco! Its one of the healthiest things for your body. Now go ahead. You need all the strength you can get."

(3)   There are many general implications that arise from this discussion about (essentially) isolationist positions in contrast with a complementarist's position, the one I wish to point out concerns various literary styles. This is extremely important with respect to how we might begin to offer our messages to the reader.

Now, some writers prefer to develop a whole and lengthy system of thought, others wish to simply and tidily put across a few well-structured points, while the discursive essay has its advocates. Some use words in a unitary and convergent way while others use them in an open and divergent manner. Each style is capable of achieving different things. It is perfectly proper for individuals to choose a style according to their own sensibility. Unfortunately, the isolationist who supports one style and disapproves of others, say with the singular view of presenting ideas simply and tidily, will not appreciate the discursive style that paints a less well defined picture (which holds at least equal richness). The simple and tidy attempt to dictate a message is infact politically powerful. The discursive writer invites the reader on a journey that does not attempt to define all the horizons, it is not a single tunnel but a network or labyrinth to be explored — but only by the adventurer and the brave. It can achieve a political success, but that is not necessarily the main purpose.

The isolationist referred to above is likely to hold such a position elsewhere, in respect to a theoretical position say. The trouble with this is that it will only lead to adversarial intellectual debates. This case in respect of theory is discussed in the text of Chapter 7, but is equally important in literary styles where, for example, the technical (simple and tidy) author writes off the discursive and diverging approach as nonrigorous, clever, metaphysical, or even mystical.

A metaphor might help here. Imagine that the discursive and artistic writer were on an exploration in some deep jungle. There are many trails to follow and thickets to break through, many dangers to face but many wonderful experiences to be had. And after some length of time there is a most beautiful experience when a small clearing is found, with huge colored butterflies, long-tailed and melodious birds bathed in shafts of sunlight, the sweet smell of tropical flowers, and curious sounds. This position was not discovered easily. 'So, what would the technical writer tell us?'

The likely advice is this. Yes, this is a quite marvelous discovery, but in order that we make this accessible to a more general audience we must cut away the jungle, destroy the paths, do away with the dangers. We must expose this beauty in a simplicity. But if the jungle is cut away, the clearing will no longer be supported by the discovered ecology. The flora and fauna will wither away and die and silence and a barren landscape will be the prize. The clearing will become a place of death and finally a desert. The technical writer just did not understand.

(4) Personally, I am quite fond of don Juan's conception of complementarism (as I understand it and as reported by Carlos Castaneda, 1987) as he attempted to explain his knowledge—named 'sorcery', although don Juan says that was not really an accurate description.

'From where the average man stands,' don Juan said, 'sorcery is nonsinous or an ominous mystery beyond his reach. And he is right—not because this is an absolute fact, but because the average man lacks the energy to deal with sorcery.'

He stopped for a moment before he continued. 'Human beings are born with a finite amount of energy,' don Juan said, 'an energy that is systematically deployed, beginning at the moment of birth, in order that it may be used most advantageously by the modality of the time.'

'What do you mean by the modality of the time?' I asked.

'The modality of the time is the precise bundle of energy fields being perceived,' he answered. 'I believe man's perception has changed through the ages. The actual time decides the mode; the time decides which precise bundle of energy fields, out of an incalculable number, are to be used. And handling the modality of the time—those few selected energy fields—takes all our available energy, leaving us nothing that would help us use any of the other energy fields.'

He urged me with a subtle movement of his eyebrows to consider this.

'This is what I mean when I say that the average man lacks the energy needed to deal with sorcery.' he went on, 'If he uses only the energy he has, he can't perceive the worlds sorcerers do. To perceive them, sorcerers need to use a cluster of energy fields not ordinarily used. Naturally, if the average man is to perceive those worlds and understand sorcerer's perception he must use the same cluster they have used. And this is just not possible, because all his energy is already deployed.'

He paused as if searching for the appropriate words to make his point.
'Think of it this way,' he proceeded. 'It isn't that as time goes by you're learning sorcery; rather, what you're learning is to save energy. And this energy will enable you to handle some of the energy fields which are inaccessible to you now. And that is sorcery: the ability to use energy fields that are not employed in perceiving the ordinary world we know. Sorcery is a state of

awareness. Sorcery is the ability to perceive something which ordinary perception cannot.' (Castaneda, 1987, p. 7–8).

(5)   For those hard-headed people who consider metaphysics a nonsense, consider this humorous sketch from the film written and directed by Woody Allen, *A Midsummer Night's Sex Comedy*. The film starts with Leopold, a professor of philosophy, addressing his last class before summer vacation.

Leopold	"Ghosts, little spirits or pixies. I don't believe in them. Do you Mr. Fox?"
Mr. Fox	"No, sir."
Leopold	"You sound like it with all your metaphysical jibberish."
Mr. Fox	"Well, I didn't mean ghosts or spirits, professor."
Leopold	"Nothing is real but experience. That which can be touched, tasted, felt or in some scientific fashion proved. We must never substitute qualitative events that are marked by similar properties and recurrences of fixed substances ... Mr. Snell!"

Mr. Snell's attention is gained.

"Since these are the last few moments before the summer vacation, I would appreciate it if you could remain awake until the last bell."

Mr. Snell	"I'm sorry, sir."
Adjacent student	"I take it you rule out metaphysics as unworthy of serious consideration?"
Leopold	"As I stated clearly in my latest paper, metaphysical philosophers are simply men who are too weak to accept the world as it is. Their theories of the so-called mysteries of life are nothing more than projections of their own inner uneasiness. Apart from this world there are no realities."

> *Another student*   "That leaves many basic human needs unanswered?"
>
> *Leopold*   "I did not create the cosmos. I merely explain it."

(6) P. B. Checkland (1978) was probably the first systems author to clearly recognize that the means-end scheme is the common defining feature of all variations of hard systems thinking. Unfortunately, Checkland has never been similarly clear with respect to the fact that switching from hard to soft systems thinking does not automatically buy immunity from positivism. An additional step is required, that is the step from an interpretivistic to a critical (critically normative) understanding of soft systems thinking (Ulrich, 1983, 1988a: the 'second' epistemological break, as argued for in this book). As Habermas (1971a, p. vii) said, 'That we disavow reflection is positivism.'

(7) A neglect that more generally is evident in his work and which has serious consequences in terms of limiting possibilities for change and this is despite his 'radical in principle' comments (see Checkland, 1981, p. 283).

(8) Let us be clear, perhaps rather belatedly, that positivism is not a type of paradigm of science in its own right. In essence, *positivism is not an approach to inquiry but a sloppy way of dealing with its assumptions and results.* It amounts to a rationality which pervades a whole paradigm. No inquirer, regardless of what science is pursued, is ever immune from falling back into positivism (e.g., in the way the means-end distinction is handled).

(9) Brian Fay's account of this debate on types of rationality is useful in that it is relatively short and easily accessible. The reader should note, however, that the book does not (and could not, according to its aims) reach the level of sophistication of Habermas' work, and does not attempt to deal with the systems debate that we are concerned with. Furthermore, there is a real danger in Fay's work of conflating radical with critical. This said, I would still recommend the book as a background read to our direct debate.

(10) Ulrich (1983, p. 237) therefore argues that:

> ...the idea of mental determinism is crucial for understanding the 'facts' of social reality in much the same way that the idea of physical determinism has been crucial for the success of the natural sciences in understanding the 'facts' of nature.

(11) For brief first introductions to Critical Heuristics, see Ulrich (1984 and 1987). Some of the underlying ideas are also summarized in Ulrich, (1977, 1980, 1981a, 1981b, 1988a, 1988b, 1989, 1991).

END OF ARGUMENT

CHAPTER 8

A BEGINNING

Exiting the argument

If I were asked to comment on what I had hoped that the argument of this book would offer the reader, then my answer would vehemently be, to show that challenge and emancipation can lead to an enriching of our intellectual and life-worlds. This I have tackled in a number of ways focusing on systems thinking. The main point from each strand of the general argument on Liberating Systems Theory is that we need to embrace complementarism and resist isolationism, and press for recognition that diversity can only be faced by unities and will destroy universals in systems thinking. This is a simple concept that of course can be found in cybernetic thinking: Ashby's Law of Requisite Variety states that only variety (diversity) can deal with variety (diversity). With the complementarist position we attempt to introduce this idea into epistemology, accepting that there have been many attempts to develop methods and theories in the face of multivarious complexities of our life-worlds and yet, not one has been found that is able to come up with full and total solutions or explanations, or is even able to point us in that direction. It would therefore be preferable to stop this search and to adopt an open and conciliatory stance that more or less says, well all right, let us consider what is being claimed by taking a critical approach that accepts that there might be legitimacies but is also honest enough to recognize that all approaches will have their limitations. As soon as this position is accepted, then universals are disposed of as totalizing and impoverished in the way that they offer one idea on rationality which must be linked to one idea on irrationality. That is not to say, of course, that a reflective view on the universal would turn up nothing at all of interest. A critical approach opens its arms to such carefully considered thinking, although despairs at the isolationism of nonreflective universalists. It is, therefore, of primary importance that we always remain skeptical and appreciate that challenge does lead to liberation, whereas subservience to any one position leads to a practical and/or an intellectual and life-world slavery. This is *alienation*. So I would hope that the argument of this book at the end of the day is simply about liberation for enrichment.

Just how this has been achieved in the preceding text is worth recapping. Very simply, I have argued for emancipation of two sorts that may also be considered as two stages: liberate and critique. What is meant here is liberation of knowledge that grows a diversity, and then critique of these various discourses in terms of a meta-unity of rationalities and an associated adequate epistemology. In this book I have made one attempt

197

at this. First, by drawing on the powerful ideas of Michel Foucault, under the label Interpretive Analytics, which offer methodological principles for fighters and resistors against assumed-as-being truths. Second, by developing the only currently realistic meta-unity as constructed by Jürgen Habermas in his knowledge-constitutive interests, that formed the basis for an adequate epistemology by which we can begin to critique truths. In this way we recognize that it is impossible to have free-floating, neutral and independent truths, but rather it is necessary that we clearly define our complementarist position, which undoubtedly has its own rules of the constitution of objects and of inclusion and exclusion according to human interests. Underlying the meta-unity are several tensions between the works of Foucault and Habermas and with each of these writers according to their own intentions there are also tensions — a necessary part, it seems, of the complementarist position.

What all this means for systems thinking has been argued through the notions of Liberating Systems Theory. There is the meta-unity of 'Liberating Systems Theory' ('LST') which relates to the liberation of systems theory (L'ST') and systems theory for liberation ('LS'T').

In fact, the liberation of systems theory is no simple matter as we have seen. First of all we have to contend with conceptual reflexivity, the unique difficulty that systems thinking suffers from. This is the tendency for systems thinkers to believe that they have at their disposal a closed set of concepts which can be used to understand and explain virtually everything. Second, there is the difficulty of showing clearly that notions of system offer both abstract richness and paradigmatic contentfulness. The initial difficulty here is to overcome the everyday contentless use that the term system has become recognized for. This can be achieved by highlighting a variety of systemic ways of meaningfully conceptualizing what we generally accept as a real external world. The important thing to remember is that the ways are metaphorical and do not at all state that this explains the world as it is. Of course, such a position has to be set against other theoretical stances, as can be done by developing views on paradigmatic contentfullness for the systems idea. At the same time we also flag the idea of different rationalities associated with differing paradigms, which is an important step in our move toward developing an adequate epistemology. Third, there is a specific need to reflect on the rise and suppression of discourse, or knowledges in the domain of systems thinking. This can only usefully be done if we are clear about our meta-position with its own rules on the constitution of objects and of inclusion and exclusion. This demands, then, that we have a well worked out adequate epistemology, for it is only by coming off the fence and making clear this position that we can begin to employ our liberating armory. In particular, we must be concerned with how untenable or impoverished epistemological positions have been assumed during the process of subjugation and domination, so we must be looking critically at the points of subjugation where the untenable or impoverished forces strike. We will want to weaken those forces by applying our own adequate epistemology at their very source.

The liberation of systems theory, then, puts out a call for its own nonneutral discourse of a liberating rationale. What is needed here is developed in the argument of this book, apparently in particular when considering systems theory for liberation. A complex argument of isolationism (in its various forms) versus complementarism led to acceptance of the latter and hence toward the development of Habermas' knowledge-constitutive interests in terms of an adequate epistemology for systems practice. This equally offers the essential ideas necessary to support all the requirements for the liberation of systems theory.

And so there we have it, one beginning for Critical Systems Thinking in the form of Liberating Systems Theory. This assumes a position of openness and conciliation, makes a liberating statement about rules for discourse analysis and has a liberating position with respect to an adequate epistemology that declares certain others to be untenable or impoverished. Of great importance, of course, is that this whole effort is declared as awaiting critical discussion and assessment.[1]

NOTES

(1) Three main issues that need to be dealt with but are not explicitly addressed in this thesis are as follows.

   (a) A concern for a critical or liberating pedagogy (for systems theory), which has effectively been addressed in the work of Freire (e.g., Freire, 1970; Shor and Freire, 1989; also Collins, 1977). This point has been brought to my attention by D. Schecter.

   (b) A concern for a critical or liberating focus on environmental issues, since the ideas of this thesis attend to the human condition without properly reflecting on Nature beyond that condition. This point has been brought to my attention by G. Midgley.

   (c) A concern for a critical or liberating study that aims to show clearly how systemic concepts can be of help to society. This point has been brought to my attention by M. C. Jackson.

TERMS AND CONCEPTS

Some critical observations

ABSOLUTISM: '...can be taken as the hall mark of positivist modern science...a natural consequence of the marriage of the Mathematical Project with the idea of progress.... Absolutism is an intuitive belief in the uniqueness of a World or Universe independent of human observers and which can be known in its independence and uniqueness by the cognitive devices of human beings.' (Fuenmayor, 1985, p. 364). A broader understanding can be grasped if we extend Fuenmayor's assumptions so that Absolutism might also mean, to know everything and know it is valid.

ANIMISM: 'The view that everything in the Universe, including even plants and nominate objects, has some kind of psychological being more or less tenuously similar to that of human and nonhuman animals. Thus it is asserted that the stone is not only an aggregate of moving molecules but has "awareness" of other bodies in, for example, attracting or repelling them or being affected along with them by gravity' (Flew, 1979, p. 14).

ANTI-FOUNDATIONALISM: See 'Foundationalism'.

ANTI-POSITIVISM: See 'Positivism'.

COMPLEMENTARISM: A position that seeks to recognize the complementary strengths of different tendencies and to align each of them with the sort of situation for which it should, in theory, provide the most suitable reasoning.

COMPLEXITY: A concept that is generally accepted as referring to the basic components of system which exist in a real world; such as elements, relationships interconnectedness, but more specifically is associated with attributes of these, or the kinds of behavior which arise because of the types of relationship. Theories of complexity of this nature have largely been developed in the life sciences. Attempts to transfer these theories to the social sciences have not been convincing, where complexity can be better understood as relating broadly to consciousness, incorporating human qualities such as values, beliefs, norms and more generally relating to psychological, cultural, and political factors. In Chapter 5, Section 4, any understanding of complexity is shown to ultimately depend on paradigmatic interpretation.

CONCEPTUAL-REFLEXIVITY: The convergent notion that a limited or finite set of concepts is sufficient for us to be able to explain the Universe and everything in it. This has a unique attractiveness in systems thinking where systems concepts might be assumed to be transportable across all disciplines and that all their difficulties can be resolved in this way. A trap for positivists.

CRITICAL HERMENEUTICS: 'Hermeneutics expanded into criticism' takes the form of a critique of systematically distorted communication (Bleicher, 1980, p. 266, attributed to Habermas).

CRITICAL SCIENCE: The science of emancipation from hidden presuppositions.

CRITICAL SYSTEMS HEURISTICS: "Rationality', according to Ambrose Bierce's usually reliable *Devil's Dictionary*, is the quality of being 'devoid of all delusions save those of observation, experience and reflection' (1958, p. 107). Critical Heuristics, or, by its full name, Critical Systems Heuristics, represents a conceptual framework for tracing some of these delusions in the realm of 'rational' social planning.

I have chosen the name Critical Systems Heuristics for this framework because it seems aptly to suggest three of its main characteristics: its critical intent against present conceptions of 'rational' planning, its employment of the systems idea for this purpose, and its heuristic rather than theoretical orientation' (Ulrich, 1983, p. 19).

CRITICAL SYSTEMS THINKING: A broad notion of critical science employed with a systems perspective.

CRITIQUE: A general term of critical thinking that has only one unchanging thesis which states that critical thinking is itself changeable. Critique in its many manifestations puts up a common opposition to instrumental rationality, because such a rationality can be linked to control in the human condition in a similar way to the idea of power in the control of the natural world. Critique takes on more specific meanings for particular schools of thought, such as the positions of Michel Foucault and Jürgen Habermas. These and other positions do show a commitment to critical analysis by dealing with subjugation and domination in respect to their different focuses; Foucault's concern is to reveal and release subjugated knowledges, while Habermas is more closely concerned with emancipation of individuals, which might be seen as one and the same in terms of liberate and critique.

DISCURSIVE FORMATION: The conception of knowledge as a living network of ideas created out of the shared subjectivities of people, but is accidental in that the living network has not arisen from a natural evolution, rather, it is a forced position. Vulnerability of discursive formations is therefore not from some natural world processes but from *possibilities of forces* being applied to consciousnesses through domination of the sources of knowledge.

EMPIRICISM: 'Usually defined as the thesis that all knowledge or at least all knowledge of matters of fact as distinct from that of purely logical relations between concepts – is based on experience. The phrase 'is based on' is sometimes replaced by 'comes from', 'derives from', or 'has its source in' – but it has to be admitted that all of these are more or less overtly metaphorical and can do little to specify just what relationship between knowledge and experience is intended. The popular appeal of empiricalism depends in interpreting the key words 'experience' in its everyday understanding, in which a claim to have experience of cows is a claim to have had dealings with mind-independent realities down on the farm. But philosophers have often so construed this key term that 'merely' to have dreams or hallucinations of cows would constitute having experience of cows.... Empiricism, then, has taken several forms...' (Flew, 1979, p. 104–105).

Although we may occasionally share the broader view of empiricism available in the above description, it is often the case in this work that empiricism refers more specifically to: (a) science pursued through measurement instruments for the collection of data from which structured models are realized and for validation, or (b) the more philosophically oriented notion of experiences being written on the mind.

ENLIGHTENMENT: 'Precisely because it does not presuppose ideal conditions of complete rationality, a 'merely' critical solution to the problem of practical reason can hope to contribute to the practical 'enlightenment' of social inquirers, planners or decision makers, that is, to help them become self-reflective with regard to the normative implications of any standard of rationality on which they may rely' (Ulrich, 1983, p. 176). 'In addition to assimilating the Enlightenment understanding of critique as oppositional thinking, the Frankfurt School have...' (Connerton, 1976, p. 20)   '...the *conditions* of possible knowledge: on the potential abilities of human beings possessing the faculties of knowing, speaking and acting' (Connerton, 1976, p. 17).

EPISTEMOLOGY: 'The branch of philosophy concerned with the theory of knowledge. Traditionally, central issues in epistemology are the nature and derivation of knowledge, the scope of knowledge, and the reliability of claims to knowledge' (Flew, 1979, p.109). Reflection on the gaining and disseminating of knowledge and on the validity of that knowledge (see 'Paradigm').

FALSE CONSCIOUSNESS: 'Around us are psuedo-events, to which we adjust with a false consciousness adapted to see these events as true and real, and even as beautiful. In the society of men the truth resides now less in what things are than in what they are not. Our social realities are so ugly if seen in the light of exiled truth, and beauty is almost no longer possible if it is not a lie' (Laing, 1967, p. 11).

'False consciousness relates to the experience of half-truths, lies, propaganda, manipulation and suppression of thought, censureship, etc... It has found its most exhausting and damning exposition in the form of historical materialism. It is here that false reflections of a 'false' reality have found their most penetrating critique - not in the sense of having an abstract set of ideas or values put against them, but by evidencing their origin in definite material conditions that add up to a state of unfreedom. The critique of the misunderstanding of self and others entails the critique of the reality that gave rise to them' (Bleicher, 1980, p. 143).

It is quite natural for us, in this thesis, to offer a complementary vision of false consciousness which typifies all nonreflective isolationists. It is that subservience to a supposed superior paradigm amounts to a state of false consciousness. So we see the importance of the liberate component of this thesis—to liberate people from what is really an alienated position (as Laing, 1967, puts it).

FOUNDATIONALISM: 'Foundationalism seeks to rest knowledge on firm, indubitable, and unshakable ground. To inform us 'in a timelessly true way what can and cannot be counted on in the edifice of human knowledge. [Anti-foundationalism supports the idea that] The move from the indubitable ideas of the individual thinking subject to the intersubjectively shared practices of actual language use seems to leave us with no 'foundations' outside or beyond the changing and contingent social practices within which such linguistic practices are actually found' (Roderick, 1986, p. 8— that in brackets added).

FUNCTIONALISM: A position that relates ontologically to realism, epistemologically to anti-positivism, and ideologically to the maintenance of social order, and conceives of the world in terms of functional units.

GENEALOGY: Genealogy is analysis of the development of humanity as a series of interpretations (arising from discursive and nondiscursive relations) emerging from a relationship between power and knowledge. It is the task of genealogy to record this.

GESTALT: 'An organized, coherent whole whose parts are determined by laws intrinsic to the whole rather than being randomly juxtaposed or associated. The concept gives its name to the 20th century school of psychology... Gestalt theory was originally set up on general principles in opposition to the prevailing psychological atomism of the empiricist traditions. But its most significant contributions have occurred in the field of psychology of perception, in virtue of a number of classic experiments designed to show that the eye naturally tends to organize, for example, a series of lines into coherent patterns. For Gestalt Theory, seeing is essentially a phenomenological process in so far as what is 'seen' is what appears to be seen rather than what may actually be there' (Flew, 1979, p. 131).

HARD SYSTEMS: 'Deals with 'problems' ...which can be formulated as the search for an efficient means of achieving a defined end' (Checkland, 1981, p. 316). What Checkland omits to say here is that traditional hard systems thinkers believe that they have the tools to tackle the whole range of managerial and organizational problems which may be encountered, and often see soft as a subset of hard. In consultancy experience I have found that UK management (and presumably Western management as such) is dominated by hard, all be it rather pragmatic, approaches.

HERMENEUTICS: '...can be loosely defined as the theory or philosophy of the interpretation of meaning... The realization that human expressions contain a meaningful component, which has to be recognized as such by a subject and transposed into his own system of values and meanings, has given rise to the 'problem of hermeneutics', how this process is possible and how to render accounts of subjectively intended meaning, objective in the face of the fact that they are marshalled by the interpreter's own subjectivity. Contemporary hermeneutics is characterized by conflicting views concerning this problem; it is possible to distinguish three clearly separate strands: hermeneutic theory, hermeneutic philosophy and critical hermeneutics' (Bleicher, 1980, p. 1). See Chapter 2, Section 3 in this text.

HOLONOMIC: Nomic—laws; holos—wholes: therefore laws of wholes.

HOLISM: '1. The contention that wholes, or some wholes, are more than the sum of their parts. One special version is organicism, urging that some systems that are not literally organisms are nevertheless crucially like organisms, whole parts can only be understood in relation to their functions in the complete and ongoing whole. 2. (In the social sciences and history) A theory that claims that society may, or should, be studied in terms of social wholes: that is, that the fundamental data of social analysis are not individuals or individual manifestations but rather societal laws, dispostions, and movements' (Flew, 1979, p. 152).

HYPOSTATIZATION: Generally, indicating that something underlies other things and acts as a support. For our purposes, hypostatization refers to '...mistaking an abstract entity for a physical one' (Bleicher, 1980, p. 269). Of main concern to us is the mistaking of the abstract notion of system for the physical idea of systems independent of the mind.

IDEAL TYPE: '...is an interpretive conceptual model. Its purpose is to serve as a conceptual system where a phenomenon may have one of its possible interpretations. It does not pretend to copy or make a 'photograph' of reality, it is rather used to highlight one point of view of a phenomenon so that the relativity and plurality of interpretations become visible. For an original insight into 'Ideal Types' and their relevance in the epistemology of Human Sciences see Weber from 1904' (Fuenmayor, 1985, p. 32). In fact the original of 1904 is referred to in this text under a later English version of 1949. It is important to move beyond such a phenomenological relativism to recognize the inherent ideological component of any ideal type (i.e., what implications are there in terms of social order and change?).

IDEOGRAPHIC: In the context of methods, where the principal concern is with an understanding of the way an individual creates, modifies, and interprets the world. Experiences are seen as unique and particular to the individual rather than general and universal. An external reality is questioned. An emphasis is placed on the relativistic nature of the world to such an extent that it may be perceived as not amenable to study using the ground rules of the natural sciences (see also Burrell and Morgan, 1979).

IDEOLOGY: See 'Paradigm'.

INSTRUMENTAL REASON: '...helps us decide how to do things... instrumental reason can only help us with technical questions such as the most efficient means to achieve predetermined ends. Rational discussion about ends and even about the value context of means, is apparently not possible' (Jackson, 1985b, p. 878).

INTERPRETIVISM: Very broadly speaking, a view that recognizes the innate subjectivity of human thought and reason. It amounts to a rationality which pervades a whole paradigm. Interpretive social theory is concerned with situations as defined through action concepts. Understanding cannot arise from observation and theory (surface and beneath the surface material analyses of traditional positivistic scientific approaches) since the human actor will have reasons, or intentions, that lie behind each action (these are not material). The interpretivist introduces the idea that a specific action concept can only be transparent in the context of a certain set of social rules, or a social practice. A third nonmaterial deeper layer that the interpretivist introduces is that of constitutive meaning. As a social practice lies behind an observation, a constitutive meaning lies behind the social practice. It is in terms of these meanings that people speak and act.

INTERPRETIVE ANALYTICS: The name given to the archaeology, genealogy, and critique of Michel Foucault by Dreyfus and Rabinow (1982). Archaeology was conceived as an analysis of the history of discursive formations explained as the anonymous systems of rules which allegedly form the conceptual and institutional conditions for the possibility of scientific statements. Genealogy was a move away from the Archaeological project and involved an abandoning of the idea of autonomy of discursive formations. This new effort attempted to account for the emergence and disappearance of discourse by an analysis of contingent and external historical circumstances which bring about an interaction of, or a contact between, discursive practices. Discourse thus now incorporates the idea of apparatuses, which are assumed to play an objective constitutive role. Critique aims to provide the possibility for discursivities, that are prevented from being 'seen or heard' or known or even formed, to be liberated. See Chapter 3 for details.

ISOLATIONISM: Where an intellectual construction holding a particular rationality is used in a totalizing fashion such that any other rationality is assumed to be irrational. A universal rationality can be found in all isolationist positions, although there are various means that isolationists adopt in order to deal with ideas and concepts from other rationalities. These range from a complete rejection to different means of absorbing these ideas. Any absorption, however, will always be characterized by a denaturing of ideas and concepts. A non-reflective isolationist is, of course, suffering from an intellectual case of false consciousness.

KNOWLEDGE-CONSTITUTIVE INTERESTS: 'There is only one way we can claim 'objectivity'—in the general sense of freedom from hidden presuppositions—for our empirical basis of rational discourse: namely, by acknowledging in each case, the knowledge-constitutive interests on which the validity and meaning of "facts" depends' (Ulrich, 1983, p.64). See Chapter 3 for details.

LEVELS OF RESOLUTION: The abstract systemic idea that a system is an interacting part of a larger system, yet itself is comprised of other interactive parts. At each level of resolution (high resolution referring to detail, low to generality) the whole is said to be greater than the sum of its parts. The concept of emergence helps to make this meaningful.

LIBERATING SYSTEMS THEORY: Liberating Systems Theory ('LST') can and should be interpreted in many ways. The pursuit of liberating systems theory (L'ST') and systems theory for liberation in the human condition ('LS'T). Three strands have so far been developed for the first: the liberation of systems theory generally from a natural tendency toward self-imposed insularity, the liberation of systems concepts from objectivist or subjectivist delusions, and the liberation of systems theory specifically in cases of internalized localized subjugations in discourse and by considering histories and progressions of systems thinking; and for the second, systems theory for liberation and emancipation in response to domination and subjugation in work and social situations.

MATERIAL CONDITIONS: Appreciation of the material conditions that shape our perception of social reality—avoiding the error of hypostatization, or mistaking an abstract entity for a real one.

METAPHYSICS: 'A central element in Western philosophy from the Greeks onwards, 'metaphysics' has meant different things' (Flew, 1979, p. 229). For our purposes, metaphysics refers to our theories (conceptions or understandings) of social reality which always go beyond that which the empirical, the phenomenal surface that we can observe, apparently tells us.

METHOD: Different modes of 'problem solving' (see 'Paradigm').

METHODOLOGY: Methodology is normative and amounts to the foundation or basis for determining the metacharacteristics of modes of 'problem solving' and inquiry methods (see 'Paradigm').

MODERNISM: 'Modernism is that moment when man invented himself; when he no longer saw himself as a reflection of God or Nature. Its historical source lies in the eighteenth century philosophy of the Enlightenment which chose Reason as the highest of human attributes...Modernism...has two versions: *Critical Modernism*...and *systemic modernism*. Systemic modernism is currently seen to be the dominant force of reason more usually expressed as 'instrumental rationality'... Critical modernism stands opposed to the cybernetic-like monolithism of systemic modernism... Despite the difference between systemic and critical forms of modernism—the one bent on the mechanization of social order; the other, on the liberation of the life-worlds—they share a belief in the intrinsically logical and meaningful world constituted by Reason as the universal firm foundation. This takes two forms: (1) that discourse mirrors the reason and order already 'out there' in the world, and (2) that there is a thinking agent, a subject, which can make itself conscious of this external order...

The key to understanding the discourse of post-modernism is the concept of *difference*: a form of self-reference in which terms contain their own opposites and thus refuse any singular grasp of their meanings, e.g., the paradox of the 'global village' in which the enlargement of the world through modern communication techniques actually makes it smaller... At the very centre of discourse, therefore, the human agent is faced with a condition of irreducible indeterminacy and it is this endless and unstoppable demurrage which postmodern thought explicitly recognizes and places in the vanguard of its endeavors' (Cooper and Burrell, 1988, p. 94–98).

NOMINALISM: The idea that reality is a product of individual consciousness, a product of one's own mind or of individual cognition.

NOMOTHETIC: In the context of methods, it is appropriate to analyze relationships and regularities between the elements of which the world is composed; the concern is the identification and definition of the elements and the way relationships can be expressed. The methodological issues are concepts themselves, their measurement and identification of underlying themes. In essence, there is a search for universal laws that govern the relaity that is being perceived. Methodologies propose systematic process and technique (see also Burrell and Morgan, 1979).

ONTOLOGY: '1. The branch of metaphysical enquiry concerned with the study of existence itself (considered apart from the nature of any existent object). It differentiates between 'real existence' and 'appearance' and investigates the different ways in which entities belonging to various logical categories (physical objects, numbers, universals, abstractions, etc.) may be said to exist. 2. The assumptions about existence underlying any conceptual scheme or theory or system of ideas' (Flew, 1979, p. 255–256). See 'Paradigm'.

PARADIGM: The word paradigm is used in a very general sense: that there are epistemological, ontological, methodological and ideological notions that are mutually influential and form into clusters, according to some worked-out argument or rationality (that may or may not be valid according to internal or external criteria).

We may begin to develop this further by defining broadly an interest in theory, where theory comprises questions about epistemology, ontology, methodology, and views on the nature of human beings. A theoretical stance along these lines can be considered to be a cohesive and integrated group of concepts and ideas from some or each of these issues areas (the process of emergence and suppression of knowledge is discussed in Chapter 2). A metatheoretical position would be about how we can operate with two or more of these theoretical stances at once. Such a view, that will be labeled complementarist in this thesis, would allow for these as ideas relating to human interests where each paradigm offers a rationality that has its legitimacies, but also has its limitations.

Methodology is normative and amounts to the foundation or basis for determining the metacharacteristics of 'problem solving' and inquiry methods. Methods are different modes of 'problem solving' or inquiry.

The notion of ideology (a politically oriented position) must be important if we are to accept anything other than neutrality in respect to social order and change, particularly when we are making observations about, or in fact carrying out, intervention.

In this sense, then, the use of the term paradigm refers to an integrated yet open intellectual framework of thought. But this statement does not go far enough because the essence of such intellectuality (as sketched about above) is normative (i.e., it is not only normative in terms of methodology being generally theoretically nonneutral and ideologically value-laden). For any method this poses particular difficulties in respect to, say, positivist, interpretivist and emancipatory intellectual frameworks. If studying any one method we would be forced to ask the question, 'Are there contrasting positions relating to that method which will give rise to meaningful interpretations of them?' 'If this were to be the case then could we realistically believe that a critique of any position can be achieved?' 'If we do carry out such a critique then can it be done impersonally and what implications does this have for understanding paradigms as such?'

PHENOMENOLOGY: '...the term referring to the method of enquiry developed by Husserl, following his own teacher Brentario. It is supposed to begin from a scrupulous inspection of one's own consciousness, and particularly intellectual processes. In this inspection all assumptions about the wider and external causes and consequences of these internal processes have to be excluded ('bracketed'). Although this sounds like a programme for a psychology of introspection, Husserl insisted that it was an *a priori* investigation of the essences or meanings common to the thought of different minds' (Flew, 1979, p. 266). Phenomenology is generally accepted as the theory which most clearly underpins the methodological work of P. B. Checkland (see 1981), although Fuenmayor (1985) gives the only rigorous account of how phenomenology can be used to construct a systems approach based on ontological and epistemological considerations. These efforts have led to a position of relativism in systems thinking and systems practice, which poses some genuine difficulties with respect to choice in 'problem solving'.

POSITIVISM: Very broadly speaking, a view that assumes objectivity and neutrality in human thought and reason. It amounts to a rationality which pervades a whole paradigm. Positivistic social theory accepts in inquiry theory-neutrality and value-freedom which are assumed to be unproblematic.

POST-MODERNISM: See Modernism.

PRAGMATISM: Has a well understood meaning as a doctrine in philosophy. In this text, however, we must not confuse this with the special connotation attached to it in terms of systems 'problem solving', which amounts to an heuristic, trial and error approach. This is expanded upon in Chapter 7, Sections 2 and 3.

PSYCHOANALYSIS: Theory developed by Sigmund Freud. '...Habermas argues that psychoanalysis reveals important methodological guidelines for the construction of a critical theory of society. For Habermas, psychoanalysis is concerned with interpretation. But unlike the hermeneutic sciences, plausible interpretations can only be constructed with the aid of explanations involving causal connections. Further, such explanations can only be constructed with reference to a general theory. Habermas distinguishes three levels in Freud's theory: (i) the metapsychological level containing the basic categories and concepts of the theory, consisting of basic assumptions concerning the connection between distorted language and pathological behaviour, for example, the theory of instincts and the id–ego–superego model; (ii) the level of general interpretation of psychodynamic development in the form of a systematically generalized narrative constructed with the aid of meta-psychology, but drawing on empirically substantive data and clinical experiences; and (iii) the level of the application of the interpretive framework to the reconstruction of individual life histories. These applications may be viewed as hypotheses generated by the theory. Verification, however, is not what it is for the natural sciences (establishing agreement concerning the results of observation and experiments in the light of predictions) or the cultural sciences (reaching consensus about an interpretation); rather it means acceptance by the individual being analysed, acceptance incorporating self-reflection that is able to overcome symptoms. Ultimately, the assessment of emancipatory reflection is a matter of practice....' (Roderick, 1986, p. 57-58).

RATIONALITY: The basis on which we interpret what we see or hear, and shapes what we do. In isolationist thought, the fundamental ideas that make a paradigm whole, meaningful, and superior. In complementarist thought, the fundamental idea that paradigms can be whole and meaningful, but none is superior as such, each one has something to offer in terms of helping to deal with our inescapable and inevitable limitations in thought.

REALISM: With this position reality is accepted as external to the individual imposing itself on individual consciousness; it is a given 'out there' and is of an objective nature.

RELATIVISM: 'The relativist recognizes: first, the importance of the social environment in determining the content of beliefs both about what is and what ought to be the case; and second, the possible diversity of such social environments. To be a relativist about value is to maintain that there are no universal standards of good and bad, right and wrong. One difficulty is to avoid saying that what is right is whatever actually is commended whenever and whatever anyone happens to be... To be a relativist about fact is to maintain that there is no such thing as objective knowledge of realities independent of the knower. The parallel difficulty here is to eschew the inconsistent claim that the relativistic thesis is itself an item of objective knowledge' (Flew, 1979, p. 303).

SCIENTISM: '...science's belief in itself; the conviction that we can no longer understand science as one form of possible knowledge, but rather must identify knowledge with science.' (Habermas, 1971a, p. 4). 'The belief that the human sciences require no methods other than those of the natural' (Flew, 1979, p. 321).

SELF-REFLECTION: Developing an awareness of one's own mind and its operations and reasoning about how and why the ideas of this mind and operation come about. Using ideas of the mind to reflect on other ideas it already possesses.

SOCIAL METAPHYSICS: The totality of relative *a priori* judgements that flow into social theories or designs but cannot be validated either empirically or logically (Ulrich, 1983).

SOFT SYSTEMS: Deals with 'problems' '...which cannot be formulated as a search for an efficient means of achieving a defined end; a problem in which ends, goals, purposes are themselves problematic' (Checkland, 1981, p. 316). Soft systemists see hard problems as a special case of soft. More generally, soft systems is concerned with the inherent subjective nature of human thought, with particular reference to the ways in which this might be dealt with in decision making and 'problem solving'. Three main protagonists are Ackoff, Checkland, and Churchman (as shown by Jackson, 1982) although these scholars differ in the methodological principles which they advocate. The soft position is associated with interpretive thinking, although only Checkland, of the three, has come anywhere near defining this dependence, or at least making explicit the link. The only clearly worked out text that carefully constructs an interpretive systems onto–epistemology, that I am aware of, is Fuenmayor (1985), who shows soft systems in the light of the Phenomenology of Husserl. Churchman, of the three, is the only one who clearly shows a bent toward critical thinking.

STRUCTURALISM: An advancement on empiricism which 'merely' is concerned with events on a material surface, considering the importance of hidden, or beneath the surface generative mechanisms that produce the surface events. Structuralism is concerned to develop theories about those mechanisms.

SUBJECTIVELY INTENDED MEANING: The meaningful component of human expression according to a 'system' of values and beliefs.

SYSTEM: An abstract organizing structure that has many different paradigmatic interpretations, some of which attach systems to processes of the world, while others attach systems to processes of consciousness. The main ideas are of a whole characterized by richly interactive parts, and this is then expanded and/or interpreted according to various paradigms.

SYSTEMS RATIONALITY: An ideal that may orient applied inquiry toward a critically rational social practice in the face of incomplete knowledge and understanding.

SYSTEMS SCIENCE: Any effort to employ a systemic outlook in doing basic or applied science according to the conventional ideas of nonreflective positivistic empirical-analytical rationality (objective data, testable hypotheses, valid modeling and so on). The plural version, systems sciences, does however indicate that we recognize alternative rationalities and therefore becomes useful if we are discussing complementarism in systems 'problem solving'.

SYSTEMS THINKING: A term that is reserved for general discussions concerning any matter of systems without holding bias for any position, rationality, and so on. Essentially, then, a neutral term in respect to paradigmatic considerations that are investigated in this book.

THEORY: The separate/related issues of ontology and epistemology.

TOTAL SYSTEMS INTERVENTION (TSI): An approach to systems based 'problem solving' reported in Flood and Jackson (1991a). Devized over a number of years, actually through academic based inquiry, but more recently by applying the ideas in consultancy activities. TSI can broadly be thought of as an approach which accepts the value of the diversity of available methods and the richness that this offers for dealing with a seemingly more varied and changeful 'social world'. Each method, on investigation, can be revealed to have a particular view on such complexities. In fact, they also assume much about the nature of the relationships between participants. The methods have been tried and tested and have been shown to work well in some circumstances, being those situations that (not surprisingly) reflect the assumptions inherent in the approaches about the nature of organizational and social contexts.

The assumptions that the methods hold can be drawn out and used to constitute a grid of 'method types'. This grid can also be constituted through the underlying metaphors that are also inherent in the methods, concerning the way social reality might be conceived (e.g., like a machine, an organism, a culture, etc.). If, then, metaphor are found to be useful in appreciating problematic situations we can claim to have made a major breakthrough. That is, the methods constitute the grid, the grid can also be understood through metaphor. Metaphor can be used to develop appreciations of problem situations, and therefore lead to reflection between problem situation and method. With this we can establish a creative approach to 'problem solving' which guides participants toward an appropriate method for intervention, for that method will assume the social context to be like the idealized metaphor that most usefully helps participants to appreciate and deal with 'the' problem situation.

TSI is based on the complementarist ideas of Chapter 7 in this book, accepting openness and conciliation. It is a pragmatization of this strand of Liberating Systems Theory, but is not a compromise. It is converted to nonexpert terms as far as is possible. See the 'Appendix'.

TRANSCENDENTAL: Transcendentalism is a mode of thought that emphasizes the intuitive and supersensuous. 'Providing the conditions for the possibility of knowledge' (Bleicher, 1980, p. 271).

UNITIES: Recognition of the strength of diversity and that differing rationalities which underpin competing paradigms may each, in their own particular way, contribute to our understanding of our being and existence. Recognition that no single universal has come near to explaining everything, that each has both legitimacies and limitations. Acceptance of tensions that inevitably arise in unities, without them we would slip into the convincing trap of universal thinking, a nonreflective false consciousness.

UNIVERSALS: Absorbing paradigms. An intellectual stance which is normally invisibly held and hence easily dominates our thoughts about our existence and being in a totalizing fashion. A state of absolute false consciousness in respect to our view of being and existing.

APPENDIX

A practical face to Liberating Systems Theory

The ideas of this book underpin a methodological body of thought which we have researched and put into practice over the last four or so years. The main work that draws these efforts together is *Creative Problem Solving: Total Systems Intervention* (R. L. Flood and M. C. Jackson, J. Wiley and Sons, 1991a). In that book Jackson and I have developed a pragmatization (without compromise) of systems approaches to 'problem solving' which reflects at a methodological level the complementarist ideas discussed in Chapter 7 of this book.

Chapter 7 offers the link to our practical efforts, but let us not forget that it is the culmination of a crafted argument and would be weakened and impoverished without the ideas that build up to it. After all, the thesis amounts to 'liberate and critique': liberate to help to critically grow a necessary diversity of ideas (necessary because a substantial variety of phenomena require equal diversity in our understanding and intervention); and critique to ensure that we adopt a critical approach to understanding legitimacies and limitations of the variety of partial views, in an open and conciliatory way. Obviously such a position of 'liberate and critique' requires that we have a means of choice, and this is founded on a focal interest in liberation. This is not radicalism. Rather, it is a well balanced scholarly activity with an interest in action.

Our Creative Problem Solving approach has been developed by putting theory into practice. The ideas have been used in many interventions with a wide variety of organizations, dealing with a range of problem contexts. Some examples of these are: Metropolitan Police Force—(a) resource allocation for policing vice in the West End of London, (b) the 'problem' of carrying offensive weapons, (c) redesign of health and welfare services; a major tourism services group—redesign in the face of pending financial disaster; PA Consulting Group—development of IT strategy; an entertainments group—redesign in the face of poor organization; etc.

In addition to this we have developed several substantial training packages. An example is a package developed for Senior Managers in British Telecom (U. K.) as part of their core training. Run eight times now (about twelve managers per course and continuing every month) we have gained substantial experience and have learnt how to effectively put the material across to 'hard nosed' managers. Creative Problem Solving has been written and structured taking on board our training experience with British Telecom and others. The material is different and challenging, and some managers remain skeptical, wanting simple systematic tools that can easily be applied in their own organizational context. Our approach argues against such forces. Generally we receive a good response.

In the remainder of this Appendix we will consider the main ideas of Jackson's and my volume. In the short space of this Appendix we can do no better than partially reproduce the Preface from that book that adequately achieves this.

In the modern world we are faced with innumerable and multifaceted difficulties and problems which cannot be captured in the minds of a few experts and solved with the aid of some super method. We are faced with 'messes', sets of interacting problems, which range from the technical and the organizational to the social and political, and embrace concerns about the environment, the framework of society, the role of corporations and the motivation of individuals. It is the argument of Total Systems Intervention that the search for some super method that can address all these problems is mistaken and must quickly lead to disenchantment. It would be equally wrong, however, to revert to a heuristic, trial and error approach to managing problems. We need to retain rigorous and formalized thinking, while admitting the need for a range of 'problem solving' methodologies, and accepting the complexities which that brings. The future prospects of management science will be much enhanced if the diversity of the 'messes' confronting managers is accepted, work on developing a rich variety of methodologies is undertaken, and the question is continually asked: 'What kind of problem situation can be managed with which sort of methodology?'

With Total Systems Intervention we offer an approach to creative 'problem solving' which hopefully enriches the way managers, decision makers and their advisers perceive the diversity of difficulties they face. We then consider currently existing systems based methodologies and organize these according to the ideal type problem situations to which they are most relevant. The key to the successful use of the Total Systems Intervention (TSI) approach, is to choose an appropriate methodology for tackling the problem situation as it is perceived, but to always recognize that other possible perceptions of that problem situation are possible. In deciding to view a problem situation in a certain way, one is making a partial representation of it. And in employing a methodology which is congruent with that partial representation, one is addressing only certain of the interacting problems in that situation. It follows that alternative perceptions of the

problem situation need constantly to be kept under review, and
alternative approaches to problem management retained in case the
problem situation should change character in the opinion of concerned
individuals. Sophisticated users of TSI will, indeed, operate
simultaneously with different views of the problem situation and with
dominant and support methodologies to sweep in both the main issue of
concern and significant side issues.

Let us now rehearse these arguments again. Consider the
following tasks:

- Optimizing the number and arrangement of supermarket check out
  points to reduce waiting time to a minimum, given certain cost
  constraints.
- Designing a petrochemical plant.
- Pollution control for water authorities.
- Structuring an organization which exists in an environment of rapid
  technological and market change.
- Assisting decision making in a worker's cooperative.
- Making decisions on police resource allocation in dealing with vice
  in a major city.
- Helping debate among adherents of different doctrinal positions in
  the Anglican Church.
- Assisting one side or the other in an industrial dispute between
  managers and workers.

These are all management problems which, we would argue require
more than commonsense to resolve. They take us beyond our limited,
everyday human information processing capabilities, and demand
treatment using appropriately designed formal procedures. Our
contention is that systems thinking (a broadly neutral term which
encompasses all systems based activities) can provide an insightful
way of understanding and dealing with such messes. Systems thinking
offers numerous powerful ways of tackling problem situations, while
employing a set of concepts that can comfortably be understood by
practicing managers and decision makers.

The other thing to notice about the tasks set out above is, of
course, their diversity. Intervention to help with these tasks must,
therefore, recognize them as diverse and contrasting. Now, it may be
thought that the systems approach itself can be accused of hiding that
diversity because it sees everything as a 'system'. An alternative use
of systems concepts is possible however, which retains the richness of
the systems idea, and its power as a means of organizing our thought,

while filling it with different types of content each of which yields a differing interpretation of problem situations. This use of the systems idea assists us in developing novel and insightful appreciations of problematic situations rather than encouraging us to see them as all the same.

Management tasks and problems often assume sufficient complexity to require a structural methodological approach to aid their resolution, and they are also very diverse in character. The logic leads us to suggest that managers must demand from management scientists equally diverse and contrasting systems based methodologies for problem management. Clearly, without access to a diversity of methods, managers would be faced with a high variety of differing 'messes' without a sufficiently rich variety in available systems approaches. Fortunately, there is a diversity of systems based 'problem solving' approaches available. Each of these has been developed, implicitly or explicitly, with a particular view on the nature of modern day complexities and how to manage them. What is needed is an overview of these various systems methods which enables them to be related to the type of problem situation each serves best. To this end we have developed some guidelines that point to the respective strengths of different systems methods and suggest when a situation favors the use of one rather than another. We achieve this by 'classifying' the most important systems approaches in a 'system of systems methodologies', which is constituted from the underlying assumptions different systems approaches make about the 'systems' with which they deal and about the relationship between the individuals concerned with the problem situation.

The 'systems of systems methodologies' stands as a rebuke to those who see the diversity of systems based approaches as representing a fragmentation and weakening of management science as a discipline and profession. It organizes tried and tested systems methodologies and shows why each works well in some situations but not in others. It reveals the strengths and the inevitable limitations of each approach. It enables an informed choice of systems methodology to be made in the light of how the problem situation is perceived and what the manager or decision maker wants to achieve.

The essence of our Total Systems Intervention (TSI) approach is to encourage highly creative thinking about the nature of any problem situation before a decision is taken about the character of the main difficulties to be addressed. Once that decision has been taken, TSI will steer the manager or analyst toward the type of systems methodology most appropriate to resolving problems of the kind identified as being most significant. As the intervention proceeds, however, so the nature of the problem situation will be continually reviewed, as will the choice of appropriate systems methodology.

In highly complex problem situations it is often best to address different aspects revealed by taking different perspectives on it, at the same time. This involves employing a number of systems methodologies in combination. In these circumstances it is necessary to nominate one methodology as dominant and others as support, although these relationships may change as the study progresses.

Having developed an understanding of the richness of systems thinking and the strength that comes from the diversity of systems methodologies, and having harnessed the two together in TSI, the task is to make sure that the practitioner has access to the most important methodologies. Our style of presentation is crucial in this respect. For each methodology Jackson and I first of all develop a broad understanding of the philosophy and main principles that underpin it. Following on from this, the methodology itself is described. We then provide a worked example, usually drawn from our own consultancy experience, which shows the application of the methodology in a practical situation. We have already suggested above that each methodology has particular strengths and limitations, and we take advantage of worked examples to highlight these in terms of (1) a specific consultancy example provided, and (2) more general observations.

A case study is also set for the reader to consider and work on. In this way we deal comprehensively with systems based 'problem solving'.

In these introductory notes we have pointed to the complexity and diversity of the difficulties that modern day managers, decision makers and 'problem solvers' face. We have also outlined a systems based approach to creative problem solving called Total Systems Intervention (TSI), as a means of facing up to this challenge.

REFERENCES

Ackoff, R. L. (1963). General Systems Theory and systems research: Contrasting conceptions of systems science. *General Systems*, 8, 117-121.

Ackoff, R. L. (1974). The systems revolution. *Long Range Planning*, 7, 2-20.

Ackoff, R. L. (1979). The future of Operational Research is past. *J.Opl.Res.Soc.*, 30(2), 189-199.

Ackoff, R. L. (1981) *Creating the Corporate Future*. J. Wiley and Sons, New York.

Ackoff, R. L. (1988). Some comments on the Flood and Jackson papers received July 1988. Personal Communication.

Albin, P. S. and Gottinger, H. W. (1983). Structure and complexity in economic and social systems. *Math.Soc.Sci.*, 5, 253-268.

Ando, A. and Fischer, F. M. (1963). Near-decomposability, partition and aggregation and the relevance of stability discussions. *Internat.Econom.Rev.*, 4, 53-67.

Angyal, A. (1941). *Foundations for a Science of Personality*. Harvard University Press, Cambridge, Mass., Ch.1, 243-261. Reprinted in F. E. Emery (ed.) (1969).

Apel, K. O. (1965). Die Entfaltung der 'sprachananalytischen' Philosophie und das Problem der 'Geisteswissenschaften'. *Phil. Jahrb.*, 72, 239-289.

Atkinson, C. J. and Checkland, P. B. (1988). Extending the metaphor "system". *Human Relations*, 41(10), 709-725.

Atthill, C. (1975). *Decisions: West Oil Distribution*. British Petroleum Education Services.

Ayer, A. J. (1971). *Language, Truth and Logic*. Penguin, Harmondsworth.

Banathy, B. H. and Banathy, B. A. (1989). 'A General Theory of Systems'— Bela Zalai (book review). *Systems Practice*, 2(4), 451-454.

Barber, B. (ed.) (1970). *L. J. Henderson on the Social Sciences: Selected Readings*. University of Chicago Press, Chicago.

Battista, J. R. (1977). The holistic paradigm. *General Systems*, XXII, 65-72.

Bauman, Z. (1978). *Hermeneutics and Social Science: Approaches to Understanding*. Hutchinson, London.

Beer, S. (1967). *Management Science*. Aldus, London.

Beer, S. (1979). *Heart of the Enterprise*. J. Wiley and Sons, Chichester.

Beer, S. (1981). *Brain of the Firm* (2nd ed.). J. Wiley and Sons, Chichester.

Beer, S. (1985). *Diagnosing the System for Organisations*. J. Wiley and Sons, Chichester.

Belsey, C. (1980). *Critical Practice*. Methuen, London.

Bertalanffy, L. von. (1950). The theory of open systems in physics and biology. *Science*, 3, 23-29.

Bertalanffy, L. von. (1968). *General Systems Theory*. Braziller, New York.

Bierce, A. (1958). *The Devil's Dictionary*. Dover Publications, New York.

Black, M. (1962). *Models and Metaphors*. Cornell University Press, Ithaca, New York.

Bleicher, J. (1980). *Contemporary Hermeneutics: Hermeneutics as Method, Philosophy and Critique*. Routledge and Kegan Paul, London.

Bogdanov, A. (1922). *Tektologia: Vseobshchaya Organizationnaya Nauka*. Izdatelstvo, ZI, Moscow.

Boulding, K. (1956). General Systems Theory – The skeleton of science. *General Systems*, 1, 11-17.

Boyd, R. (1979). Metaphor and theory change: What is metaphor and metaphor for? In, A. Ortony, (ed.), *Metaphor and Thought*. Cambridge University Press, Cambridge.

Bunge, M. (1977). Levels and reduction. *Am.J.Physiol.*, 233(3), R75-R82.

Burrell, G. (1988). Modernism, post-modernism and organisational analysis 2: The contribution of Michel Foucault. *Organisation Studies*, 9(2), 221-235.

Burrell, G. and Morgan, G. (1979). *Sociological Paradigms and Organisational Analysis*. Heineman, London.

Cannon, W. B. (1932). *Wisdom of the Body*. Norton, New York.

Carr, E. H. (1964). *What Is History?* Penguin, Harmondsworth.

Castaneda, C. (1987). *The Power of Silence: Further Lessons of Don Juan*. Blackswan, Falmouth.

Caws, P. (1967). Science and system: On the unity and diversity of scientific theory. *General Systems*, 12, 3-12.

Checkland, P. B. (1978). The origins and nature of "hard" systems thinking. *J.Appl.Sys.Anal.*, 5, 99-110.

Checkland, P. B. (1979). Techniques in "soft" systems practice. *J.Appl.Syst.Anal.*, 6, 33-40.

Checkland, P. B. (1980). Are organisations machines? *Futures*, 12, 421-424.

Checkland, P. B. (1981). *Systems Thinking, Systems Practice*. J. Wiley and Sons, Chichester.

Checkland, P. B. (1988a). The case for "holon". *Systems Practice*. 1(3), 235-238.

Checkland, P. B. (1988b). Images of system and the systems image. *J.Appl.Syst.Anal.*, 15, 37-42.

Checkland, P. B. (1988c). Churchman's '"Anatomy of System Teleology" Revisited'. *Systems Practice*, 1(4), 377-384.

Checkland, P. B. (1989). 'Systems Research Methodological Problems: Selected Papers From Yearbook 1969-81; and Systems Research II: Methodological Approach to Systems Research II'—J. M. Gvishiani (ed.) (book review). *Systems Practice*, 2(4), 454-458.

Churchman, C. W. (1968a). *Challenge to Reason*. McGraw-Hill, New York.

Churchman, C. W. (1968b). *The Systems Approach*. Delacorte Press and Dell Publishing, New York.

Churchman, C. W. (1970). "The Artificiality of Science," a review of Herbert A. Simon's "The Sciences of the Artificial" (book review). *Contemporary Psychology*, 15, 385-386.

Churchman, C. W. (1971). *The Design of Inquiring Systems, Basic Concepts of Systems and Organisation*. Basic Books, New York.

Churchman, C. W. (1977). A philosophy for complexity. In H. A. Linstone and W. H. Simmonds (eds.), *Managing Complexity*. Addison-Wesley, Reading, Mass.

Churchman, C. W. (1979). *The Systems Approach and Its Enemies*. Basic Books, New York.

Churchman, C. W. (1981). *Thought and Wisdom*. Intersystems Publications, Seaside, California.

Churchman, C. W. Ackoff, R. L. and Arnoff, E. L. (1957). *Introduction to Operations Research*. J. Wiley and Sons., New York.

Clemson, B. (1984). *Cybernetics: A New Management Tool*. Abacus Press, Tunbridge Wells.

Clemson, M. and Jackson, M. C. (1988). Evaluating organisations with multiple goals. *OR Insight*, 1(2), 2-5.

Colins, D. E. (1977). *Paulo Freire: His Life, Works and Thought*. Paulist Press, New York.

Connerton, P. (ed.) (1976), *Critical Sociology*. Penguin, Harmondsworth.

Cooper, R. and Burrell, G. (1988). Modernism, post-modernism and organisational analysis: An introduction. *Organisation Studies*, 9(2), 221-235.

Cornock, S. (1978). The structure of the systems paradigm. In R. Trappl and G. Pask (eds.), *Progress in Systems and Cybernetics*. J. Wiley and Sons, New York.

Courtois, P. J. (1977). *Decomposability: Queueing and Computer System Application*. Academic Press, New York.

Courtois, P. J. (1985). On time and space decomposition of complex structures. *Comm. A.C.M.*, 28, 590-603.

Courtois, P. J. and Semal, P. (1975). Bounds for the positive eigenvectors of non-negative matrices and for their approximation by decomposition. *J.A.C.M.*, 31, 804-828.

Daellenbach, H. G. George, J. A. and McNickle, D. C. (1983). *Introduction to Operations Research Techniques* (2nd ed.). Allyn and Bacon, Boston, Mass.

Dando, M. R. and Bennett, P. G. (1981). A Kuhnian crisis in Management Science? *J.Opl. Res.Soc.*, 32, 91-104.

Derrida, J. (1972). *Margins of Philosophy*, (translated from French by A. Bass). University of Chicago Press, Chicago.

Derrida, J. (1980). The law of genre. *Glyph*, 7, 202-229.

Derrida, J. (1981). *Dissemination* (translated from French by B. Johnson). Athlone Press, London.

DeVries, R. P. and Hezerwijk, R. (1978). Systems theory and the philosophy of science. *Annals of Systems Research*, 7, 91-123.

Downing Bowler, T. (1981). *General Systems Thinking: Its Scope and Applicability*. North Holland, Amsterdam.

Dreyfus, H. L. and Rabinow, P. (1982). *Michel Foucault: Beyond Structuralism and Hermeneutics*. Harvester Press, Hemel Hempstead.

Ellis, R. K. and Flood, R. L. (1987). Management of technological change: Systems theory or systems technology? *Problems of Constancy and Change*. International Society for General Systems Research, 270-277.

Emery, F. E. (ed.) (1969). *Systems Thinking, Volumes 1 and 2* (Volume 2 first published in 1981), Penguin, Harmondsworth.

Espejo, R. (1979). Information and management: The cybernetics of a small company. *Working Paper*, 125, University of Aston Management Centre, UK.

Espejo, R. (1987). Cybernetic method to study organisations. *Problems of Constancy and Change*. International Society for General Systems Research, 323-336.

Espejo, R. and Harnden, R. (eds.) (1989). *The Viable Systems Model*. J. Wiley and Sons, Chichester.

Fairtlough, G. (1989). Systems practice from the start: Some experiences in a biotechnology company. *Systems Practice*, 2(4), 397-412

Fay, B. (1975). *Social Theory and Political Practice*. George Allen and Unwin, London.

Feibleman, F. and Friend, F. W. (1945). The structure and function of organisation. *Philos.Rev.*, 54, 19-44.

Flew, B. (ed.) (1979). *A Dictionary of Philosophy*. Pan Books, London.

Flood, R. L. (1985). *Quantitative Modelling of Fluid-Electrolyte, Acid-Base Balance for Clinical Application*. PhD. thesis, City University, London.

Flood, R. L. (1987). Complexity: A definition by construction of a conceptual framework. *Systems Research*, 4(3), 177-185.

Flood, R. L. (1988a). Systems and Control Encyclopedia: M. Singh (ed.) (book review). *Systems Practice*, 432-436.

Flood, R. L. (1988b). The need for a substantive soft systems language. *J.Appl.Sys.Anal.*, 15, 43-47.

Flood, R. L. (1989a). Six scenarios for the future of systems 'problem solving'. *Systems Practice*, 2(1), 75-100.

Flood, R. L. (1989b). Archaeology of (systems) inquiry. *Systems Practice*, 2(1), 117-124.

Flood, R. L. (1990). Liberating Systems Theory: Towards Critical Systems Thinking. *Human Relations*, 43(1), 49-76.

Flood, R. L. and Carson, E. R. (1988). *Dealing with Complexity: An Introduction to the Theory and Application of Systems Science*. Plenum, New York.

Flood, R. L. and Gaisford, P. (1989). Policing vice in the West End: A systemic perspective points to a multi-agency approach. *OR Insight*, 2(3), 10-15.

Flood, R. L. and Gregory, W. (1990). Systems: Past, present and future. In Flood, R. L. Jackson, M. C. and Keys, P. (eds.) *Systems Prospects: The Next Ten Years of Systems Research*, Plenum, New York, 55-60.

Flood, R. L. and Jackson, M. C. (1988). Cybernetics and organization theory: A critical review. *Cybernetics and Systems*, 19, 13-33.

Flood, R. L. and Jackson, M. C. (1989). Editorial. *Systems Practice*, 2(2), 151-153.

Flood, R. L. and Jackson, M. C. (1991a). *Creative Problem Solving: Total Systems Intervention*. J. Wiley and Sons, Chichester.

Flood, R. L. and Jackson, M. C. (1991b). *Critical Systems Thinking: Directed Readings*. J. Wiley and Sons, Chichester.

Flood, R. L. and Robinson, S. A. (1988). Analogy and metaphor and systems and cybernetics methodology. *Cybernetics and Systems*, 19, 501-520.

Flood, R. L. and Robinson, S. A. (1990). Whatever happened to General Systems Theory? In Flood, R. L. Jackson, M. C. and Keys, P. (eds.) *Systems Prospects: The Next Ten Years of Systems Research*, Plenum, New York, 61-66.

Flood, R. L. and Ulrich, W. (1990). Testament to conversations on critical systems thinking between two systems practitioners. *Systems Practice*, 3(1), 7-29.

Flood, R. L. Carson, E. R. and Cramp, D. G. (1986). Validation of a large scale simulation model of fluid volume maintenance in man. *New Peaks in Simulation.* Reno: Society for Computer Simulation, 427-432.

Flood, R. L. Stupples, D. W. and Charlwood, F. J. (1988). A biomedical application of nearly completely decomposable matrix theory. *Biomed.Meas.Infor.Contr.*, 2(4), 222-230.

Foucault, M. (1974). *The Archaeology Of Knowledge,* (translated from French by A. M. Sheridon-Smith). Tavistock, London. Originally published as *L'Archéologie du savoir* by Editions Gallimard in 1969.

Foucault, M. (1979). *The History of Sexuality: Volume 1. An Introduction,* (translated from French by R. Hurley). Penguin, Harmondsworth. Originally published as *La Volonté de savoir* by Editions Gallimard in 1976.

Foucault, M. (1980). *Power/Knowledge: Selected Interviews and Other Writings 1972-1977,* C. Gordon (ed.). Harvester Press, Brighton.

Fraser, N. (1981). Foucault on modern power: Empirical insights and normative confusions. *Praxis International,* 1, 272-287.

Freire, P. (1970). *Pedagogy of the Oppressed* (translated from Portuguese by M. Bergman Ramos). Continuum, New York. Originally published in 1968.

Freud, S. (1973). *Sigmund Freud. Two New Introductory Lectures in Psychoanalysis.* Penguin, Harmondsworth.

Freundlieb, D. (1989). Rationalism v irrationalism? Habermas's response to Foucault. *Inquiry,* 31, 171-192.

Fuenmayor, R. (1985). *The Ontology and Epistemology of a Systems Approach.* PhD. thesis, Lancaster University, Lancaster.

Giddens, A. (1976). *New Rules of Sociological Method.* Hutchinson, London.

Goodheart, E. (1984). *The Skeptic Disposition in Contemporary Criticism.* Princeton University Press, Princeton.

Gordon, C. (1979). Other inquisitions. *Ideology and Consciousness,* 6,

Gorelik, G. (1975). Principal ideas of Bogdanov's "tektology": The universal science of organisation. *General Systems,* 20, 3-13.

Habermas, J. (1970). *Zur Logik der Socialwissenschaften.* Materialien, Suhrkamp, Frankfurt am Main.

Habermas, J. (1971a). *Knowledge and Human Interests* (translated from German by J. J. Shapiro). Beacon Press, Boston. Originally published as *Erkenntnis und Interesse* by Suhrkamp Verlag in 1968.

Habermas, J. (1971b). *Toward a Rational Society,* (translated from German by J. J. Shapiro). Beacon Press, Boston. The first three essays originally published in *Protestbewegung und Hochschulreform* by

Suhrkamp Verlag in 1969, the first and third essays were abridged for the English edition by the author; and the last three essays were originally published in *Technik und Wissenschaft als 'Ideologie'* by Suhrkamp Verlag in 1968.

Habermas, J. (1976). On systematically distorted communication, *Inquiry*, 13, 205-218.

Habermas, J. (1985). *Der philosophische Diskurs der Moderne*. Suhrkamp Verlag, Frankfurt.

Hamwee, J. (1986). Personal communication.

Hawkins, S. (1988). *A Brief History of Time: From the Big Bang to Black Holes*. Bantam Press, London.

Honneth, A. (1985). *Kritik der Macht*. Suhrkamp Verlag, Frankfurt.

Hoos, I. (1972). *Systems Analysis in Public Policy: A Critique*. University of California Press, Berkeley.

Horkheimer, M. (1968). *Critical Theory: Selected Essays* (translated from German by M. J. O. O'Connell and others). Herder and Herder, New York. Excerpts published in *Critical Sociology*, P. Connerton (ed.) (1976). Originally published as Traditionelle und kritische Theorie, *Zeitschrift für Sozialforschung*, 6, 245-294.

Husserl, E. (1950). *Die Krisis der europäischen Wissenschaften und die transzendentale Phänomenologie*, in *Gesammelte Werke*. Martinus Nijhoff, Hague.

Jackson, M. C. (1982). The nature of soft systems thinking: The work of Churchman, Ackoff and Checkland. *J.Appl.Sys.Anal.*, 9, 17-28.

Jackson, M. C. (1985a). Social systems theory and practice: The need for a critical approach. *Int.J.Gen.Syst.*, 10, 135-151.

Jackson, M. C. (1985b). The itinerary of a critical approach... 'Critical Heuristics of Social Planning': W. Ulrich (book review). *J.Opl.Res.Soc.*, 36, 878-881.

Jackson, M. C. (1987a). Present positions and future prospects in Management Science. *OMEGA*, 15(6), 455-466.

Jackson, M. C. (1987b). New directions in Management Science, In M.C. Jackson and P. Keys (eds.), *New Directions in Management Science*. Gower Press, Aldershot.

Jackson, M. C. and Keys, P. (1984). Towards a system of systems methodologies. *J.Opl.Res.Soc.*, 35, 473-486.

Jenkins, G. (1969). The systems approach. *J.Syst.Eng.*, 1(1), 3-49. Reprinted in *Systems Behaviour*, J. Beishon and G. Peters (eds.) (1972), Harper and Row, London.

Jones, L. M. (1978). The conflicting views of knowledge and control implied by different systems approaches. *J.Appl.Syst.Anal.*, 5, 143-148.

Kant, I. (1934). *Critique of Pure Reason* (translated from German by J. M. O. Meiklejohn). Dent, London. See also (translated from German by N. Kemp Smith), Humanities Press, New York. Originally published in 1781, with a second edition in 1787.

Keeney, R. L. and Raiffa, H. (1976). *Decisions with Multiple Perspectives: Preferences and Value Tradeoffs.* J.Wiley and Sons, New York.

Kiss, I. (1989). Forerunners and backwardness—guest editorial. *Systems Practice,* 2(4), 413-417.

Klir, G. (1985). *Architecture of Systems Problem Solving.* Plenum, New York.

Koehler, W. (1938). *The Place of Values in the World of Fact.* Liveright. Excerpt from Chapter 8, 314-328, reprinted in F. Emery (ed.) (1969).

Korzybski, A. (1958). *Science and Sanity* (4th ed.). The International Non-Aristotelian Library Publishing Co., Lakeville, Conn.

Kuhn, T. (1970). *The Structure of Scientific Revolutions* (2nd ed.). University of Chicago Press, Chicago.

Kuhn, T. (1977). *The Essential Tension: Selected Studies in Scientific Tradition and Change.* University of Chicago Press, Chicago.

Laing, R. D. (1967). *The Politics of Experience and the Bird of Paradise.* Penguin, Harmondsworth.

Laszlo, E. (1972). *Systems View of the World.* Braziller, New York.

Leaning, M. S. (1987). Systems and Control Encyclopaedia: M. Singh (ed.) (book review). *Institute of Measurement and Control - Interfaces,* 21(5), 150.

Lilienfeld, R. (1979). *The Rise of Systems Theory.* J. Wiley and Sons, New York.

Lowi, T. J. (1969). *The End of Liberalism.* Norton, New York.

Lorenzer, A. (1970). *Sprachzerstörung und Rekonstruktion.* Suhrkamp Verlag, Frankfurt, 72-92. Originally translated from German by T. Hall and reprinted in P. Connerton (ed.) (1976), 134-152.

Luhman, N. (1971). Moderne System Theorien als Form gesamtgesell-schaftlicher analyse, In J. Habermas and N. Luhman, *Theorie der Gesellschaft oder Sozialtechnologie.* Suhrkamp, Frankfurt.

Luhman, N. (1973). *Zweckbegriff und Systemrationalität.* Suhrkamp, Frankfurt.

Mangham, I. (1979). *The Politics of Organisational Change.* Associated Business Press, London.

Marsh, J. L. (1988). The post-modern interpretation of history: A phenomenological hermeneutical critique. *J.British Society for Phenomenology,* 19(2), 112-127.

Mason, R. O. and Mitroff, I. I. (1981). *Challenging Strategic Planning Assumptions: Theory, Cases and Techniques.* J. Wiley and Sons, New York.

Mattesich, R. (1978). *Instrumental Reasoning and Systems Methodology: An Epistemology of the Applied and Social Sciences.* D. Reidel, Dordrecht.

Maturana, H, M. (1980). Autopoiesis: Reproduction, heredity and evolution. In M. Zeleney (ed.), *Autopoiesis, Dissipative Structures and Spontaneous Social Orders.* AAAS Selected Symposium 55, Westview Press, Boulder, Colo.

Maturana, H. M. and Varella, F. G. (1975). *Autopoietic Systems.* Biol. Comp. Lab. Res. Rep. 9.4, University of Illinois, Urbana. Reprinted in H. M. Maturana and F. G. Varella (eds.) (1980).

Maturana, H. M. and Varella, F. G. (1980). *Autopoiesis and Cognition: The Realization of the Living.* Reidel, Dordrecht.

Midgley, G. (1989a). A brief introduction to critical systems theory and practice. *Occupational Psychologist,* 9 (Dec.) 3-7.

Midgley, G. (1989b). Critical systems and the problem of pluralism. *Cybernetics and Systems,* 20, 219-231.

Miller, J. G. (1978). *Living Systems,* McGraw–Hill, New York

Milne, A. A. (1926). *Winnie the Pooh.* Methuen, London.

Mingers, J. (1984). Subjectivism and soft systems methodology: A critique. *J.Appl.Syst.Anal.* 11, 85-104.

Mingers, J. (1989). An introduction to autopoiesis: Implications and applications. *Systems Practice,* 2(2), 159-180.

Morgan, G. (1986). *Images of Organisation.* Sage, Beverly Hills, Ca.

M'Pherson, P. K. (1974). A perspective on systems science and systems philosophy. *Futures,* 6(3), 219-239.

M'Pherson, P. K. (1980). Systems engineering: An approach to whole system design. *Radio Electron. Eng.,* 50(11/12), 545-558.

M'Pherson, P. K. (1981). A framework for systems engineering design. *Radio Electron. Eng.,* 51(2), 59-93.

Norris, C. (1982). *Deconstruction.* Methuen, London.

Naughton, J. (1977). *The Checkland Methodology: A Reader's Guide* (2nd ed.). Open University Press, Milton Keynes.

Naughton, J. (1979). Anti-GST: An evolutionary manifesto. *Proceedings of Silver Anniversary Meeting of the Society for General Systems Research.* London, August.

Oliga, J. C. (1986). Methodology in systems research: The need for a self-reflective commitment, In J. A. Dillon Jr. (ed.), *Mental Images, Values, and Reality.* Society for General Systems Research, Louisville, Ky.

Oliga, J. C. (1988). Methodological foundations of systems methodologies. *Systems Practice*, 1(1), 87-112.

Pepper, S, (1942). *World Hypotheses*. University of California Press, Berkeley and Los Angeles.

Petrie, H. G. (1968). The strategy sense of methodology. *Philosophy of Science*, 248-257.

Radnitzky, G. (1970). *Contemporary Schools of Metascience. Volume 2: Continental Schools of Metascience*. Scandinavian University Books, Göteborg.

Reed, M. (1985). *Redirections in Organisational Analysis*. Tavistock, London.

Reynolds, P. A. (1971). *An Introduction to International Relations*. Longman, New York.

Rhodes, D. D. (1985). Root definitions and reality in manufacturing systems. *J.Appl.Syst.Anal.*, 12, 93-100.

Ricoeur, P. (1975). Phenomenology and hermeneutics. *Noûs*, 2(1).

Robb, F. F. (1989). Cybernetics and suprahuman autopoietic systems, *Systems Practice*, 2(1), 47-74.

Robinson, S. A. (1990). *The Utility of Analogy in Systems Sciences*. PhD. thesis, City University, London.

Roderick, R. (1986). *Habermas and the Foundations of Critical Theory*. Macmillan, Basingstoke.

Roethlisberger, F. J. and Dickinson, W. J. (1939). *Management and the Workers*. Harvard University Press, Cambridge, Mass.

Rosenhead, J. (1984). Debating systems methodology: Conflicting ideas about conflict and ideas. *J.Appl.Syst.Anal.*, 11, 79-84.

Shor, I. and Freire, P. (1987). *A Pedagogy for Liberation*. Bergin and Garvey, South Hadley, Mass.

Simon, H. (1962). The Architecture of Complexity. *Proceedings of the American Philosophical Society*, 106, 467-482.

Simon, H. (1969). *The Sciences of the Artificial*. MIT Press, Cambridge, Mass.

Simon, H. and Ando, A. (1961). Aggregation of variables in dynamic systems. *Econometrics*, 29, 111-138.

Singh, M. (ed.) (1987). *Systems and Control Encyclopaedia, Volumes 1 to 8*. Pergamon, Oxford.

Smart, B. (1983). *Foucault, Marxism and Critique*. Routledge and Kegan Paul, London and New York.

Smart, B. (1985). *Michel Foucault*. Ellis Horwood, Chichester.

Strickland, G. (1981). *Structuralism or Criticism? Thoughts on How We Read*. Cambridge University Press, Cambridge.

Suppe, F. (ed.) (1974). *The Structure of Scientific Theory* (2nd ed.). University of Illinois Press, Urbana.

Tomlinson, R. (1987). Operational research and systems analysis: Science in action, applicable mathematics or social engineering? In R. Trappl (ed.), *Cybernetics and Systems 1986*. Reidel, Dordrecht.

Troncale, L. (1986). Knowing natural systems enables better design of man-made systems: The linkage proposition model. In R. Trappl (ed.), *Power, Autonomy, Utopia: New Approaches Toward Complex Systems*. Plenum, New York.

Trusted, J. (1981). *An Introduction to the Philosophy of Knowledge*. Macmillan, Basingstoke.

Ulrich, W. (1977). The design of problem-solving systems. *Management Science*, 23, 1099-1108.

Ulrich, W. (1980). The metaphysics of design: A Simon-Churchman 'debate', Interfaces, 10(2), 35-40. Reprinted and slightly expanded in J. P. van Gigch (ed.), *Decision Making about Decision Making: Metamodels and Metasystems*. Abacus Press, Tunbridge Wells, 1987, pp. 219-229.

Ulrich, W. (1981a). Systemrationalität ind praktische Vernunft-Gedanken zum Stand des Systemansatzes. Introduction to: Churchman, C. W. *Der Systemansatz und seine 'Feinde'*. Haupt, Berne, pp. 7-38.

Ulrich, W. (1981b). A critique of pure cybernetic reason: The Chilean experience with cybernetics. *J.Appl.Syst.Anal.*, 8, 33-59.

Ulrich, W. (1983). *Critical Heuristics of Social Planning: A New Approach to Practical Philosophy*. Haupt, Berne.

Ulrich, W. (1984). Management oder die Kunst, Entscheidungen zu treffen, die andere betreffen. *Die Unternehmung*, 38, 326-346.

Ulrich, W. (1987). Critical heuristics of social systems design. *Eur.J.Opl.Res.*, 31, 276-283.

Ulrich, W. (1988a). Systems thinking, systems practice, and practical philosophy: A program of research. *Systems Practice*, 1(2), 137-163.

Ulrich, W. (1988b). Churchman's 'process of unfolding' – its significance for policy analysis and evaluation. *Systems Practice*, 1(4), 415-428.

Ulrich, W. (1989). Systemtheorie der Planung. In N. Szyperski (ed.), *Handwörterbuch der Planung*, Poeschel, Stuttgart, Germany, cols. 1971-1978.

Ulrich, W. (1991). Toward emancipatory systems practice. In R. L. Flood and M. C. Jackson (eds.) (1991b).

Van Gigch, J. and Stolliday, I. (1980). Epistemological foundations of the system paradigm. In F. R. Pichler and F. de P. Honika (eds.), *Progress in Systems and Cybernetics*. Hemisphere, Washington.

Varella, F. G. (1979). *Principles of Biological Autonomy*. Elsevier, North Holland, New York.

Warfield, J. (1976). *Societal Systems: Planning, Policy and Complexity*. J. Wiley and Sons, New York.

Warfield, J. (1984). Principles of Interactive Management. *Proceedings of the International Conference on Cybernetics and Systems*. IEEE, New York.

Weaver, W. (1968). Science and complexity. *American Science*, 36, 536-544.

Weber, M. (1949). "Complexity" in social science a social policy. In E.A. Shills and H. A. Finch (eds.), *The Methodology of the Social Sciences*. Free Press, New York, pp. 72-111. Originally published as Die Objektivität sozialwissenschaftlicher und sozialpolitischer Erkenntnis, *Archiv für Sozialwissenschaft*, 19, 22-87, in 1907. Reprinted in M. Weber, *Gesammelte Aufsätze zur Wissenschaftslehre* (3rd ed.), J. Winckelmann (ed.), J. C. B. Mohr, Tübingen, 1968.

Wittgenstein, L. (1922). *Tractatus Logico–Philosophicus* (translated from German by C. K. Ogden). Routledge and Kegan Paul, London and New York.

Wittgenstein, L. (1953). *Philosophical Investigations* (translated from German by G.E.M. Anscombe). Basil Blackwell, Oxford.

Woodburn, I. (1985). Some developments in the building of conceptual models. *J.Appl.Syst.Anal.*, 12, 101-106.

Zeleney, M. (1987). 'Cybernetyka'. *Int.J.Gen.Syst.*, 13, 289-294.

Zola, É. (1962). *Thérèse Raquin*. Penguin, Harmondsworth.

INDEX

A

absolutism 5, 177, 180, 203
animism 73, 92, 203
anti-foundationalism 16, 17, 19, 20,
  21, 22, 203
anti-positivism 83, 203, 207
anti-reflexivity x, 23, 31,59, 63, 66
archaeology 15, 26, 42, 43, 48,139,
  140, 141, 142, 209

C

complementarism x, 27, 30, 35,
  38, 40, 41, 51, 110, 136, 137, 138,
  139, 142, 143, 152, 154, 161, 162,
  183, 184, 185, 187,197, 199, 203,
  217
complexity vii, xii, 67, 71, 72, 81, 82,
  83, 84, 88, 89, 90, 99, 100, 101,
  103, 104, 105, 106, 108, 109,
  123,135, 143, 150, 151, 152, 155,
  156, 160, 203, 226, 227
critical hermeneutics 19, 21, 204, 208
critical science 174, 176, 177, 204
critical systems heuristics 99, 191,
  152, 177, 178, 179, 204
critical systems thinking xi, 26,
  113, 141, 184, 199, 204
critical theory xi, 5, 27, 30,35, 37,
  38, 46, 47, 48, 63, 178, 179, 180,
  214
critique ix, x, xi, 3, 4, 5, 17, 20,
  21, 22, 26, 31, 35, 43, 44, 45, 46,
  47, 48, 49, 50, 51, 52, 53, 99, 104,
  113, 119, 120, 130, 162, 165, 166,
  176, 177, 204, 205, 206, 209, 210,
  213, 223
cybernetics vii, 5, 18, 74, 78, 79, 97,
  98, 184

D

discursive formation 26, 42, 43, 44,45,
  48, 49, 99, 104,115, 119, 205, 209,
  210

E

empiricism 19, 205, 216
enlightenment 52, 163, 205, 211
episteme 42, 43
epistemological break 25, 66, 71, 73,
  74, 81, 91, 92, 93, 99, 101, 103,
  104, 105, 135, 163, 165, 166, 177,
  190
epistemology 29, 35, 36, 38, 42, 49,
  50, 65, 66, 68, 76, 82, 83, 84, 86,
  92, 98, 99, 100, 101, 103, 104, 113,
  121, 123, 130, 135, 137, 143, 144,
  153, 154, 161, 162, 163, 164, 165,
  168, 170, 175, 181, 182, 184, 197,
  198, 199, 206, 208, 213, 216, 217

F

false consciousness 15, 21, 28, 101,
  103, 163, 164, 174, 176, 178, 179,
  181, 165, 206, 210, 218, 219
foundationalism 16, 17, 18, 19, 20, 21,
  22, 206
functionalism 93, 161

G

genealogy 15, 26, 42, 43, 49, 50, 115,
  119, 207, 209, 210
general systems theory vii, xi, 23,
  26, 47, 59, 60, 64, 66, 67, 68, 73,
  101, 113, 119, 120, 121, 122, 123,
  124, 125, 126, 127, 128, 129,
  130,151, 184

H

hermeneutics 15, 18, 19, 22, 38, 174,
  207, 208
holism 5, 23, 59, 73, 74, 93, 98, 151,
  167
hypostatization 173, 208, 211

I

ideographic 209
ideology 14, 28, 29, 30, 47, 50, 83,
    103, 135, 161, 181, 185, 209, 213
imperialism 136, 137, 140, 142, 143,
    147, 148, 153, 161
instrumental reason 28, 48, 168, 169,
    209
interactive management 145, 150, 151
interactive planning 151
interpretive analytics ix, xi, 22, 23,
    32, 35, 41, 46, 47, 48, 49, 50, 54,
    64, 71, 99, 104, 120, 130, 198, 209
interpretivism 3, 31, 38, 93, 161, 163,
    165, 166, 170, 175, 178, 181, 209
isolationism vii, 3, 27, 30, 37, 48, 136,
    137, 139, 140, 142, 143, 146, 147,
    148, 155, 161, 162, 184, 197, 199,
    210

K

knowledge-constitutive interests ix,
    xi, xii, 21, 23, 27, 30, 31, 32, 35,
    36, 37, 38, 39, 40, 41, 47, 48, 50,
    51, 52, 54, 135, 162, 163, 174, 198,
    199, 210

L

liberating systems theory ix, xii, 3,
    4, 6, 13, 14, 15, 16, 23, 27, 28, 31,
    32, 35, 47, 48, 50, 51, 53, 113, 197,
    198, 199, 210, 218

M

material conditions 101, 164, 165,
    172, 173, 176, 178, 179, 181, 206,
    211
meta-unity ix, 32, 35, 47, 48, 50, 51,
    54, 197, 198
metaphor 15, 24, 25, 42, 63, 66, 71,
    72, 76, 77, 78, 79, 80, 82, 84, 86,
    88, 89, 90, 91, 92, 99, 100, 104,
    115, 141, 148, 149, 150, 151, 152,
    187, 218
metaphysical 123, 157, 177, 187, 189

metaphysics 20, 99, 100, 101, 211
methodology 14, 19, 27, 30, 42, 62, 66,
    90, 92, 96, 98, 107, 124, 127, 129,
    135, 136, 137, 138, 139, 140, 142,
    143, 147, 148, 149, 151, 152, 154,
    159, 160, 161, 175, 179, 211, 213,
    224, 226, 227
modernism 21, 211

N

nominalism 83, 212
nomothetic 212

O

ontological break 19, 76, 120
ontology 37, 66, 76, 82, 83, 84, 92, 95,
    98, 103, 135, 137, 143, 153, 157,
    212, 213, 217
operations research vii, 150

P

paradigm 6, 14, 21, 23, 27, 28, 35, 39,
    65, 83, 99, 100, 117, 118, 119, 127,
    128, 138, 139, 140, 148, 153, 154,
    157, 158, 160, 161, 184, 185, 190,
    198, 203, 206, 209, 211, 212, 213,
    214, 215, 217, 218
phenomenology 19, 214, 216
positivism 3, 4, 37, 38, 44, 46, 65, 83,
    120, 128, 163, 165, 166, 168, 169,
    170, 173, 181, 190, 214
post-modernism 21, 212, 214
pragmatism 136, 138, 143, 146, 147,
    161, 214
psychoanalysis 21, 123, 214

R

rationality 5, 6, 21, 28, 30, 31, 36, 46,
    47, 48, 49, 74, 80, 103, 104,120,
    144, 163, 164, 165, 166, 169, 170,
    172, 197, 215, 217
realism 207, 215
reflexivity 24, 43, 59, 63, 64, 65, 120,
    129, 136, 198, 204
relativism 103, 175, 209, 214, 215

S

scholars of union 21, 23, 32, 53
scientism 44, 163, 216
social metaphysics 216
soft systems methodology (SSM) vii,
    29, 61, 92, 95, 96, 142, 175
strategic assumption surfacing and
    testing (SAST) 151
structuralism 14, 18, 22, 25, 46, 114,
    117, 216
system dynamics vii, 184
systems analysis 150
systems engineering 141, 150, 159,
    184
systems practice 165
systems rationality 104, 163, 164,
    165, 176, 180, 217
systems science vii, 5, 61, 88, 100,
    101, 105, 117, 118, 119, 121, 124,
    163, 167, 168, 180, 217

T

total systems intervention xi, 81,
    217, 223, 224, 226, 227
totalization 51, 52
totalizing ix, 22, 30, 32, 197, 219
transcendental 17, 18, 19, 36, 38, 39,
    49, 156, 177, 218

U

unites ix, 14, 22, 23, 32, 60, 218
universals x, 67, 68, 123, 129, 130

V

viable systems model 79, 150